Export Marketing Strategy

Export Marketing Strategy

Tactics and Skills That Work

Shaoming Zou

University of Missouri

Daekwan Kim

Florida State University

S. Tamer Cavusgil

Georgia State University

Export Marketing Strategy

Copyright © Business Expert Press, LLC, 2009.
All rights reserved. No part of this publication may be reproduced, stored in a retrieval system, or transmitted in any form or by any means—electronic, mechanical, photocopy, recording, or any other except for brief quotations, not to exceed 400 words, without the prior permission of the publisher.

First published in 2009 by
Business Expert Press, LLC
222 East 46th Street, New York, NY 10017
www.businessexpertpress.com

ISBN-13: 978-1-60649-008-2 (paperback)
ISBN-10: 1-60649-008-7 (paperback)

ISBN-13: 978-1-60649-009-9 (e-book)
ISBN-10: 1-60649-009-5 (e-book)

DOI 10.4128/9781606490099

A publication in the Business Expert Press International Business collection

Collection ISSN (print) forthcoming
Collection ISSN (electronic) forthcoming

Cover design by Artistic Group—Monroe, NY
Interior design by Scribe, Inc.

First edition: April 2009

10 9 8 7 6 5 4 3 2 1

Printed in the United States of America.

Abstract

Export is the oldest form of international marketing and is still one of the most popular strategies for a firm to reach foreign markets. For many firms, exporting is an important strategic initiative for growth and a vital part of their business operations. Without success in exporting, many firms may not survive or prosper in the intensely competitive marketplace. Unfortunately, successful export marketing is not easy, and many firms lack a good understanding of the fundamentals of effective export marketing strategies and operations. This handbook of export marketing strategy presents a comprehensive and practical guide for firms interested in participating and succeeding in export marketing. Drawing on their sustained research in export marketing and knowledge of the literature, the authors introduce a systematic process for a firm to assess its readiness to export, identify and select viable export markets, explore suitable forms in which to enter foreign markets, develop an effective export marketing plan, work with export facilitating firms, set an export budget, manage the supply chain and logistics in exporting, analyze foreign cultures, adapt the product and promotion, set export prices, receive payment for exported products, and manage and control export transactions. They cover various aspects of a successful export marketing program, discuss detailed tasks and considerations involved in each aspect, and present a set of practical guidelines for firms to follow when making export marketing decisions. The book balances strategic considerations with operational issues and theoretical rationales with practical applications. By reading this book, managers will master the art and science of successful exporting and learn a strategic approach to helping their firms succeed in export marketing.

Keywords

Export, export marketing strategies, successful export marketing, export fundamentals, practical export guide

Contents

CHAPTER 1

Introduction: Export Marketing Strategy

Upon completing this chapter, you should be able to

- understand the importance of exporting to your firm's business performance;
- understand the determinants of export performance, especially the importance of export marketing strategy;
- follow an export marketing strategy framework to develop suitable marketing strategies for your export venture in a foreign market.

Importance of Exporting

In a globalized market, exporting plays an important role in a firm's growth and profitability. With trade barriers coming down, advances in telecommunication, transportation, and data processing technologies, and increasing global travel, exporting is no longer the privilege of large multinational corporations. In fact, a large number of small and medium-size firms have become active and dynamic exporters in the global market in the last few decades (Katsikeas, Bell, & Morgan, 1998). Increasingly, exporting is becoming a very important strategic initiative in the growth of many small and medium-size firms. For many firms, exporting is a vital part of their business operations. Without success in exporting, many firms may not survive in the saturated domestic market.

Determinants of Export Performance

Yet success in export marketing is by no means easy for small and medium-size firms. While many firms have succeeded in internationalization, examples of failure in export marketing are easy to find (Cavusgil, Knight, & Riesenberger, 2008). To be successful in internationalization and in export marketing, firms need to conduct a careful assessment of their readiness to export, go through the learning process of internation-alization, develop effective export marketing strategies that suit the for-eign markets, and implement the strategies effectively.

Past research in export marketing has identified a number of deter-minants of export performance. These include internal organizational factors such as management's commitment to exporting, international experience, human and financial resources, research and development (R&D) capabilities, product uniqueness, and organizational structure, and external environmental factors such as competitive intensity, cultural differences, market structure and turbulence, and government restric-tions/regulations (Katsikeas, Piercy, & Ioannidis, 1996; Zou & Stan, 1998). However, the most important determinant of export performance has been found to be a firm's export marketing strategy (Cavusgil & Zou, 1994; Zou & Stan, 1998). It has been established that the fit between a firm's export marketing strategy and its internal organizational character-istics and external market characteristics is what ultimately determines its export performance (Cavusgil & Zou, 1994). This framework is sum-marized in Figure 1.1.

Export Marketing Strategy and Export Performance

According to the above framework of determinants of export perfor-mance, external market/industry characteristics and internal firm and

Figure 1.1. A framework of determinants of export performance.

Internal Characteristics

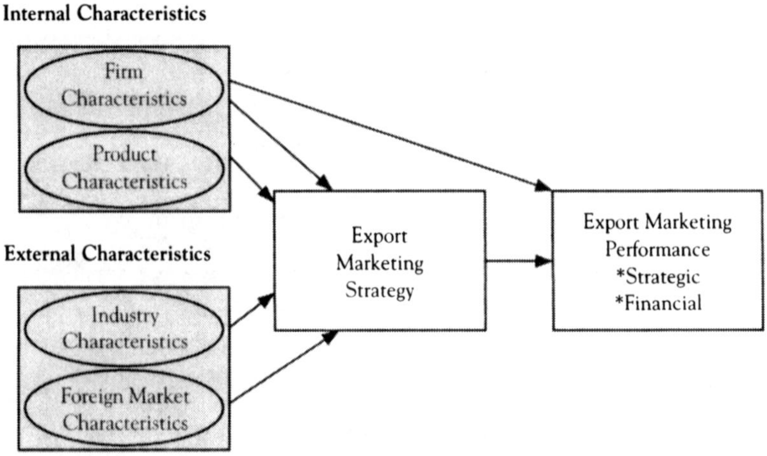

product characteristics impose pressure for a firm to respond in its export venture. A firm that can respond with effective export marketing strategy that fits the internal and external environments will experience improved export performance.

Export performance can be assessed along two different dimensions: strategic and financial (Zou, Taylor, & Osland, 1998). Strategic export performance can be viewed as the extent to which a firm's strategic objectives of exporting are achieved in the foreign market. When a firm decides to export, it may set some strategic objectives such as setting up a strategic foothold in the important foreign markets, gaining competitive advantages through market diversification, exploiting the product and technological strengths in the foreign market, increasing market share, preempting competition, gaining international experience, and building brand awareness and brand equity in foreign markets (Cavusgil & Zou, 1994). Achievement of such objectives will enhance the firm's strategic market position and increase its competitiveness, leading to long-term business success.

A firm may also set financial objectives when it decides to export. These may include increasing sales of existing products, making profits through exporting to foreign markets, and reducing the cost via increasing the scale. Accomplishing these objectives will lead to improved financial performance of the firm. Depending on the situation of the firm, strategic export performance or financial export performance may be the focus of the firm's export ventures.

The framework suggests that when a firm's export marketing strategy fits its internal environment and external environment, its strategic export performance and financial export performance will be improved. To achieve a good fit of export marketing strategy to the internal and external environments, a firm can engage in a conscious effort to adapt its marketing strategies to these environments. In other words, adaptation is a central means to achieve a fit between export marketing strategy and the firm's internal and external environments (Cavusgil, Zou, & Naidu, 1993). The adaptation may involve various components of the firm's marketing strategy, including market targeting, brand positioning, product promotion, distribution, and pricing.

Product adaptation is a key export marketing strategy that influences a firm's export performance (Cavusgil & Zou, 1994). In a foreign market, political/regulatory, cultural, and economic environments can be very different. Product standards, safety standards, and technical specifications in foreign markets can be quite different from those in the domestic market. In order to market a product successfully in the foreign market, an exporter needs to properly adapt its product to the foreign market's requirements. Sometimes the product may be culture specific or unique to domestic market demand. To market it successfully in the foreign market, the product also needs to be adapted to make it more appealing to foreign market demand. There are two types of product adaptation that can be pursued by exporters: mandatory adaptation and discretionary adaptation (Czinkota & Ronkainen, 2002). Mandatory product adaptation is the minimum level of adaptation of a product in order to make the product acceptable in the export market. It may be prompted by the local regulatory environment or physical and educational characteristics. Discretionary product adaptation, on the other hand, is pursued at the exporter's discretion to make the product more appealing to customers in the export market. It is usually done by the exporter to gain a competitive advantage over its rivals in the export market.

Promotion adaptation is another major export marketing strategy that is important to export performance. Laws and regulations about advertising, cultural values and norms, and advertising infrastructure in the foreign market can be very different from those in the domestic market (Cavusgil et al., 2008). As a result, effective advertising in the domestic market may not work well in the foreign market, leading to the need to adapt the advertising's theme, message, media, and evaluation in the foreign market. Sales promotion may also need to be adapted to fit the foreign environment. In many countries, the retailing structure is dominated by small and independent stores, making it hard for exporters to use coupons to promote sales. In some countries, face saving is an important value in the culture, making price discounts, coupons, and rebates ineffective for promoting sales because consumers may shy away from these tools in their effort to project a positive affluent image. Language difference also makes it necessary to adapt the firm's advertising and promotion (Czinkota & Ronkainen, 2002).

Adaptations to channels of distribution may be necessary in some foreign countries due to unique local distribution structures. Indeed, most countries in the world still lack the modern American type of large-scale distribution channels in which mega-retailers and chain stores dominate retail sales. In these countries, long and inefficient distribution channels with multiple levels of wholesaling and small-scale retailing are prevalent (Czinkota & Ronkainen, 2002). In addition, cultural differences also lead consumers to shop in different types of outlets. To succeed in such markets, exporters must adapt their distribution strategy to fit the characteristics of the export market.

Price adaptation may be necessary in order to market a product effectively in foreign markets. There are several factors that may necessitate price adaptation. First, the added costs of exporting, such as international freight charges, insurance, tariffs and duties, and exporting specialists, have to be covered in order for export ventures to be profitable, leading to possible price increases. Second, the long and less efficient distribution channels in many foreign markets may increase the price of exported products to foreign consumers due to distributors' margins and higher costs of transportation and storage. To control such price increases, exporters may have to reduce their quoted price to foreign importers/distributors to remain competitive. Third, product adaptation and promotion adaptation that are necessary to market the product in the export market require investment that need to be recovered through price adaptation. Exporters may consider charging a higher price to cover such investments. Finally, income levels in many export markets may be relatively low or competition may be intense. Consumers may not be able to afford the regularly priced products or have competing products to choose from. As a result, the price of the exported product may have to be reduced to make the product viable in foreign markets (Cavusgil, 1988).

In addition to export marketing strategy, a firm's internal organizational resources and capabilities may also have a direct effect on its export performance. Top management commitment, international experience, organizational and financial resources, and competencies in product and process technologies can all directly influence export performance (Zou & Stan, 1998). In fact, successful exporters are those that have considerable top management commitment, international experience, and organizational and financial resources, and superior competencies in product and process technologies. Exporting represents a significant commitment by a firm to enter the international market. A firm with high-level management commitment to exporting, adequate staff with international experience, and sufficient financial resources is more likely to meet the demand of export market development and avoid prematurely aborting export operations in the face of temporary market turmoil (Aaby & Slater, 1989). In the long run, successful exporters must develop and sustain distinctive competencies in product development and process improvement, as the export market will become mature and competition will catch up. Moreover, exporters must capitalize on their gained experience in an export market by expanding their operations and establishing themselves as dominant competitors in the export market.

Development of Export Marketing Strategy

Given the importance of export marketing strategy in determining a firm's export performance, it is very important that a systematic process be followed to develop an export marketing strategy that is properly adapted to the firm's internal and external environments. To be effective, an exporter should conduct a thorough Strengths, Weaknesses, Opportunities, and Threats (SWOT) analysis before deciding on the degree of adaptation of its marketing strategy for the export market. Specifically, the following are examples of a firm's strengths, weaknesses, opportunities, and threats in the foreign market (Czinkota & Ronkainen, 2002):

Strengths

- A strongly differentiated product
- Distinctive competencies in the industry
- Strong brand name and reputation
- An attractive customer base
- Superior intellectual capital and international experience
- Innovative marketing capabilities
- Quality management
- Technological and financial resources
- Cross-cultural competencies
- Strong alliances with foreign partners

Weaknesses

- Lack of distinctive competencies
- Higher costs or weak differentiation
- Weak brand and customer base
- Weak distribution network
- Lack of intellectual capital and international experience
- Limited financial resources
- Lack of cross-culturally competent personnel
- Lack of strategic vision

Opportunities

- Rising demand, especially from the export market
- Existence of underserved market segments in the export market
- Opportunity to utilize existing skills and resources in the export market
- Falling trade barriers and attractive foreign markets
- Opportunity to increase scale from foreign operations
- Possibility of exploiting a relationship with foreign business partner or government officials

Threats

- Intense competition in the foreign market
- Slowing market growth
- Growing bargaining power of foreign businesses or governments
- Shift in customer demand
- Costly new government regulations
- Likely entry by formidable competitors into the foreign market
- Technology changes fast in the industry

After a careful SWOT analysis, the firm should seek to adapt its marketing strategies in such a way as to capitalize on its strengths, overcome its weaknesses, exploit opportunities, and avoid threats. In other words, a firm should align its strengths with market opportunities when adapting its marketing strategies to the export market. Once a close fit is achieved between its export marketing strategy and its internal and external environments, its export performance will be improved (Cavusgil & Zou, 1994).

The Objectives of This Book

In this book we seek to present a comprehensive guide for firms interested in participating and succeeding in export marketing. Drawing on the authors' sustained research stream in export marketing and our knowledge of the export marketing literature, we will introduce a systematic process for a firm to assess its readiness to export, identify and select viable export markets, explore suitable forms to enter foreign markets, develop an effective export marketing plan, work with export facilitating firms, set an export budget, manage the supply chain and logistics in exporting, analyze foreign cultures, adapt the product, adapt the promotion, set export prices, get paid in exporting, and manage export transactions. We attempt to cover various aspects of a successful export marketing program, discuss the detailed tasks and considerations involved in each aspect, and present a set of practical guidelines for firms to follow when making export marketing decisions.

By reading this book, business managers will master the art and science of successful exporting and understand the complete process and decision-making tasks involved in export marketing. More importantly, they will learn a strategic approach to helping their firms participate in exporting, develop properly adapted export marketing strategies, manage export operations, and improve export performance. Eventually they will help their firms survive and prosper in the ever-changing global market environment.

Throughout this book we attempt to balance strategic considerations with operational issues in export marketing. We also balance the theoretical rationales with practical applications of export marketing knowledge. Readers with different levels of knowledge and preparation in export marketing should benefit from this book by focusing more or less on certain chapters. To our knowledge this is the first comprehensive book focused specifically on export marketing strategy and operations. We believe it will be an invaluable addition to the export marketing literature.

CHAPTER 2

Assessing Company Readiness to Export

Upon completing this chapter, you should be able to

- understand the importance of internal assessment of your firm's strengths and weaknesses prior to launching an export venture;
- develop and recommend a framework and methodology for assessing a company's internal strengths and weaknesses prior to formulating a strategy for going international;
- suggest approaches that could reduce the impact of export-related weaknesses and correct some deficiencies.
- understand the microcomputer-based decision support tool: CORE (COmpany Readiness to Export).

Why Should You Assess Company Readiness to Export?

Exporting requires company resources, including management commitment, human resources, capital, research and development (R&D) efforts, and production capacity. Therefore it is important to assess whether you have resources available to meet the commitment exporting requires. There is no point in trying to implement an export strategy if the company is barely meeting its existing resource commitments. A common mistake made by some companies is to become involved in exporting without adequate preparation and assessment of their readiness to export. In such companies, managers' expectations from exporting are often unrealistic, and insufficient thought is given to undertaking export development tasks in a systematic manner. In these cases, the results may be disappointing and the company may decide not to reenter export markets later because of earlier setbacks (Cavusgil, 1993).

Most marketing managers are thoroughly familiar with their domestic markets. They know their competitors, and the strengths and weaknesses of their products. They understand who their customers are and what is required to sell to them. In contrast, their information about overseas markets and conditions for success is often incomplete and sometimes misleading (Czinkota, 1991). The dangers are obvious: companies run the risk of committing manpower and resources to exporting without first assessing their strengths and weaknesses. As a result, their export activities could have a detrimental impact on their overall business performance.

Therefore managers are advised to assess their internal and external business environments before making a commitment to exporting. An internal assessment can show the level of export operations that can be supported by the company's existing resource pool. This helps in making a realistic and achievable commitment to export operations.

Then Who Should Export?

Successful exporters have a strong strategic rationale for going international. This is known as strategic intent. It is the company's first "road map" toward its longer term objectives (Miller, 1993b). This strategic intent statement includes a list of the company's initial objectives and strategies for going international.

Before a company decides to go international, there are a number of factors to be considered. Demand for a company's products in international markets is only one indicator of growth potential. Other alternatives might seem more attractive compared to the exporting option. Consider the following questions:

- Can your company sell more in the domestic marketplace?
- Is the profit potential of increasing domestic sales higher than that of export sales?
- Can resources for foreign market development be freed without endangering your domestic market position or long-term prospects for the home market?

As a rule of thumb, exporting is likely to pay off if the company has a successful domestic business, sound financial basis, an effective R&D effort, experienced and flexible management, and is operating profitably (Miller, 1993b). Rarely is exporting a suitable way in the long run to improve the overall situation of a company already beset by stagnating or decreasing sales, shrinking profit margins, or financial troubles in the home market. However, if a company's sales are saturating the home market, which means there is a steady demand without strong growth potential, such demand can be boosted by exporting products to overseas markets where the products are new in local consumers' eyes. In other words, proactive exporters are more likely to be successful than reactive exporters (Czinkota, 1994).

Analyzing Your Company's Ability to Export

The strengths and weaknesses of your company have to be analyzed through an internal audit. The focus of this audit is to determine your company's key strengths and weaknesses in the following areas (Cavusgil, Knight, & Riesenberger, 2008):

- Competitive capability in the domestic market
- Motivation for going international
- Commitment of top management to the export cause
- Organizational readiness
- Product readiness
- Company resources

Thoroughly assessing these areas before any external market research is conducted will allow you to assess the level of commitment you should make toward exporting.

Competitive Capability in the Domestic Market

Before embarking on expansion of a business into foreign markets, it is extremely important that the company be competitive in its domestic market. This domestic competitiveness can be called "defensive competitiveness," which means the ability to compete in the domestic market against the best global competitors.

This is important because only a competitively successful company in its home market will be able to export successfully. Because of globalization, chances are very good that your competitors in the home market will also be your competitors in the export market. Until and unless your organization and its product offerings have the strength to gain and retain a domestic share of the market, exporting is not likely to be a very attractive option.

Domestic competitive ability is determined by evaluating the following factors (Peter & Donnelly, 2007):

- Your company's customer base
- Sales and distribution structure
- Business experience
- Market share in categories that you compete in
- Sales revenues
- Number of employees
- Growth prospects
- Budgeting and financial systems within your organization

Figure 2.1. Key success factors for exporting.

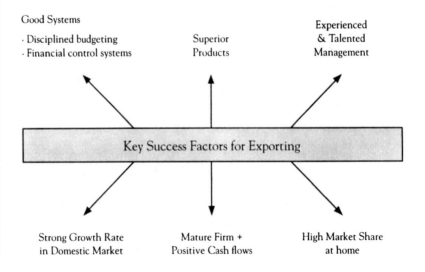

The quality and diversity of experience in your management team is also an important variable for determining your competitiveness. Typically successful exporting companies have strong management teams, internationally comparable and competitive products, and sustained positive cash flow for a long period. Compliance with the following principles will do much to ensure defensive competitiveness:

- A company will be better prepared to embark on international operations if it has expanded its operations nationally in its domestic market and has not restricted sales to local or regional markets.
- The more complex the network of sales representation and distribution channels in the domestic market, the more ready will a company be to deal with that complexity in foreign markets.
- If the company has been in business for many years and resists venturing into foreign markets, its chances of success in foreign markets will be lower because the company is *risk averse*.
- The more competitive a company is in its domestic market, the better its chances of success in foreign markets.
- The larger the company is in its domestic market, the better the chances of success in foreign markets.
- A strong growth rate in the domestic market is an indicator of dynamism, which enhances the chances of success in foreign markets.
- Success in foreign markets requires disciplined budgeting and financial management. If a company has already developed and implemented these systems, its chances of success in foreign markets are greater.
- A company's product line should provide superior value in features, benefits, and pricing compared to its principal competitors.
- Best results are attained in foreign markets when the company has passed its earliest growth stages and has evolved into a professionally managed, mature firm.
- Among all the factors required for success in foreign markets, few are more important than a company's cash resources. Therefore it is important that a company demonstrate a recent history

of positive cash flow from domestic operations that will finance foreign market entry initiatives.

Motivation for Going International

The exporting company must have a strong strategic intent for going international. Haphazard forays into export markets through filling unsolicited orders, using excess production capacity, seasonal balancing of capacity, and simply supplementing domestic sales through export orders are insufficient for long-term export success. Entering international markets is a long-term strategic initiative. It requires compelling and proactive motivations derived from the company's business environments and competitive positions in the market. A solid and sustainable position cannot be attained by short-term, profit-oriented forays into in foreign markets. In fact, research has found that proactively motivated exporters focus on marketing strategy adaptation, customer satisfaction, and competitive advantage, which are vital to success in the export market. In contrast, exporters that react to their negative business situations in the domestic market and look to alleviate their poor position through exporting often place their emphasis on the mechanical and operational details of exporting. Such exporters are unlikely to satisfy their customers in foreign markets and attain long-term export success (Czinkota & Ronkainen, 2002). However, sporadic exporting may be a starting point that can lead to the development of a full-scale exporting venture.

Successful exporters have one or more of the following as their key objectives (Burton & Schlegelmilch, 1987):

- Expanding into key markets
- Enhancing competitiveness by acquiring market knowledge
- Extending the life cycle of existing products by launching them in new markets
- Diversifying risk by selling in foreign markets
- Exploiting proprietary knowledge and technology
- Improving long-term return for the company by tapping profitable markets
- Long-term sales and operations expansion
- Preempt competitors' moves into global markets

Commitment of Top Management to the Export Cause

Why Is Commitment Important?

Exporting is not a quick fix for improving company profitability. Success-ful exporting requires a certain degree of long-term commitment and sac-rifice of short-term profits. Thus management commitment is considered key by most experienced exporters. Unless a company and its manage-ment are committed to exporting and are willing to invest time, money, and manpower, chances of success are very slim (Zou & Stan, 1998). Isolated interest from the management in exporting without sufficient support can be self-defeating.

Top managers must be committed to the export objective. This commitment has to be translated into a solid long-term strategy for the company's export effort. Management should be willing to invest in the exporting business and sacrifice short-term gains for longer term gains from export activities, increasing the viability of its export success. Evalu-ation of the following factors should yield important insights into the commitment level of a company's top management team (Cavusgil & Nevin, 1981; Zou & Stan, 1998):

1. The greater the willingness to risk current profits and return on investment in the short to medium term, the greater the likelihood of success in foreign markets.

2. If a company is willing to become more of an "insider" in foreign markets by establishing subsidiaries in some of those markets, its chances of success will be greater than those who prefer to sell through middlemen.

3. The longer a company is willing to wait to break even on its invest-ment in building foreign markets, the greater the likelihood of success.

4. If a company is willing to use law firms in foreign countries, par-ticularly those well versed in the laws of that country or region, it is more likely to succeed in foreign markets than those companies that insist on using their current attorneys exclusively.

5. It is important that top management view exporting as a regular activity with aggressive levels of targeted exports, rather than just an occasional activity.

6. When a company targets a high percentage of its total sales for foreign markets (greater than 30%), it is more likely to succeed than those companies targeting only a very small percentage.

7. Companies that place strategic emphasis on developing strong market shares in key global markets are more likely to succeed in foreign markets than those that focus on maximization of profitability or return on investment.

8. The greater the funding that the company makes available for expansion into foreign markets, particularly in the area of market research and market development, the greater its chances of success.

9. The greater the human resources (part time and full time) the company commits to its international operations, the greater its chances of success. This applies to senior managers and operations personnel.

10. The more detailed and thorough the planning and budgeting for foreign markets, the greater the chances for success.

11. A willingness to compensate international personnel at a level comparable to the best in international trade positions will help ensure that a company attracts the best people for those positions, and therefore is likely to be more successful than those companies paying less than competitive salaries and benefits.

Trade-Offs Between Domestic and Export Operations

One of the early hazards of exporting is the tendency for the export management function to become isolated from the domestic side and be assigned a lower priority. When this occurs, senior management is not always well informed regarding the details of the export process, nor are they aware of the opportunities available to aggressive exporting companies.

It is important that export opportunities be properly balanced with domestic opportunities in both the short and long term, with proper allocation of the company's resources. For instance, exporting may take a little longer to develop than a new domestic program, but the returns may be greater over time. Therefore management must decide if they are willing to sacrifice short-term expenditures for long-term profits (Cavusgil et al., 2008). Unfortunately many companies have only short-sighted quarterly goals to meet, which dissuade them from making exporting commitments. Therefore, to make an exporting commitment usually requires that management balance out its short- and long-term interests and goals.

Most companies consider new domestic ventures at a top management level. All new ventures in the home market have active participation from one or more top managers. Exporting requires the same level of attention and participation. Some companies regard exporting as either a method for alleviating declining domestic sales or an outlet for excess production. Such approaches create an impression that exporting is a "second class" activity conducted by "second class players." This attitude can never lead to the creation of a successful export-oriented business.

Management commitment is a constantly changing element of the exporting process. The degree of commitment may be increased or decreased depending on feedback information and market situations. Feedback information is crucial for the postexport audit. Feedback can be in the form of customer and management opinions and performance measurements, both financial and nonfinancial.

Organizational Readiness

Organizational readiness assessment explores and documents your company's strengths and weaknesses. Key internal factors that need to be evaluated as part of your company's self-assessment are human resources, export experience, financial resources, manufacturing capacity, marketing expertise, marketing intelligence, technical knowledge, and planning and systems for going international (Aksoy & Kaynak, 1994).

The important point for management to realize is that exporting is no different from any other business activity. It requires thought, research, and planning, and it starts with commitment. Aggressively entering the exporting arena requires at least the same degree of effort and follow-through necessary to implement any domestic venture.

Assessing Human Resources

Human resources involved in exporting require some level of familiarity with the importing country and foreign customers. International experience and cultural and linguistic familiarity can prove to be sources of competitive advantage. Experience in dealing with trade facilitators (banks, law firms, freight forwarders, and research firms) can also prove to be very useful. In addition, training in cross-cultural effectiveness directed at target markets is one of the greatest contributors to success in foreign markets. International success also requires experience and expertise in building trust-based relationships with overseas partnering firms and their managers (Bello & Williamson, 1985). Successfully managing all these activities requires specialized managerial talent within your organization.

If you have no employees with export experience, you have two options. First, you could choose to train and develop suitable employees. These individuals, regardless of their level of responsibility, should be extremely familiar with the company, its products, its organizational structure, and its management attitudes. These people should also have the required technical knowledge about the products to achieve their objectives. Training and development can be acquired through seminars, exporting organizations, or other training opportunities.

It is desirable to find motivated individuals who really want to learn and apply exporting processes and principles. Often these people will be from the domestic marketing department and may have handled unsolicited foreign orders.

The second choice is to hire an export manager who is already trained and experienced in exporting. This may cost more but may allow you to launch the export program more quickly. Regardless of where you recruit your export personnel, it is important to provide adequate compensation. Compensation for services should include an incentive factor that will reward superior job performance.

Export Experience

A practical way to begin your internal evaluation is to assess past exporting or international experience. If your company has no past experience in exporting or very limited experience, it may be possible to review previous sales inquiries or requests for product information from abroad.

Such information may prove to be a valuable link to international markets. Simplistic as it sounds, it is often meaningful to first study your own company's records. Firms that have neither export know-how nor inquiries from abroad can learn about export opportunities from outside sources.

Financial Resources

Launching an exporting venture will place additional demands on the capital resource pool of the firm. This capital will be required to finance increased inventories and receivables for your international business. Therefore your company must have sufficient funds available to start an export venture. New costs can include (Cavusgil, 1988)

- overcoming barriers such as compliance with standards and regulations;
- legal fees;
- international market research;
- foreign travel;
- transportation, insurance, and tariffs;
- product modification;
- warranty and after-sales service provisions;
- participation in trade fairs and exhibitions.

Knowledge of tariff and nontariff barriers is also important, as it affects the landed cost of your products in the importing country. International operations are also affected by foreign exchange risk. Understanding foreign exchange dynamics and developing appropriate strategies to deal with these risks is of crucial importance to the success of an international business venture.

Managers also need to understand and develop an appreciation for the various risk hedging tools available to international business managers through financial intermediaries. There is a significant degree of uncertainty involved with entering a new market. It is important to get reliable and timely cost information to reduce this level of risk. Identifying sources of information and assessing their reliability is a key step in the process of generating a cost picture of the new international business. A basic commitment to an export venture may require a minimum of $250,000 of start-up capital to finance market visits, research, product sampling, and other related activities.

Manufacturing Capacity

It is important to determine if your company has enough manufacturing capacity available to meet export demand in addition to your domestic demand. Spikes in export or domestic demand could lead to a situation where relationships with either foreign or local customers are endangered. Manufacturing capacity decisions are also related to unit landed costs in the importing country and structural arrangements with your overseas partners.

It is possible to have overseas partners contribute to the value addition process by shipping in bulk or by implementing other logistical postponement strategies (including mixing, final packaging, and labeling).

Marketing Expertise

Knowledge of export markets, customers, channels, and competitors can be an invaluable asset for your organization. The ability to commission and interpret focused market research can provide insights into your customers' needs (Craig & Douglas, 1999).

A well-developed and mature marketing organization provides a strong base from which to launch international market ventures. Technical marketing skills can be applied across markets, and expertise in this area is a strong source of competitive advantage for most companies based in developed countries.

Gathering Market Intelligence

Gathering foreign market intelligence is a key component of organizational readiness. Foreign market product and logistical costs; knowledge of legal, financial, political, social, and trade barriers; assessments of foreign competitors and their product/market strategies; and an accurate appraisal of the benefits and risks involved in exporting are crucial to export success. It is also important to know where to look for information. The ability to leverage publicly available information can save a lot of time, effort, and money.

Technical Knowledge

Proprietary product or process knowledge is a strong competitive advantage. You have to systematically analyze the strengths and weaknesses of your organization to discover its distinctive competencies. Leveraging these competencies will result in a strong competitive posture in your export market.

Distinctive competencies can be product or process based. Product-based competencies will have a strong technological base, whereas process-based competencies can be a mix of people, systems, knowledge, and environmental factors. The core identifier of a competency is that it results in an attribute that is important from the customer's viewpoint, and the competency is something that you do better than your competitors. The superior performance of this process leads you into a position of competitive advantage.

Planning and Systems for Going International

The important point for management to realize is that exporting is no different than any other business activity. It requires thought, research, and planning, and it starts with commitment. Aggressively entering the export arena requires at least the same degree of effort and follow-through that is necessary for implementing any domestic venture. Three key questions need to be answered at a strategic level before top management can decide to make an exporting commitment:

1. What does the company want to gain from exporting?
2. Is exporting consistent with other company goals?
3. What are the costs and benefits of exporting?

Strong managerial commitment and talented personnel do not signify an organizational readiness to export. Even companies that attach great importance to professional management practices in their domestic businesses often neglect to follow these same principles in their international business.

There must be a desire on the part of management to work hard and develop systematic plans. The very uncertainties of exporting make planning all the more necessary. You must have the resources necessary to develop such plans. Money, management commitment, production capacity, and R&D capabilities are all relevant issues for consideration. Access to such resources is a prerequisite if exporting is to prove a viable strategy (Czinkota & Ronkainen, 2002).

The export effort has to be supported through an exporting organization, specific export sales targets, time-phased profitability goals, and investment schedules. Export planning and control processes should be integrated into the existing systems of the firm (Hill & Still, 1984). Developing an export plan is very important. This plan is a statement of facts, constraints, goals, and strategies. It is also an action plan in the sense that it lays down specific and measurable objectives along with their time schedules. An effective export plan should, at a minimum, answer the following questions:

1. What products will be exported, and what modifications will they require?
2. Which countries will be targeted as export opportunities?
3. What customer segment will be targeted in each country? Which marketing and logistical channels are appropriate for targeting each segment?
4. What special challenges (may include import controls, cultural and social factors, government policies) do we face in each market? How do we plan to meet these challenges?
5. How will we determine our product's export price?
6. What specific operational steps need to be taken and when?
7. What are the time frames associated with the export plan?
8. What personnel and company resources will be dedicated to exporting?

9. What will be the cost in time and money for each element of the export plan?
10. How will the results of our venture be evaluated and used to modify and tune future action?

The export plan should be in a written form, providing the following clearly identifiable benefits:

- Provides clarity in terms of expressing strengths and weaknesses
- Establishes accountability and responsibility
- Can be used to seek external and internal financing
- Can be used in obtaining formal management commitment

Product Readiness

Managers may find that particular product attributes that are appreciated in the home market may not be so appealing to foreign customers and may therefore have to be modified. Product readiness considers adaptations of products in terms of redesigning the product, adding or eliminating features, refining attributes, and changing specifications or components (Hill & Still, 1984). Perhaps repositioning the product might also help. Different positioning across international markets can accommodate different social, cultural, and behavioral patterns.

What Determines Product Success?

Typically products that have been successful in the U.S. market will be successful in other similar markets or in places where similar needs exist (Zou & Stan, 1998). Similar markets are defined as markets which have almost the same level of education, wealth (per capita income), and level of infrastructural development. In addition, similar markets have compatible social, cultural, geographical, climatic, and environmental dimensions. Other markets may require some form of product modification for export. Product or packaging modifications may be required to accommodate one or more of the following factors (Cavusgil et al., 2008):

- Climatic and environmental factors
- Social and cultural factors

- Local availability of raw materials
- Low wage costs
- Local substitutes
- Low local purchasing power
- Lack of foreign exchange in the importing country
- Government import controls
- National safety and health standards
- Manufacturing, storing, shipping, and handling considerations

Rules of Thumb That Determine Product Success

Although the job of product planning for exporting is often complicated by the peculiarities, preferences, and legal requirements of the markets served by the company, you can safely count on three rules of thumb (Cavusgil & Zou, 1994; Hill & Still, 1984):

1. A high-technology product or one that is produced from an unusual process dominated by the firm's R&D tends to be successful. Proprietary knowledge provides a strong source of competitive advantage.
2. Product compatibility with the local market is important. For example, developing countries demand essential manufactured goods, while more industrialized countries demand capital goods and a variety of consumer products and services.
3. Highly adaptable products that are flexible in operation, durable, and dependable stand a good chance of exportability because such products can easily accommodate the needs of multiple markets.

Product Functionality Assessment

It is helpful to place oneself in the position of a foreign customer and attempt to identify what would be desirable from their point of view. What kind of features are important to this product? As a result of this investigative process, managers are likely to come up with various ways of improving and enhancing product appeal. Sometimes this may be as simple as a packaging adaptation.

An assessment of your product's practical functions is important. The purpose of this step is to thoroughly understand the basic need that your product fulfills both within the domestic market and in various foreign markets. This assessment starts with the question, "What does your product do and what needs does it satisfy?" Regardless of whether you are a manufacturer of an industrial, commercial, or consumer product, this question should be addressed first. Answer it in terms of the product's main advantages and disadvantages compared to competitive products or alternative ways of filling the same basic need. Perhaps through a simple modification in an existing product, new market opportunities abroad can be realized. In each country and each situation, different needs might have to be met before exporting becomes a successful venture (Miller, 1993a).

Product Support

Customers have to be provided with information and training on using your products. After-sales service, training, and information are key elements of a product support strategy. Your product offering can be embellished by enhancing the product through better customer service and after-sales support. This is something that is often forgotten. However, if the firm is in the business of selling an industrial product, satisfactory after-sales service is essential in a foreign market. Delivery can also be an important selling point. In addition to these factors, credit and financing terms can be used effectively to attract customers (Czinkota & Ronkainen, 2002).

Logistical support is an essential element in selling your products successfully in foreign markets. The weight, density, and storability of your products have to be assessed to determine its cost competitiveness from a transportation cost standpoint. Logistical costs can add significantly to the landed cost of the product and therefore must be carefully assessed. These costs can include packaging, shipping, storage, insurance, and obsolescence-related expenses.

Product Line Strategies

It may be worthwhile and less expensive to manufacture certain products for export only. Quite a few companies have built successful export businesses by reactivating discontinued products for international markets. Often technologies that are considered old or declining in industrialized countries may be new for developing countries and may offer a cheaper mode of obtaining that particular technological competency. Different products can be at different stages in the product life cycle across different markets.

It is important to determine the popularity of your products abroad. A good measure for this is its percentage share of total exports. If products similar to yours have a high percentage share of the product category then you are in a strong position to start exporting. International trade statistics such as those found in the National Trade Database (NTDB) offer a useful resource base to carry out this kind of analysis.

Accuracy of the Assessment

It is important to obtain a clear and accurate picture of your company. Distortions of your company's resources will result in a wrong decision in assessing an export market. Often cultural bias and researcher incompetence are responsible for distorted information and misrepresentation of production capacity, R&D level, financial position, and most importantly, the company's viability. If you doubt the accuracy, sufficiency, or interpretation of the facts assembled, you should seek outside assistance from those who have the training and experience to guide the audit. Consensus of opinion should be attained wherever possible.

There is a software package called CORE that is designed to help managers assess their company readiness to export. It is a structured, PC-based decision support tool that can enhance the quality of your internal self-assessment process. After performing your internal audit, you should be able to more accurately and realistically set assess your company's domestic and exporting objectives.

What If There Are Weaknesses Identified in the Assessment?

If your self-assessment uncovers weaknesses, there are some strategies that you should consider to enhance your readiness to export. These suggestions can be grouped into two categories: organizational readiness and product readiness.

Improving Organizational Readiness

Fortunately there are numerous ways to improve the readiness of your organization to export:

- Involve members of your staff in export workshops and seminars.
- Participate in trade missions and overseas trade shows sponsored by the U.S. Department of Commerce.
- Exhibit your products to foreign business people visiting your market.
- Participate in industry trade shows.
- Learn about the experiences of successful exporters.
- Mail product literature and promotional videos to selected potential customers or distributors in the language of their country.
- Respond promptly to inquiries and leads from abroad.
- Seek advice and assistance from relevant agencies and intermediary organizations such as international banks and trading companies.
- Seek joint venture opportunities.

It should be pointed out that many companies profitably engage in exporting despite some initial weaknesses and limitations. You may venture into exporting with some problems and still succeed, but it is important to understand what these problems are and work to eliminate them.

Improving Product Readiness

Just like organizational readiness, companies can improve the readiness of their products for export. Consider the following to improve product readiness (Cavusgil, 1993):

- Product adaptation, redesign, and modification
- Packaging adaptation
- Repositioning the product to meet different needs

- Stressing product benefits through customer service, delivery, trademarks, and product warranty
- Development of new products

About CORE

CORE, a PC-based tool for assessing a company's readiness to export, has been used successfully by thousands of individual managers and export assistance agencies across the globe. CORE is designed to provide an evaluation of internal company strengths and weaknesses in the exporting context. It is especially useful for small and medium-size businesses that are considering exports for the first time. CORE assesses a company's current situation and makes recommendations on export-related tasks.

CORE has been designed as an expert system. The program guides the user through a series of questions concerning the organization and its products. It then compares responses against the profile of an ideal

Figure 2.2. The CORE Process.

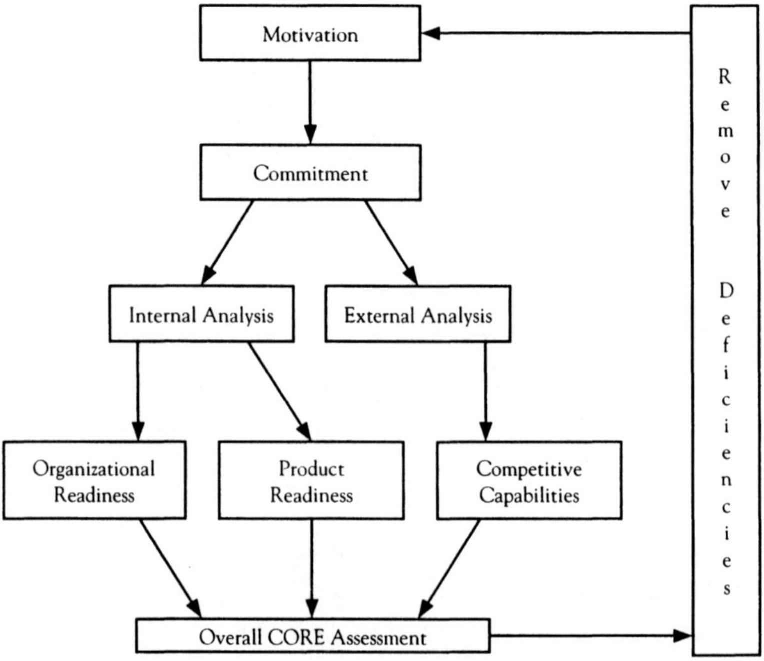

exporter. The user's potential strengths and weaknesses are highlighted and explained. Ratings of organizational and product readiness are generated, and alternative courses of action are recommended for engaging in export operations.

CORE was developed on the basis of substantial research into the characteristics of successful export businesses. It also reflects the collective opinions of numerous exporting experts and seasoned business executives.

All versions of CORE were developed by S. Tamer Cavusgil, professor of marketing and international business and Executive Director of the International Business Center at Michigan State University. Instrumental in the development process were Toni Vazquez and Myron M. Miller, international business consultants. Mr. Miller now serves as executive-in-residence at Michigan State University.

The U.S. Department of Commerce adopted CORE as one of its principal training tools. The U.S. and Foreign Commercial Service has used CORE in its field offices throughout the country. This project is known as the Export Qualifier Program. International trade specialists in these offices have been trained in the use of this tool to counsel client companies. The U.S. Small Business Administration has also adopted this software as a training and decision support tool. CORE software can be purchased by contacting the Instructional Media Center, Marketing Division, Michigan State University, P.O. Box 710, East Lansing, MI 48826-0710; Tel: 517-353-9229; Fax: 517-432-2650; E-mail: imc05@msu.edu.

CHAPTER 3

Researching and Selecting Export Markets

Upon completing this chapter, you should be able to

- determine market attractiveness using systematic, quantitative, and qualitative screening of country measures;
- understand the components of market attractiveness;
- understand why export market potential assessment is important;
- conduct export market research;
- follow the process in assessing global market opportunities;
- use various sources of information.

Few of us know even simple facts about the geography, culture, and economy of countries other than our own. Even fewer people have at their fingertips details that tell whether their goods will sell in a particular foreign market. Therefore potential issues in exporting must be carefully researched and evaluated before the decision is made to enter a foreign market.

You can probably bypass market research if there is little at stake. An example of this is a firm that chooses simply to respond to unsolicited orders from foreign customers. However, when the risks are substantial, it is essential to clarify certain potential issues before committing greater resources.

In some cases, companies know what specific markets they want to investigate when they sponsor market research, and they provide sufficient funds to cover field research in each market. However, very often they do not have any particular markets in mind when they conduct the research and such market research is thus aimed at identifying markets that are most promising. In still other cases, they ask for research on more markets than, given the budget, can be investigated in depth.

Export market research should answer the following key questions (Cavusgil, 1985, 1993; Craig & Douglas, 1999):

- Which countries offer the best prospects?
- In which foreign markets can a company's products be sold profitably?
- Does the foreign market require any modification of the product?
- What distribution channels and arrangements should be employed in selling to a particular country?
- How sensitive is market demand to product price?
- What should the landed and retail prices be?
- What sales volume and margins can be expected in each market?
- What performance criteria should be used to monitor company activity in each foreign market?

Perhaps the most important concern of export market research is the identification of attractive foreign markets for company products and the assessment of sales potentials in each selected market. The other major purpose of export market research relates to distribution: the identification, selection, motivation, and evaluation of foreign distributors and agents.

For many firms the first two tasks are the most problematic, and many marketers view them as the primary challenges of export marketing. Although substantial resources may be expended for export marketing research, managers note that they have yet to develop a "perfect" procedure for dealing with these two tasks. An approach that appears suitable for one market may not be satisfactory for another.

In most firms, the process of analyzing foreign market opportunities is fairly unstructured. The importance placed on foreign market opportunity analysis is strongly related to the emphasis placed on exporting. That is, if firms place a low level of importance on exporting, then export market opportunity analysis suffers.

The process of export market opportunity analysis usually evolves from one person's handling of the job or from a series of exporting "change agents" (Czinkota & Ronkainen, 2002). Many companies employ experienced international marketing people who have a good grasp of the potential for their industry in different countries around the world. Others find it difficult to hire or train individuals for international positions.

The following attributes characterize identification and analysis of foreign market opportunities by companies (Miller, 1993a):

- Identifying and analyzing new foreign market opportunities are unplanned and performed sporadically.
- The importance and complexity of foreign market research are underestimated.
- Their export market research activities are carried out without written procedures and clear definition of responsibilities.
- Most research reports on foreign markets stay with middle management, suggesting that top management attaches little importance to export market research.

Subjectivity in Export Market Research

Export market research is generally more subjective and less precise than domestic market research for several reasons. First, executives usually attribute the difference to the limited experience of managers in conducting export market research and the difficulties encountered in gathering relevant, accurate, and timely information. The nature and complexity of export market research is very much a function of a company's international involvement and the risks it encounters. When the amount at stake is marginal, managers prefer to make decisions on the basis of limited research, aided by judgment calls.

Second, the stage of company internationalization is also a significant determinant of the nature and complexity of export market research. The extent of international involvement, which varies from opportunistic to fully committed exporting, dictates the nature of research and the types of information to be gathered.

Third, many company executives admit that export research is most useful when it is ongoing and systematic. However, some companies view export market research as an intermittent activity and approach it haphazardly (Craig & Douglas, 1999).

Effective Export Market Research

Most firms can do export market research that renders fruitful outcomes. However, it requires resources and commitment from the management. The following questions in conducting export market research should be posed in order to gain tangible benefits (Cavusgil, 1985):

- Has management developed an export marketing program with accompanying market research tasks?
- Does management understand that foreign market research is an ongoing activity?
- Have procedures been developed to monitor, evaluate, and correct export marketing performance?
- Has the firm provided the means for timely warning of pertinent changes in foreign markets?
- Does the export market research seek the most specific information concerning the firm's products?
- Is mature judgment being applied to the facts developed by the export market research efforts?

Specific export market research tasks should be identified within the framework of an overall export marketing plan. The company should ensure that the necessary information for monitoring, evaluating, and correcting export activity is made available to management through such efforts.

Importance of Management Judgment in Export Market Research

It is also important for management to recognize that export market research is no substitute for judgment. Market researchers should always attempt to understand the reason behind the events and bare facts. In order to understand future developments, they must know not only what has happened, but also why it happened. They also should investigate the implications of current and past trends for their company and its sales.

Furthermore, export market research should always search for specific information concerning the company's products. Market demand for a type of product, such as medical equipment, should not be confused with the potential demand for a specific brand.

Since the number of world markets to be considered by a company is very large, it is neither possible nor advisable to research them all. Thus a firm's time and money is spent most efficiently and effectively in a sequential screening process. This process eliminates many unsuitable countries from the large number of available alternatives.

Most companies have not developed a formal procedure for analyzing foreign market opportunities. Some experienced exporters employ an approach that tends to support the value of such a sequential process as follows (Cavusgil, 1985; Craig & Douglas, 1999):

> Stage One: Preliminary screening/country or region selection
> Stage Two: Analysis of industry market potential
> Stage Three: Partner choice and structuring the relationship
> Stage Four: Assessing company sales potential

Stage One: Preliminary Screening/Country or Region Selection

The first stage in this sequential screening process for the company is to select the more attractive countries that it wants to investigate in detail. At this preliminary screening stage, factors at a broad level are usually used, relying mostly on secondary data sources including Internet sources and government publications. Typical factors that are usually considered include the demographic/physical environment, political environment, economic environment, and social/cultural environment.

Demographic/Physical Environment

The demographic and physical environments of potential markets are probably one of the most popular factors firms consider in evaluating the potential market size and feasibility. The following variables are usually found to be helpful:

- Population size, growth, and density
- Urban and rural distribution of population
- Climate and weather conditions

- Shipping distance
- Product-significant demographics
- Physical distribution and communication network
- Natural resources

Political Environment

Even if the demographic/physical environments of a market are attractive, it is probably quite difficult for a firm to enter a market that is politically unstable. It is possible that the government may be practicing unfair regulations against foreign firms or protecting domestic industries and firms. Thus assessing the soundness of the political environment should be carried out considering the following variables (Cavusgil, Knight, & Riesenberger, 2008):

- System of government
- Political stability and continuity
- Ideological orientation
- Government involvement in business
- Government involvement in communications
- Attitudes toward foreign business (trade restrictions, tariffs, nontariff barriers, bilateral trade agreements)
- National economic and development priorities

Economic Environment

A country may be demographically promising and politically sound, but entering the country is yet to be justified in terms of economic strength. Without enough buying power from consumers, businesses, and the public sector, your firm's products may have limited appeal. Demand for your products should be assessed based on the following variables:

- Overall level of development
- Economic growth: GNP, industrial sector growth
- Currency: inflation rate, availability, controls, stability of exchange rate
- Balance of payments

- Per capita income and distribution
- Disposable income and expenditure patterns

Social/Cultural Environment

Even though the social/cultural environment may not play an eminent role in the beginning of an export venture into a market, it may result in formidable long-term obstacles. The following factors should be considered:

- Literacy rate, educational level
- Existence and size of the middle class
- Similarities and differences in relation to home market
- Language and other cultural considerations

Once the relevant criteria for screening countries have been identified, company executives can assign weights to them, based on the relative importance of each criterion from the company's perspective, and then compare countries. This comparison provides a basis for selecting a group of countries on which to focus further research (Cavusgil, 1997).

The export marketer will eliminate some foreign markets from further consideration on the basis of this preliminary screening. An example would be the absence of comparable or linking products and services, a deficiency that could hinder the potential for marketing company products.

The country/region choice is a strategic choice with very long-term consequences. It requires much learning about the country, and later abandonment of this choice might be very costly. One approach to regional market choice is to use "gateway" countries. These countries offer more receptive environments and can be used as a base for launching business operations in other surrounding/similar countries. Typical examples of gateway countries include

- Hong Kong → China
- Australia → New Zealand
- Finland → Russia
- Turkey → central Asian republics

Stage Two: Analysis of Industry Market Potential

Once several attractive countries have been selected for further study, the firm is ready for the second stage of the screening process. This stage involves assessing the industry-level market potential for each selected foreign market. At this stage, the company will be interested in determining the present and future aggregate demand for the industry within the selected markets. The factors to be studied at this stage include market access, product potential, and local distribution and production potential (Cavusgil, 1997).

Market Access

Information about trade barriers, tariffs, and duties can be gleaned from government contacts and publications. It is important to remember that trade barriers are often linked to the form of the product or the level of value addition. Therefore there is some flexibility in structuring operations so that favorable financial outcomes can be obtained. For example, final assembly or repackaging in the importing country can lead to a lower import duty classification. Useful information having to do with market access includes the following:

- Limitations on trade: tariff levels, quotas, trade barriers
- Documentation and import regulations
- Local standards, practices, and other nontariff barriers
- Patents and trademarks
- Preferential treaties with trading partner countries
- Legal considerations: investment, taxation, repatriation, employment, code of laws

Product Potential

Indicators of population, income levels, and consumption patterns should be considered. Useful information having to do with product potential includes

- customer needs and desires;
- product consumption;

- exposure to and acceptance of the product;
- availability of complementary products;
- industry-specific key indicators of demand;
- attitudes toward products of foreign origin;
- the number of competitors (the U.S. Department of Commerce tracks market shares for many different industries across a number of countries in its *Market Shares Report*);
- competitive strengths, weaknesses, and offerings.

Local Distribution and Production Potential

In addition, statistics on local production trends along with imports and exports of the product category are helpful for assessing industry market potential. Often an industry will have a few key indicators or measures that will help them determine the industry strength and demand within a foreign market. A manufacturer of medical equipment, for example, may use the number of hospital beds, the number of surgeries, and public expenditures for health care as indicators to assess the potential for its products. Some of these indicators include

- local production;
- the amount and growth of imports;
- conditions for local manufacture;
- regional and local transportation facilities;
- the availability of manpower;
- potential local manufacturers;
- potential foreign manufacturers;
- existing distributors/agents of foreign manufacturers;
- potential distributors who carry my products;
- any discriminatory measures of local government.

Stage Three: Partner Choice and Structuring the Relationship

An effective partner can play a very important role in determining your success in a foreign market. Your company's sales potential is sometimes inextricably linked to the business strategy and approach of your business partner. Great products can remain limited in market share if your local distributors are not aggressive enough, do not have the resources to expand their reach, or are using ineffective sales techniques. Therefore selecting the right partners is a critical decision. The partner selection process includes examining and deciding on the following factors (Bello & Williamson, 1985; Cavusgil et al., 2008):

1. What type of partner are you looking for (distributor, franchisee, licensee, contractor, freight forwarder, or service provider)?
2. What are your selection criteria for this partner?
3. What is the candidate selection process?
4. How does the choice of a partner impact your company's sales potential in the foreign market?

Selecting Partners Using Decision Support Software

Managers often find themselves with no criteria to use in selecting potential partners. This process could be further exasperating if the decision maker or firm has no substantial previous experience in foreign partner selection. To help managers who are uncomfortable with the section process, the Center for International Business Education and Research (CIBER) at Michigan State University has developed a number of computer-based decision support tools that can help in the partner selection process. Details about this software can be obtained from the Instructional Media Center, Marketing Division, Michigan State University, P.O. Box 710, East Lansing, MI 48826-0710; Tel: 517-353-9229; Fax: 517-432-2650; E-mail: imc05@msu.edu or administrator@ciber.msu.edu.

Partner Selection Criteria

Just like potential domestic business partners, your foreign business partners should exhibit the following characteristics (Cavusgil et al., 2008; Czinkota & Ronkainen, 2002):

• Financially sound and resourceful
• Competent management with an aggressive outlook
• Willing and able to invest in your business

- Good knowledge of your industry, and should offer functional complementarities
- Known in the marketplace and well connected
- Committed in the long run
- Good reputation

However, in an international partnership, ideal foreign partners should have the following additional characteristics to help you do business locally:

- Substantial experience in the industry
- Well-developed distribution channels
- Local market knowledge
- Previous work experience with foreign partners
- Trustworthiness

Partnering Agreement

There are a number of factors that have to be considered in forming the relationship with a foreign partner:

- What should be your legal relationship to the partner?
- Do we want a formal agreement?
- Should there be a courtship period?

If there is to be a legal agreement, its contents should be in terms of

- mutual tasks and responsibilities;
- method of compensation;
- decision-making autonomy;
- exclusive territory;
- dispute resolution;
- termination clauses.

Cultivating the Partnership

It is in your best interest to maintain a good, long-term relationship with your foreign partners. Disruptive relationships may result in additional costs associated with new partner recruiting and training. Also, it is usually time-consuming to recruit and train new partners, leading to loss of business. The most unwanted consequence of switching partners is potential disclosure of core business competences to the old partner (Bello & Williamson, 1985; Czinkota & Ronkainen, 2002). Also, remember that your old partners could be your future competitors after the relationship. Therefore your firm needs to put every effort into maintaining a good relationship with foreign partners. You can do a number of things to make your partnership more effective. These include assessing your partner's expectations, building a successful relationship, implementing practical performance measurement, and future planning.

Assessing a Partner's Expectations

- What will the partner get out of this relationship?
- Do we have a realistic understanding of his expectations?
- What can we do to help him achieve his objectives?

Building a Successful Relationship

- What can we do to ensure a successful relationship?
- How do we build trust and cultural empathy?
- How can we provide our partner with technical and managerial support?
- What can we learn from failed/unsuccessful partnerships?

Implementing Practical Performance Measurement

- What criteria should we use to measure satisfaction/performance in this venture?
- How should we monitor the relationship?

Future Planning

- What plans shall we make for the future of this relationship?
- Under what conditions can the relationship be terminated? By whom?

Effective collaborative arrangements translate into success in foreign markets. Therefore it is important that senior management is fully involved in the process of partner selection and that an appropriate collaborative strategy is chosen and implemented.

Stage Four: Assessing Company Sales Potential

The fourth stage of the screening process involves assessing company sales potential in those countries that prove promising based upon earlier analyses. The issues that must be addressed at this stage include forecasting sales volume, landed cost, cost of internal distribution, and other determinants of profitability.

Forecasting Sales Volume

Company sales potential depends on factors such as

- partner capabilities;
- access to distribution;
- competitive environment;
- pricing and financing;
- human/financial resources available;
- market penetration timetable;
- company risk tolerance;
- special local links, contacts, and capabilities.

Sales volume forecasting can be effectively carried out when the following factors are adequately measured:

- Size and concentration of customer segments
- Projected consumption statistics
- Competitive pressures
- Expectations of local distributors/agents

Landed Cost

Exporting products to a foreign market incurs extra costs that managers usually do not consider for the domestic market. Therefore estimating landed cost turns out to be quite complicated. The following should be considered in estimating landed cost:

- Costing method for exports
- Domestic distribution costs
- International freight and insurance

Cost of Internal Distribution

Internal distribution refers to the activities carried on after the product reaches the target country. Related costs include

- tariffs and duties;
- value-added tax;
- local packaging and assembly;
- margins/commissions allowed for the trade;
- local distribution and inventory costs;
- promotional expenditures.

Other Determinants of Profitability

Other determinants of profitability include

- price levels of local competitors;
- competitive strengths and weaknesses;
- credit practices;
- current and projected exchange rates.

Competitive information in the foreign market is often very valuable in determining export prices, and hence export profitability. To help project sales, factors such as quality, design, sizing, and packaging should also be compared to competitive offerings. Typical methods available for gauging company sales potential include

- field research;
- survey of end users and distributors;
- trade audits;
- competitor analysis;
- gauging the qualifications of the partner;
- test marketing and extrapolation.

Sales Forecasting Techniques

Country attractiveness and potential assessments deal with what can be achieved in a market. Forecasts incorporate conditions existing in the market and are statements of what is likely to happen given the present situation. Forecasting requires a number of technical skills that are useful in most markets. The most commonly used forecasting techniques are product life cycle (PLC) analysis, judgmental forecasts, the Delphi method, time series extrapolation, and regression-based forecasting (Cavusgil et al., 2008; Czinkota & Ronkainen, 2002).

Product Life Cycle Analysis

Your products might be at different stages of the PLC in different countries. Therefore each market will have a different level of sales potential associated with the stage of the PLC. It is useful to compare similar markets and analyze the lessons learned from markets that were entered earlier.

One of the techniques used is called the "build-up" method. In this method, various people who are knowledgeable about the market are consulted and their opinions about segments, size, and potential are gradually built up to form an assessment of the market. Given that these estimates are subjective, it is important for you to gather information from different sources to cross-check the reliability and validity of these estimates.

Judgmental Forecasts

Some of your products may not have any sales history for a related or similar market. In such a case, judgmental forecasting assumes importance. Even with forecasts obtained through other techniques, judgmental forecasting helps in adding some rigor to the analysis.

One common way of conducting a judgmental forecast is to obtain separate forecasts from each member of your management team and then pool this information. It is important to add the opinions of overseas staff and reliable external sources (management consultants, partners) to the forecast. In addition, all data sources should be provided to the participants.

The Delphi Method

One commonly used method for conducting judgmental forecasting is the Delphi method. In this method a group of experts goes through a series of rounds of numerical forecasting. Participants are provided each others' feedback at the end of each round. The process leads to a convergence of opinions. The main disadvantage of this process is that sometimes good opinions can be "driven out" by bad opinions if the participants are stubborn.

Time Series Extrapolation

Time series numbers are based on the history of sales for a particular product category in a country. In a time series analysis, statistical procedures are applied to the data set to uncover the inherent trends within the data. The following are key assumptions for this analysis:

- The data are available.
- The past is an indicator of the future.
- Statistics provide a better picture than judgmental analysis.

Extrapolation is a statistical process in which past data points are projected into the future. The main disadvantage of this form of forecasting is the excessive reliance on numerical techniques that might not present an accurate picture of actual market conditions.

Regression Analysis

This is a statistical technique that is used to identify and define relationships between different independent and dependent variables. The objective is to define the relationship between the dependent variable and the independent variables in the form of an equation. This equation can then be used to calculate forecasted values of the dependent variable. A number of computer-based statistical packages also include regression analysis.

As part of the competitor analysis, it is important to also forecast your company's share of the market. Forecasting market share requires an understanding of the local and international competitive environments as well as the internal strengths and weaknesses of your company.

Much of the information needed for the first and second stages of opportunity analysis can be gathered through desk research (e.g., documentary sources, international business publications, and so on). In contrast, the third and fourth stages, selecting a partner and estimating company sales and profitability, often require field research.

The final decision to enter a market cannot be based on secondary data alone. It is important for top managers to develop a feel for the market. A personal visit to the country is therefore essential. Once in the foreign country, it is advisable to try and observe the culture; markets; consumer patterns; and social, political, and economic climates.

Some primary data collection usually will be undertaken in the foreign market, sometimes with the assistance of market research firms. One of the best ways to gather this information is to visit potential foreign end users and distributors. Industry trade shows and fairs are also useful in sizing up the competition and in meeting potential distributors. Advertisements can be placed in trade journals. Value surveys and direct mail campaigns to end users and distributors can also be useful.

Companies can obtain export market research data from a variety of other sources. These include the U.S. Department of Commerce (U.S. DOC) and other governmental agencies; international organizations such as the Organization for Economic Cooperation and Development (OECD), United Nations Food and Agriculture Organization (FAO), United Nations Conference on Trade and Development (UNCTAD), and the General Agreement on Tariffs and Trade (GATT); service organizations such as banks; export trading companies, trade associations, and world trade clubs; as well as a multitude of private research organizations and their publications.

Assistance programs from the U.S. DOC are varied to suit the needs of companies at different stages of internationalization. These include business counseling, new product information service, agent/distributor services, trade opportunities programs, catalog exhibitions, trade missions, and many others.

Approaches That Work

There are some practical approaches to identifying foreign market opportunities (Cavusgil, 1993; Miller, 1993a):

- Use existing distributors as a source of information about developing market opportunities.
- Direct promotion to prospective distributors or other customers.
- Participate in overseas trade fairs and shows.
- Follow major contractors around the world.
- Use trade audits for assessing market potential.

Distributors as a Source for Identifying Foreign Market Opportunities

Companies, large and small, experienced and inexperienced, have learned that perhaps the best way to identify market potentials is to use their foreign distributor/agent contacts. Because of their local market presence, familiarity with customer needs, and contact with governmental agencies, distributors are often the best source of valuable and timely information about market developments. Consequently the more experienced companies tend to shift much of their opportunity analysis and identification functions to capable distributors and representatives. In addition, they establish fairly formalized communication channels for a free and frequent flow of information from those closest to the market back to headquarters.

Advertising Directed to Prospective Distributors or Other Customers

Many companies have found it useful to generate inquiries and subsequent orders by advertising their products in trade journals, directories, or other publications. Still others engage in direct mail campaigns in order to uncover potential markets.

Managers are pleasantly surprised to find that English-language American trade journals often circulate in foreign countries and thus reach prospective customers. Unsolicited inquiries often result from these publications, as well as from favorable word-of-mouth publicity generated by satisfied customers.

Participation in Trade Fairs

A related approach to delineating foreign market opportunities is through attendance at foreign trade fairs and shows. In some cases, thousands of buyers from around the world congregate at international trade fairs for specific industries. Companies generally rate trade fairs high in effectiveness. With the assistance of the U.S. DOC, even small companies with limited resources can participate.

According to an executive at Research Products, Inc., of Madison, Wisconsin, trade fairs are "one way that anyone trying to make assessments of foreign markets can gain a tremendous amount of information."

Following Other Suppliers Around the World

A few companies have been able to expand their supplier relationships with some of their domestic customers to overseas markets. These customers typically are large multinationals involved in contract manufacturing, turnkey operations, or foreign production abroad. Thus it is often desirable to explore the possibility of supplying multinational customers in overseas projects. For example, Snap-on-Tools, of Kenosha, Wisconsin, regularly identifies large construction projects abroad where American companies are involved. It then contacts these companies with an offer to supply tools.

Trade Audits

A technique that is especially suitable for consumer goods companies is the use of trade audits. With trade audits, a company attempts to size up the market potential from the perspective of the channel members. Parker Pen Company, of Janesville, Wisconsin, has refined this approach and finds it very useful in its international market research.

After conducting a thorough, sequential analysis of export market opportunities by using both quantitative and qualitative measures, your company will be able to move on to the next step in internationalization:

structuring your own internal functions so that you will be able to successfully begin and continue exporting.

Exhibit: Master Questionnaire to Discover Facts about a Foreign Market

I. Country

A. Background

- Where is your proposed market?
- What is the physical size of the market?
- What is the population of the market?
- What is the climate?
- What is the geography and terrain?

B. Economy

- What are the major industries and sources of income?
- How much trade exists between your country and this market?
- What is the current balance of payments situation? What was it in the recent past?
- What is the country's gross national product?
- What is the unemployment rate?
- What percentage of employed workers are skilled?
- Is the economy stable?
- Is local capital available?
- What is the annual inflation rate now? In the recent past?

C. Government

- What is the current form of government?
- How are decisions reached?
- What is the government's attitude toward your country? The citizens' attitude?
- How volatile is the political situation?

- Has this country ever nationalized, frozen, or expropriated foreign assets?
- Does this country have a good credit record?
- What current tariffs exist? Trade quotas? Other restrictions?
- What other trade peculiarities exist in dealing with this country?
- What are the laws regarding taxation and repatriation of income?
- What are the foreign ownership laws?
- Overall, what other barriers to market entry exist?
- Is this country a part of a regional trade alliance?

D. Miscellaneous

- What is the national language? Do regional dialects exist?
- What is the language of the business community?
- What is the literacy level?
- Are competent translation services available?
- What percentage of the population enjoys electric power?
- What are the electrical characteristics (voltages, etc.)?
- How developed is the national transportation network?
- What are the principal modes of moving freight? Costs?
- Are efficient harbor and port facilities available?
- Are free trade zones nearby? Local warehousing facilities?
- What is the demographic profile of the population?
- What are the ethnic origins of the population? Does conflict or class rivalry exist?
- What are the significant differences in business and social customs in the country as compared with those in your own country?
- What is the general reputation of this country as a marketplace?

II. Industry

A. Product

- How many units of product are manufactured locally? At what dollar value?
- What are the total imports of product? What are the total exports?
- For what uses is the product manufactured?
- Are there variations in usage?
- Do industry and performance standards exist? What are they?
- What product attributes are common industry-wide?
- Is there full product acceptance? How recent?

B. Market Structure

- Is this a concentrated industry? Competitive?
- What are the relative market shares?
- What main industries use the product?
- What are their respective market shares?

C. Trends

- What was output for the last 5 years? Exports? Imports?
- What was usage for the last 5 years? Projected usage?
- What was the trend in user industries for the last 5 years?
- What is the technological level of the industry in general? In the user industries? Do constraints exist?
- What are the projected sales for the product?
- What are the short-term growth prospects for the industry overall? Long-term prospects?

III. Marketing

A. Media

- What types of advertising are generally used? Average costs? Intensity level? Importance in the marketing mix?

- Are there local advertising agencies available? How diverse are their capabilities?
- What are the major trade periodicals? Are they widely read?
- Are trade fairs and exhibitions held regularly?
- Is direct marketing a viable technique? Are support services available?
- What other sales promotion techniques are used?
- What about general marketing support services like photography, graphic arts, printing, and so on?
- What seems to be the most effective method or channel of communication?
- How much information is carried by salesmen? What is their relative importance?

B. Distribution Channels

- What are the most popular methods of distribution?
- What are the various distribution levels?
- What is the average inventory carried at each level?
- What storage facilities usually exist at each level?
- What is the average delivery time of product between distribution levels?
- What are the average per-unit distribution costs between levels?

C. Customers

- Who is the typical customer for your products?
- Where is the customer located? What is the customer's job function?
- When does the customer usually buy? At what quantity?
- What aspects of the product influence the customer's decision?
- Does a buying decision require a consensus? If so, who are the key buying influences?
- How important is price in the buying decision? Have widely recognized price points developed?

- What are the customer's preconceptions about the product? Performance expectations?
- Who are potential new customers for your products?
- What advantages or disadvantages do you possess over a customer's present suppliers?
- Are customer buying habits regular and predictable? How are buying plans developed for the future?

D. Backup Services

- What extra services does the customer expect? What services does the customer need?
- How easy is it to set up repair and maintenance facilities? Are trainable personnel available?
- What marketing assistance do agents/distributors expect? What services do they need?

IV. Competition

A. Basic Data

- Who are your major competitors? Number of branches? Locations?
- What are their respective market shares?
- Which are from your country, local, other? Rank in number employees and total sales?
- When did they enter the market? With what level of success?
- How sharp is their organization? Strengths? Weaknesses?
- Do competitors have a built-in edge over you such as a tax break or special status? If so, what is it?
- What are some possible short- and long-term objectives for your competitors? What is their research and development capability?
- What competitors are avoiding the market? Why?
- Are new competitors preparing for market entry?

B. Marketing Considerations

- Describe competitors' sales organizations.
- What is the relationship with agents and distributors?
- What is the pricing structure? Discounts? Allowances? Warranty?
- How are advertising, product literature, and general sales promotion handled?
- Do competitors regularly participate in trade fairs and exhibitions?
- What financing and credit terms does the competition offer?
- How is product distribution handled? Structure? Methods? What are shipment and delivery lead times?
- How is repair and maintenance service handled?
- Is advisory or application assistance provided? Free of charge?
- How well has the competition responded to changes in the marketplace?

C. Product

- What are the individual products supplied by each competitor?
- How complete are their product lines?
- Are their products imported or made locally? Is there a reason for this?
- How do their products compare in quality, performance, durability?

(Adapted from Jack H. Atkinson, *Export marketing manual: A results-oriented guide for the eighties*. Charlotte, NC: MacKenzie-Koch Associates, 1981 [from black binder in CIBER].)

CHAPTER 4

Exploring International Entry Modes

Upon completing this module, you should be able to

- understand the process of internationalization;
- list and explain various modes of foreign market entry and expansion;
- explain the process, advantages, and disadvantages of each mode of market entry;
- identify the characteristics of alternative methods of foreign market entry;
- use the framework presented to decide on an appropriate foreign market entry mode.

The entry mode that your company uses to penetrate a foreign market will have a long and lasting impact on the success of your business and on its operations in that market (Agarwal & Ramaswami, 1992). In the past couple of decades, increased globalization, the opening of traditionally closed markets, and the emergence of new organizational forms of market entry have heightened managers' awareness of the entry mode choice decision.

Entry mode selection and implementation is an integral and crucial part of the firm's internationalization process. First, let's take a look at different modes of entry managers can consider.

Most companies follow an internationalization process that can be divided into three main stages (Cavusgil, Knight, & Riesenberger, 2008; Czinkota & Ronkainen, 2002):

1. Experimental involvement: At this stage the company is an intermittent exporter. Typically the firm exports to one or two geographically close markets. Whenever a company takes an exporting initiative at

this stage, it will export to countries that are psychologically closest to its domestic market.

2. Active involvement: At this stage the company systematically begins identifying foreign markets for export. International business is given importance in the overall priorities of the company and specific resources are devoted to developing international business opportunities.

3. Global involvement: At this stage the company has developed a broad spread of international business activities. The company seeks and develops competitive advantages through the configuration of its international activities. Coordination of the company's international business is undertaken at a global strategy level.

Companies can employ three broad approaches to selling their products in foreign markets. These methods of selling products in foreign markets are called the modes of foreign market entry. Within the three broad categories of foreign market entry modes, companies can choose from a wide variety of business arrangements. The three broad classifications are direct selling, indirect market entry, and direct company presence.

Direct Selling

In direct selling situations, your company interacts with the customer directly or through someone who represents your organization. There are several options available to you as an exporter to establish direct sales channels using representatives/agents, distributors/importers, or overseas retailers.

Representatives/Agents

An agent is a person who represents your organization. Typically agents or representatives are responsible for selling your products but are not directly responsible for the payment of goods. A representative might carry several similar lines and can sell them to customers through catalogs or manufacturer's samples.

Once a representative has obtained an order, it is your firm's responsibility to check the overseas customer's credit and payment history, as the representative is not taking title to the goods. Most legal experts advise that you should use the term representative rather than agent, as some legal systems (including that of the United States) treat an agent as someone who directly represents your organization and is responsible for its actions.

Distributors/Importers

Distributors and importers take title to the goods sold to them and then sell them along the channel to the next customer. Distributors can have varying levels of involvement in implementing your marketing strategy. Some of them might help with advertising and sales promotions, while others have a dedicated sales force that provides service to customers and helps in establishing point of sale displays.

A distribution arrangement can be especially beneficial if your product has a strong brand name and established demand in a particular market. If this is not the case, then extensive communication is required with customers (based on the nature of the product), requiring greater manufacturer involvement.

Overseas Retailers

Sales to foreign retailers are mostly for consumer goods. One major advantage of this method is that the price of goods can be kept low because no significant intermediaries are involved. Some storeowners actually might want the services offered by an agent, including ordering, following up on orders, and taking care of claims. As the role of some intermediaries in this method increases, selling directly to overseas retailers becomes less attractive.

Indirect Market Entry

An indirect market entry mode means that your company uses an intermediary to sell your products in a foreign market. In most cases, this intermediary is an export trading company (ETC) based in the exporter's country (Cho, 1987).

Indirect Exporting

One method of foreign market entry is through the use of domestic intermediaries. The most notable form of indirect exporting is through the use of an export trading or management company. Such intermediaries are known as export management companies (EMCs) or export trading companies (ETCs).

What Are the Advantages of Exporting Through an EMC?

Using an EMC has the following advantages (Cho, 1987; Czinkota & Ronkainen, 2002):

- An EMC can select products that are most needed in different countries. They have the ability to choose from a wide variety of product lines.
- An EMC can sell a wide variety of complementary product lines.
- An EMC can ship container loads of mixed products and save on logistics costs.
- An EMC can effectively mediate the fluctuating supply of and demand for seasonal products.
- Exporting through an EMC can provide critically needed leverage and lower costs to a small business that wants to establish a foreign market presence. An EMC can also assume credit and financial risks for the manufacturer.

Export Management Company

An EMC represents various complementary and noncompeting manufacturer's product lines with whom it has agreements over various time periods in foreign markets. The EMC can either be compensated on a commission basis or it may take legal title to the products that it sells. Basically the EMC functions as an outsourced export sales department for a manufacturer. The EMC identifies appropriate markets, establishes local channels of distribution, and helps in implementing marketing communication plans in foreign markets.

A manufacturer using an EMC is making domestic sales. Foreign buyer-related risks are assumed by the EMC. However, such arrangements can vary depending upon the agreement between the manufacturer and the EMC. Some manufacturers might want to establish customer relationships and carry out marketing campaigns on their own to maintain a higher degree of control over the selling process.

Export Trading Company

The ETC is very similar to the EMC, however it has a much diminished client relationship. An ETC typically conducts its business on a case-by-case basis. The ETC concept implies less responsibility toward the supplier or buyer. Each transaction is a separate entity, although there are still economies of scale in dealing with large volumes and multiple product lines. Most ETCs take title to the goods they sell.

Because ETCs deal in a number of product lines represented by multiple manufacturers, there are antitrust considerations associated with their operations. ETCs are protected against antitrust legislation through the Export Trading Company Act. This act allows ETCs to apply for an Export Trade Certificate of Review through the U.S. Department of Commerce. This certificate provides immunity against antitrust prosecution in certain areas.

Advantages and Disadvantages of Using an EMC/ETC

The advantages are (Cavusgil et al., 2008; Cho, 1987) the following:

- Faster and less costly entry into foreign markets
- Better focus on exporting while your company assigns priority to its domestic market
- An opportunity to learn the methods of exporting
- Reduced business and market risk along with the advantage of dealing with an experienced partner

The disadvantages are the following:

- Loss of control over marketing and after-sales service strategies
- Competition from other product lines of the EMC
- The added margins of the EMC, which increase the final prices for the customer

- Reluctance on the part of some foreign buyers to deal with a third party intermediary
- The EMC might neglect your product line compared to others that offer higher profit margins

What Is Licensing?

A license is permission given by one firm to another to allow the latter to engage in a business activity otherwise legally forbidden to it. Broadly speaking, licensing typically involves the transfer of intellectual and proprietary knowledge from your firm to a partner. This knowledge might include the following elements:

- Product and process technology
- Design
- Trademarks, logos, and brand names

A licensing agreement is a contractual arrangement allowing the partner access and usage rights to your firm's proprietary knowledge for a product or process. The contract should clearly spell out what is being licensed and under what terms and conditions. The licensor receives a compensation called a royalty, which can be a fixed amount, vary as a percentage of sales, or be a combination of both.

There are two distinct forms of licensing. A company can agree to allow another firm to manufacture its products using the original brand name or it can create a new one. From the licensor's standpoint, making a product under the licensee's name is less risky than allowing the use of the licensor's brand name. However, giving the licensee flexibility to use a new brand name also might give away proprietary knowledge and control over that knowledge.

The Reasons for the Growth in Licensing Agreements

Licensing among firms has been growing rapidly. Some of the reasons for this growth include the following (Cavusgil et al., 2008):

- It is an effective response to protectionism by country governments.
- Small high-technology firms can easily go international using this route.
- Rising R&D costs make cross-licensing an economically attractive option.
- Shorter product life cycles demand quicker responses, thereby reducing incentives for long-term R&D.
- Emergent industries such as semiconductors and biotechnology are increasingly dependent on licensing.

Advantages and Disadvantages of a Foreign Market Entry Strategy Based on Licensing

Advantages of licensing include the following:

- Licensing is the fastest way to enter a protected market. Most governments offer some sort of protection to domestic manufacturers. In markets where there are high barriers to entry, it might be feasible for a manufacturer to license production of its products to a local company.
- Licensing requires minimal investment, as the licensee, in most cases, is already a well-established local manufacturer.
- The licensee has a sales and distribution network that can be used to sell your products locally.

Disadvantages of licensing include the following:

- Foreign manufacturers might not adhere to the quality standards that you have established for your products.
- The licensee may turn into a future competitor.
- Countries vary in the level of protection that they provide to patents and intellectual property. Typically, developing countries and transitional economies have lax enforcement of patent and intellectual property protection.

Franchising

Franchising provides a greater level of control over the selling processes of your products than exporting. A franchising arrangement allows the franchisee the right to manufacture and sell your products along with your brand name.

The franchiser provides a variety of services to the franchisee. These can include management help and training, access to proprietary product and process knowledge, access to selected suppliers, and the use of advertising for a well-established brand. Most franchising agreements are of a longer duration and are based on a stronger relationship than agreements with foreign distributors.

When Is Franchising a Good Option?

1. A strong product line with well-known brand names in many foreign markets is a good candidate for franchising. Leveraging the strength of your brand equity will provide economies of scale and scope for your firm.

2. There is similarity in marketing needs in the foreign country compared to your home country. Franchising typically involves replicating standard processes or "recipes" for success. This is only workable if there are sufficient similarities in needs of consumers, offering standardization potential of a firm's offerings. Franchising works particularly well across horizontal segments in different countries. These are segments with similar tastes, income levels, and psychographic profiles in many seemingly different country markets.

3. The franchisee has to invest in the business, therefore the capital needs for franchising businesses are not as great. Developing an effective network of franchisees requires helping to start a string of small and medium-size businesses. The replicable franchising operation has to be stripped down to a level where the economics of investment and operating costs make sense for the small business owner.

4. A large proportion of the raw materials or ingredients required for making your products must be available locally. Franchising arrangements require local manufacture of your products, which will lead to a large number of manufacturing locations. This adds logistical

and supply-related complexity to the business. Importation of raw materials and supplies can greatly increase the costs of your products and can make prices uncompetitive in the foreign market.

5. Given the fact that there will be a large number of franchisees, there should be some economies of scale in the manufacturing of small batches of the product. For example, fresh hamburgers have a limited batch size, based on the consumption rate. There would be little economies in manufacturing large quantities, as most would go to waste due to spoilage.

Management Contracts

A management contract represents an arrangement that allows another firm to manage your foreign activities on behalf of your company. The managing company has the same role as a multinational's local team running a subsidiary operation. Typically a management contract would include the day-to-day running of a business, including managing all the functional areas (marketing, finance, operations, and human resource management). However, management contracts do not allow the managing foreign firm to make capital investment or financing (debt/equity) decisions.

Management contracts are often found supplementing other international business arrangements. For example, a management contract could be associated with licensing, a turnkey project, or a joint venture. The disadvantage of a management contract is that it does not allow your firm to build an entrenched market position in the foreign country. Most management contracts are concentrated in particular industries such as the hospitality and transportation industries.

What Is the Compensation Structure and Time Frame for Management Contracts?

Most management contracts have complex, multilayered compensation structures. They are combinations of flat fees along with incentives and variable charges. Sometimes the compensation is based on the time period of the contract. Management contracts in the hotel and hospital management business can be for periods of up to 20 years.

Turnkey Contracts

A turnkey contract is an arrangement in which a contractor is responsible for setting up a facility from start to finish. The facility may be a factory, an infrastructure project such as a highway or bridge, or a technical facility such as an oil rig.

In a turnkey operation, the contractor is responsible for all activities that are part of establishing the facility as a fully functioning unit. This can include design, engineering, provision of technology, civil works, installation and commissioning of equipment, and seeing the project through the startup phase. A large number of turnkey projects are handled by engineering firms.

Contract Manufacturing/International Subcontracting

This arrangement is based on subcontracting manufacturing of your company's products to an offshore manufacturer. Most multinational companies resort to this arrangement to take advantage of lower labor costs in developing countries. There is an element of transfer of technology and know-how in these arrangements. This transfer of technology is covered under a separate licensing agreement.

Contract manufacturing has gained importance with the development of export processing zones (EPZs) by a host of developing and developed countries. EPZs are special zones set up by the local government to encourage export-intensive industry. These zones are mostly free from customs regulations and tariffs. EPZs also provide infrastructure for conducting business to both local and foreign firms.

Direct Company Presence

A company can decide to establish its own presence in a foreign market. This strategy can be motivated by a number of economic and strategic factors. Some of the common methods of directly establishing a market presence are joint venture, wholly owned subsidiaries, and strategic alliances.

Joint Ventures

Joint ventures are a form of partnership between two firms to create a new legally independent entity to achieve the common objectives of the involved partners. There could be equity participation in the joint venture. However, involved firms often make contributions of various resources, such as financial investment, technology, and know-high, and even management skills, depending on the agreement. Some of the advantages of joint ventures include the following:

- Joint ventures may represent an alternative to staying out of a "closed" market.
- In a fast-changing global environment with rapid technological change and large capital requirements, small firms may find joint ventures an easy way to build a global business presence.
- Joint ventures can be used to gain access to technology, channels of distribution, or suppliers. In this sense they can also be used to preempt your competitors from gaining access to these resources.

Wholly Owned Subsidiaries

Companies form wholly owned subsidiaries in a foreign market when they need to control foreign business operations very closely. The reasons for this high degree of control could be related to marketing, manufacturing, or protection of proprietary knowledge. Sometimes multinational corporations need tight controls to respond effectively when implementing global strategies, which might not always have a locally optimal outcome associated with them. Successfully implementing global strategies requires a high degree of coordination. Wholly owned subsidiaries can be marketing companies, manufacturing companies, or any other combination of value-adding activities.

Strategic Alliances

In forming a strategic alliance, two or more firms form a strategic collaboration that is typically nonequity based, pooling together the resources and strengths of the various players, and furthering their strategic business development objectives. Increased global competition, rapidly surfacing international opportunities, and shortening product life cycles are some of the factors responsible for the tremendous growth in strategic alliances over the last few years.

Corporate alliances have evolved as a competitive ploy to enhance market power and establish a hold on supply chains. Smaller companies have used them to build defenses against larger, global players. Larger firms have used alliances to redefine the way business is carried out and realize tremendous efficiencies from closer cooperation with supply chain partners. The widespread use of information technology has served as a key enabler in making these alliances successful.

Entry Decision Criteria That Work

There are some criteria that managers use when deciding upon a mode of entry for a foreign market. These criteria fall into two broad categories: economic criteria, which are related to financial considerations, and strategic criteria, which determine the global coordination and configuration of the company's international business operations (Osland & Cavusgil, 1996). Specific strategic criteria include the locus of control, resource commitment, resources transferred, motivation, and other relevant dimensions of foreign market entry modes.

Locus of Control

The degree of control of foreign business activities is a critical factor in determining the success of the international venture. Effective control mechanisms allow the following:

- Implementation of strategies
- Coordination of global actions
- Resolution of cross-national disputes in an optimal manner
- Sharing of resources and profits

Increased control also leads to deeper levels of commitment to the foreign business venture. This, in turn, produces higher risk and escalated costs. In order to gain control, firms have to commit resources to control systems. In general, a higher level of ownership in a foreign enterprise renders a higher degree of control over its operations. Therefore the highest degree of control is offered by wholly owned subsidiaries.

Resource Commitment

Resource commitment is tightly linked to the question of control. The greater the firm's resource commitment, the higher the level of control desired. In addition, higher levels of control will necessitate the allocation of resources to information and control systems. Resource commitment also flows from the business strategy of the firm: strategically important ventures will have access to a larger share of the firm's resource pool. Thus export typically requires the lowest level of resource commitment, while wholly owned subsidiaries as a mode of market entry require the highest level of resource commitment.

Resources Transferred

Different foreign market entry modes require varying degrees of transfer of resources. The largest transfers occur in the cases of wholly owned subsidiaries. Here, capital, technology, and management are transferred from the parent to the subsidiary organization. Other less intensive methods require lower levels of resource transfer. For example, licensing requires the transfer of technology and proprietary knowledge, whereas joint ventures might require both capital and management transfers along with the transfer of technology.

The resource transfer issue is also closely related to control and resource commitment issues. Sometimes it becomes necessary to transfer resources to establish a strong negotiating position with the local government. Many developing country governments expect foreign companies to invest in the host country, thereby creating infrastructure and generating employment in addition to transferring technology and management skills.

Motivation

A number of potential benefits can motivate firms to enter foreign markets (Burton & Schlegelmilch, 1987; Cavusgil, 1993):

- Access to the attributes of a market or a partner. For example, a potentially attractive market or a technologically sophisticated partner.
- Achievement of economies of scale by selling in international markets, allowing the firm to sell larger volumes of its products worldwide.
- Learning by producing and selling in lead markets or by forming joint ventures or alliances in the R&D area.
- Diversifying business risks by operating in a larger number of negatively correlated markets.
- Shaping competition by raising entry barriers, fixing prices, or gaining a first mover advantage.
- Taking advantage of a "closed" market situation by entering into a collaborative arrangement with a local partner.

Differing motivations will lead to different foreign market entry modes. The choice of an entry mode and the structural arrangement of a business in a country will vary as the motivations of the firm entering a market change over time.

Other Relevant Dimensions of Foreign Market Entry Modes

There are other factors that affect a firm's foreign market entry modes, including time limitations, space limitations, and payment methods (Cavusgil et al., 2008).

Time Limitations

Each market entry mode has its own time limitations. Licensing and franchising agreements have time frames built into them. This contrasts with foreign direct investment and exporting operations, which have no time barriers associated with the business arrangement.

Space Limitations

Space limitations are concerned with the geographical area within which the business arrangement is valid. Licensing, franchising, and joint ventures are all valid only within a certain geographical territory.

Government regulations also might affect the space limitations of a business arrangement.

Payment Methods

Various international business arrangements have a number of payment methods associated with them. Fees, royalties, dividends, and profit sharing can be part of complex structures that are used to compensate the parties involved in an international business venture. Countertrade, which uses alternative means of payment in lieu of monetary payment, can be another mechanism for carrying out transactions. Companies have to evaluate three dimensions of these payment methods:

1. The cost of using a particular payment method
2. The control aspects of using a payment method
3. The flexibility associated with a payment method

Decision Factors of Foreign Market Entry

Your company's choice of a foreign market entry mode is governed by a number of internal and external factors, including product-related factors, market-based factors, and organizational factors (Zhao, Luo, & Suh, 2004).

Product-Related Factors

Your company has to answer the following product-related questions to select a mode of entry effectively:

- What is the nature and range (in terms of product line width) of your product offering for the foreign market?
- What marketing strategies are appropriate for this product given its stage in the product life cycle within that market?
- Will the products require any adaptation? If yes, how extensive?
- What advantages can a foreign-based partner bring to selling this product?

Each of these questions has implications for your foreign market strategy. These considerations are linked to the broader issues of control and resource commitment in the foreign market. Wider product offerings, new products, and high levels of adaptation require a far more involved approach than selling a few products that are well established.

Market-Based Factors

Each country market presents a unique marketing challenge for your organization. Therefore you have to consider the following market-related factors before making a foreign market entry decision:

- What marketing strategies are appropriate for your target segment?
- What are the available distribution channels? Are they appropriate?
- What is your "psychic distance" from the market?
- How much experience does your firm have in similar markets?
- What is the geographic spread of your firm's international business operations (number of countries, locations)?
- What is the relative priority of each country market in terms of revenues, profits, or business strategy?

Your answers to these questions will provide guidelines for the kind of market entry strategy that your firm should pursue in a particular country. Once again, your responses to these questions need to be viewed in the larger context of the characteristics of foreign market entry modes.

Organizational Factors

Communication with foreign operations and control of overseas business activities are major concerns in international business. Financial management, marketing decisions, and human resource management issues create a lot of organizational stress. There is always the trade-off between the local and the global optima, with local management supporting the country operation's local interests.

If manufacturing or selling the product requires assets that will be dedicated to the business, then your firm would prefer to retain a high degree of control over its foreign operations. This is in line with the theory that whenever there is asset specificity in the business relationship, the probability of a display of opportunism by the partner is higher, and therefore firms prefer to internalize such activities.

Complex or proprietary technology can also lead to a higher level of internalization of activities. Complexity leads to problems in the valuation and transmission of knowledge. High levels of R&D are associated with the generation of proprietary knowledge and are also linked with higher control-oriented strategies for foreign market entry.

CHAPTER 5

Partnering Strategies

Upon completing this chapter you should be able to

- appreciate the critical role of partnering in international business;
- understand the conceptual basis of business collaboration;
- explain frameworks for business strategy and partner fit analysis;
- understand the monitoring and control strategies available to you as an exporter;
- identify successful partnerships;
- structure effective partnership agreements;
- identify reasons why partnerships fail.

In today's business environment, international marketing activities play an important role in the success of companies. Managing cross-national marketing relationships creates unique challenges for companies because their foreign partners can operate in different political, cultural, legal, and economic environments.

Not many companies today can develop, manufacture, and market their products all by themselves. Increasingly firms seek partnerships to offer value-added products and services to their customers (Osland & Cavusgil, 1996). When a company needs strengths that are different from its own internal strengths, it needs to develop relationships with partners who can offer these complementary strengths. Today, global markets are resembling a landscape of extended networks where firms are collaborating in almost all functional areas to meet unique customer needs. Effective partnering has emerged as a key competitive strength.

For export marketing, local partners in foreign markets often play a crucial role, as exporters are often not familiar with the local business environments and thus local partners fill the local knowledge void of the exporters (Bello & Williamson, 1985). Yet international partnering remains relatively unfamiliar territory for most managers. Given its "soft" nature and because it is primarily based on human relationships, it is hard to structure, monitor, and measure effective partnering. In this chapter we will attempt to develop and present broad guidelines that can help managers in making strategic choices related to international partnering.

Most exporters cannot control their partners through ownership. An exporting strategy renders ownership in foreign-based enterprises unviable. Therefore most exporting firms have to achieve their organizational objectives through arms-length contractual agreements. This arrangement is different from ownership-based structures such as joint ventures and strategic alliances.

Partnering in international business is based on the firm's overall global competitive strategy. The two key dimensions of a company's international strategy that should be considered in international partnering are the following:

1. The international configuration of the firm's value-adding activities such as inbound logistics, manufacturing, outbound logistics, sales, and marketing
2. Coordinating a firm's worldwide activities in order to gain economies of scale and scope

Partnerships allow the company to outsource or perform in collaboration with other firms' value-adding activities that it would have had to perform by itself otherwise. Therefore a firm makes configuration choices by deciding which activities will be performed in what manner and by whom. Coordination implies gaining from economies of scale and scope in performing value-adding activities. Naturally, widely spread out activities outsourced to a large extent are difficult to coordinate.

The costs and benefits of a partnership can be understood by viewing them in the perspective of the firm's value chain. A value chain activity is performed by a partner whenever there is a situation in which the partner can perform the task better than your firm. For example, local distributors in a foreign market will have a better understanding of local market conditions and will have developed relationships with retailing establishments, giving them a competitive advantage. Thus most exporters are likely to benefit from working with local partners.

Potential Strategic Benefits of Partnerships

Partnerships can be based on expectations of the following strategic benefits (Cavusgil, Knight, & Riesenberger, 2008; Kogut, 1988):

- One benefit is gaining economies of scale. Firms, as part of a value chain, can decide to divide value-adding activities among themselves, with each partner focusing on one or more tasks and thereby gaining economies of scale.
- Firms can gain access to knowledge, capability, and technology through partnerships. This is especially relevant where there are asymmetries between firms in terms of these resources. Partnerships can be formed to gain access to distribution channels, product and process technology, or capital. These partnerships offer advantages in terms of lower cost and, more importantly, greater speed to market for your firm.
- Partnerships spread out risks among the partnering firms. Neither partner bears the full risk of the ensuing partnership, thereby reducing the level of risk to which your firm is exposed.
- Partnerships can affect competitive patterns. Partnerships result in deciding who competes with whom and on what basis. Partnerships can be used as a strategic lever to favor competition in your firm's favor. Partnerships can even be used to facilitate collusion.

Partnerships succeed when both partners can see clear benefits from the relationship. However, it is not necessary that the benefits be the same for all partners. Each partner may be extracting different benefits from the relationship.

Strategic Costs of Partnering

The costs of partnerships can be classified into three main categories: costs of coordination, erosion of competitive position, and weakening of your firm's bargaining position.

Costs of Coordinating a Partnership

Coordination between partners requires management time and resources. There are often differences between how partners view their interests in terms of a particular value-adding activity. This could lead to situations where the partners are reluctant to reach solutions that might be beneficial to both partners. For instance, there are always forces for localization of marketing practices rather than standardization from foreign business partners, and these often lead to higher costs of coordinating international strategies.

Global strategies require higher levels of coordination and are therefore more expensive to implement. The greater the similarity in the interests of the partners, the lower the costs of coordinating because the need for monitoring and control systems will be reduced.

Erosion of Competitive Position

Partnerships can change the balance of power by transferring knowledge, technology, and skills from one partner to another (Inkpen & Beamish, 1997). One consequence of this movement of competence can be the creation of new competitors or a loss in strength of traditional competitors. Competitive considerations contribute to increasing the costs of coordinating a partnership. Suspicions about your partner's motives might lead to higher costs of monitoring and control. Take those multinationals from emerging markets like LG and Samsung. They relied on Western technologies for production of their main product lines decades ago. As they have learned from their Western partners, they have become formidable competitors of these firms. Interestingly, they have grown to control the Western market today. Partnering and transferring core business competences can render short-term as well as long-term benefits. However, some serious long-term loss of competitive position should also be considered.

Weakening of Your Firm's Bargaining Position

The benefits or value created as a result of the partnership have to be divided among the partners. Therefore the stronger partner (this can be due to investment in specialized assets, the size or market power of the firm, or specific technology and skills) will gain a larger share of the benefits. This unequal arrangement is because of the weaker firm's adverse bargaining position.

Identifying Ideal Partners

Exporters should carefully assess the qualifications of foreign partners. To minimize the uncertainties and costs associated with identifying a new partner, many exporters look for ways to start new business ventures with existing partners. Existing successful partnerships can provide a springboard for your business by building on past successes in partnering. However, the implications of expanding existing relationships should be examined, as it may lead to an increase in your dependence on the local partner. Therefore, unless your partner base is already well diversified, the implications of increasing your dependence should be carefully assessed. That is, although using existing partners has advantages, it is sometimes safer to diversify your partner base just in case things do not work well with existing partners. It is always better to have other options available.

If you believe it is your better option to go with a new partner, there are three attributes that should be considered when determining the choice of a "right" partner for your organization: compatibility, capability, and commitment (Cavusgil et al., 2008; Czinkota & Ronkainen, 2002).

Compatibility

The ability to work together with your partner is a critical factor for the success of a partnership (Cavusgil et al., 2008). The compatibility between you and your partner's firm must have enough strength and resilience to withstand changing market and environmental conditions. Many organizations talk about firm-to-firm partnerships in terms of marriage. This alludes to the fact that compatibility and the ability to resolve differences are crucial in a prosperous partnership.

Determining the Compatibility of a Potential Partner

- Seek comparability in size and resources if possible. Imbalanced matches could result in problems such as an unreasonable level of dependence or low bargaining power, especially if the local partner is stronger in areas critical to the venture. This does not necessarily mean that the two partners are expected to be comparable in every aspect of business, as companies are often built upon the premise of leveraging the strengths of the other company through partnering. It simply means that your company should strive to have reasonable power in bargaining, and such power often comes from comparable size and resources.

- It is important to determine your strategic fit with the partner. This includes examining the goals and motivations of the partner firm, identifying the resource contributions of the partner to the relationship, and assessing the partner's strengths and weaknesses. A clear and comprehensive understanding of the partner's intentions and abilities leads to realistic expectations from the partnering firm.

- There are likely to be differences between the corporate cultures of the two organizations. However, it is important to assess if these differences are manageable. It is especially important to assess the impact of these differences on the outcomes your firm is seeking from the partnership.

- Besides organizational culture, management policies, procedures, and the structures of the two organizations are also critical variables that need to be examined. Levels of centralization, product and promotion policies, and attitudes toward customer service should be investigated before your partnership agreement is finalized.

- Objective analysis of the partner's market standing is also important. Trends in market share growth, profitability, and costs must be analyzed to arrive at a true picture of the partner's past accomplishments and future potential. The partner organization's image and reputation are also very important for your business success.

- Your partner's legal environment also impacts the partnership. You must understand the legal risks and obligations of your partner, including any unionization of labor, minimum wages, and agreements with employees.

- You need to evaluate the financial strength of your prospective partner. The structure of ownership, liquidity, relationships with local financial institutions, and risk orientation are all relevant factors to investigate.

- The safety, health, and environmental policies of your partner may be major concerns for some businesses. Especially when dealing with businesses in developing countries, it is important to determine that there are appropriate monitoring and control systems in place. Any unwanted incident in these areas could have a catastrophic impact on your corporate reputation and image.

The Importance of Trust in Partnerships

Successful corporate partnerships are not always based on a strategic fit between organizations or on business interests. Sometimes a good relationship between two key personalities from two organizations can lead to success. Therefore it is important to realize that "mutual trust" is probably the single most important variable that determines the success of a partnership.

Trust is especially important at senior management levels. There can be disagreements and problems at lower levels of the organization, but mutual trust between top managers of both organizations can help in ironing out petty differences and retaining the strategic thrust of the partnership.

Capability

Understanding your partner in terms of its business capabilities and competencies will also help you develop a good working relationship with the foreign partner, as it will help form a reasonable level of expectation in your organization. Thus you should strive to identify the core competencies of your prospective partner. Your goal is to seek a partner who will compensate for your weaknesses and lack of reach in the foreign market. Key factors that need to be analyzed include

- market strength and share;
- financial capability;
- marketing skills and experience;

- experience in marketing foreign products and product lines similar to yours;
- distribution assets and capability;
- relationships in the local marketplace;
- skill levels in technology relevant to your products and competence in related selling processes.

Considerations of a partner's capability have to be traded off against the concern that today's partner might turn out to be tomorrow's competitor. The partner should not be so strong as to be able to extract an unfairly large share of the benefits from the partnership.

Commitment

Besides compatibility and capability, there also must be commitment from both sides behind the relationship. This commitment is the core that will allow both firms to weather storms encountered as part of the relationship. There are two questions that can indicate the level of commitment of your prospective partner:

1. Is the partnership affecting a strategic asset or area of the partner's business? Is it based on a star product line or high-performing business area? Naturally managers are more committed to key business areas than to nonperforming product lines.
2. What and how high are the barriers to exit for the prospective partner? Higher barriers to exit will lead to greater levels of commitment from the partner.

For an illustration, consider the Ford-Mazda partnership. In 1979, Ford bought 25% of Mazda Motor Corp. Since then, the two companies have established a web of cooperative projects. While Ford focuses on light trucks such as its Ranger, Mazda engineers Ford's small cars and markets them under its own nameplate. During the four years since 1990, Mazda suffered great losses and turned to its American partner. Three senior executives at Ford were dispatched to Mazda to help the company weather the storm. With the assistance of its partner, Mazda realized a profit of $44 billion in 1993.

Structuring the Partnership

In April 1997, AT&T reported that its net income for the first quarter of the year fell 24% compared with the same period in 1996. The reason for this decline was AT&T's failure to implement an appropriate partnering strategy. Without clear objectives and goals, AT&T entered into collaborative activities of World Partners and Unisource. A lack of aligned economic interests of the partners resulted in a loosely structured alliance. Because of this, joint efforts were unable to meet the uniform quality standards required in contractual provisions, resulting in dismal performance. Obviously it is in your best interest to structure the relationship in a way such that your firm's management can directly influence the decision making of the foreign partner. Alternatively you can create an environment whereby, even without direct influence, the actions of your foreign partner are not detrimental to the interests of your firm. How then do you create a partnership structure that protects your interests? There are two broad strategic approaches available to accomplish this objective.

Manipulation of Material Incentives

Through the manipulation of material incentives your firm can alter the behavior of a partner through threats of punishment and promises of rewards. Partners in a business relationship try to maximize their individual gains, which can sometimes be detrimental to the interests of the other partner.

A necessary condition for the exercise of influence by the exporting firm over a foreign partner's decision making through manipulation of material incentives is that the former has something that the latter needs. This creates a business environment in which the foreign partner has to be dependent on the exporter, and there must be interdependence between the parties.

In most international relationships, both parties are dependent on each other to a certain extent, and the degree of dependence of the two parties may not be equal. Hence the concept of interdependence is useful in understanding such relationships. Interdependence between two entities is defined as the degree to which the objectives of the two parties are realized based on each other's resources and skills.

There are two aspects to interdependence: amount and symmetry. The amount of interdependence between two firms will be high if both partners are highly dependent on each other. Symmetry of interdependence refers to the balance of dependence between two firms. If one partner needs the benefits derived from the relationship more than the other, the relationship is asymmetrical.

Interdependence between the two parties creates a "mutual holdup" or a "mutual hostage" condition, whereby it becomes costly for either party to take action that would be detrimental to the interests of the partner because of the fear of retaliation. Thus objectives can be achieved in exchange relationships through bilateral credible commitments.

The amount and symmetry of interdependence can also be manipulated in cross-national business relationships. For instance, in most cross-national relationships, there is usually a transfer of products, technology, and know-how between the firms. Both partners are dependent on each other for some aspects of their business.

There are two distinct approaches for achieving interdependence that is favorable for the exporter:

1. Vulnerability interdependence: In this approach, interdependence is increased through the transfer of technology and product know-how to the foreign partner.
2. Sensitivity interdependence: This is the "mutual holdup" approach, whereby interdependence is increased through mutual investments in assets specific to the business. This approach leads to intertwined interests and therefore higher levels of interdependence.

With the manipulation of material incentives the exporter can also change the substantive beliefs of the foreign partner. This limits the foreign partner's potential to take action that might be detrimental to the exporter.

Changing Substantive Beliefs

This approach focuses on changing the belief system of your foreign partner to be more compatible with your organization's business interests. This can be done through education of the foreign partner's key employees. This approach will ultimately lead to the convergence of objectives between the exporter and its foreign partner, barring any peculiar circumstances.

Maintaining the Relationship

Formality

Formality in a relationship is defined as the degree to which the continuing functioning of the relationship between two partners is governed by written/prescribed rules and regulations. From the exporter's perspective, formal structure allows greater influence and control over the foreign partner's decision making. However, formal structure also leads to frustration.

With limited autonomy and self-control, the foreign partner may manifest its frustration with aggressive behavior toward the exporter. Such outcomes are detrimental to the quality of the relationship and increase the foreign partner's motivation for opportunistic behavior and withholding information from the exporter.

Amativeness

Amativeness of the relationship is defined as the degree to which a firm adapts the terms of the contract and functioning of the partnership to the business practices of the partner firm's organization/country. The exporter can either impose its corporate norms on the relationship with its foreign partner or it can adopt the foreign partner's norms into the relationship. Naturally, imposing your own norms on the partner will not be viewed as desirable by the partnering firm. On the other hand, adapting your firm's norms to take into account the foreign partner's practices will influence the partner's belief system and will create a framework that allows creation of new relationship-specific norms, thus minimizing the motivations of the foreign partner to take actions detrimental to your business interests.

Control Systems

The purpose of a control system is the regulation of activities to ensure that they conform to established expectations. There are three dimensions of control that need to be incorporated into a cross-national business relationship: extent of control, focus of control, and type of control mechanism.

Extent of Control

The extent of control in the relationship is determined by the locus of the decision-making process in the relationship. If the exporter makes all key marketing decisions, the extent of control is very high. However, delegation of marketing decisions to the foreign partner leads to a loss in the extent of control.

Focus of Control Activities

This dimension explains the organizational activities that are subject to control. In a particular relationship the focus of control might be marketing, finance, or human resource-related activities, or any combination of organizational activities. However, in our case, which deals specifically with exporting situations, we are primarily concerned with marketing and related financial activities.

Each relationship has a scope of activities that are important to the success of that relationship. It is these activities that are the focus of planning and control activities. In the case of most exporters, these are related to marketing, sales, and distribution.

Type of Control Mechanisms

The type of control mechanism that an exporter uses to monitor the behavior of its partners can be classified as formal versus informal controls, and behavior versus outcome controls (Czinkota & Ronkainen, 2002).

Formal Versus Informal Control Systems

Formal controls are defined as management initiated mechanisms that are designed to regulate organizational activities to ensure their conformance to established expectations. Within formal controls systems, organizations can choose either process or output controls. Process controls focus on influencing the means that the foreign partner uses to achieve certain ends. The focus here is on the activity rather than the results. Output controls, on the other hand, control the final output of the process (e.g., the sales volume of a foreign partner).

Informal controls are unwritten, organizational culture-based mechanisms that influence individual or group behavior in organizations. Another difference between formal and informal control systems is in their information requirements. Information requirements for the exporter in implementing a formal control system are prices and business rules, whereas in an informal control system the informational requirements are the common traditions and beliefs between the partners in the relationship.

Behavior- Versus Outcome-Based Control Systems

Behavior-based control systems attempt to monitor the behavior of the foreign partner and the means used by the foreign partner to achieve desired ends. These controls require direct personal surveillance and high levels of management direction and intervention in the activities performed by the foreign partner.

Outcome-based control systems operate on specified performance measures such as sales generated and market share achieved. These systems are also called performance control systems. In outcome-based controls, little monitoring is done by the exporter and the foreign partner's performance is evaluated on objective measures.

Choosing the Right Control Systems

Different control systems require different levels of the exporter's time and resources. The decision to use a given type of control is a function of the ability and willingness of the exporter to invest the required time and resources to implement one or more controls. Furthermore, the exporting firm has to decide whether it needs to use one control approach or a combination of approaches.

Research has shown that if a firm relies on formal controls, it will use a combination of process and output controls. However, if a company relies more on behavior-based controls, it is likely to use process-based controls along with trying to influence the organizational culture and values of the foreign partner.

- The greater the amount of interdependence between the firm and its foreign partner, the more likely it is that the firm will use process and social controls rather than output-based controls over its foreign partner.
- The greater the symmetry of interdependence between the firm and its foreign partner, the more likely it is the firm will use process and social controls rather than output-based controls over its foreign partner.
- The greater the level of formality in the relationship between the firm and its foreign partner, the more likely it is that the firm will use process and output controls rather than social controls over its foreign partner.
- The more a firm adapts its relationship to the norms of the foreign partner's firm/country, the more likely it is the firm will use social control rather than process or output controls over its foreign partner.

Generally speaking, high uncertainty leads to lower levels of economic performance. Likewise, higher quality relationships lead to better economic performance, and higher degrees of vertical control have a positive effect on economic performance. On the other hand, opportunistic behavior by the foreign partner contributes to lower levels of economic performance.

In most international relationships, both parties are dependent upon each other to some extent, resulting in interdependency. This means each involved party is likely to seek some benefits from the relationship, including, but not limited to, exclusive market information, reliable customer service in the local market, a well-developed network with local government officials, advanced technology, management skills, and so on (Bello & Williamson, 1985). These benefits sought after can be better realized when the partners are well integrated in various dimensions. Here are some tips to help maintain a good relationship with foreign partners:

- Partners must be integrated with the company's business information systems. Integration leads to sharing of information both from the company to the partner and vice versa. Information from the partner can provide product and market feedback and intelligence. Close coordination of activities also allows partners to meet critical customer needs (problem solving, consulting, and after-sales service) with the exporter's support.
- Partners, especially distributors, can provide customers a variety of value-added services locally. These can include support in product selection, financing schemes, consulting, and training in the use of products and systems.
- Successful partnerships are based on trust. This is particularly important for international partnerships, as they involve geographic separation as well as cultural barriers. Trust is based on sharing benefits, continuity in relationships, and excellent communication between the exporter and the foreign partner.
- Recognize that partners closer to customers understand their needs better than your organization and are better equipped to meet those needs in a timely and satisfactory manner. Such partners are also important sources of customer feedback, which can contribute to redesigning products or product innovations.
- Eliminate the "us" versus "them" mentality. Consider your partners as part of your organization, striving for common goals and seeking synergies to better achieve profitability targets.
- Involve partners in your company's quality improvement, cost reduction, and other strategic initiatives.
- Establish clear expectations in the relationship. There should be clear rewards for the partner. A set of rules should be implemented at the start of the relationship and adhered to over the long term. The partner must realize that whatever investment they make in this relationship will be beneficial for them.
- The partner must value its relationship with your organization and view it as a strategically important business relationship.
- You must stand by your business partners during economic or market downturns. This is critically important to build loyalty and trust. Attempts to gouge partners will lead to lower levels of

trust and poorer economic performance of the partnership over the long run.

- Provide support to your partners. Successful exporters provide management and technical support to their foreign partners in areas such as marketing, finance, and logistics. This support can also involve training the partner's personnel to upgrade their skills.

- Establish honest, full, and frequent communication. Effective two-way communication is a cornerstone of successful partnerships. It is important to keep your partner fully informed of all major company decisions and policies.

- Your company must establish routine contact with the partner. On these occasions, managers should review strategy, product plans, and functional area policies. Regular sharing of strategic and operating information will lead to better understanding between the two organizations.

- The senior management of your partner organization should have access to top managers within your organization. Accessibility leads to better communication and fewer misunderstandings.

- There will always be sources of friction within the partnership. However, your company needs to develop mechanisms to resolve these conflicts. It is important to respect the partner's interests and to reach decisions that serve the mutual interests of both parties.

- You and your partner's organizations must share the same business mission and vision for the future. Strategic consensus can help in ironing out operating problems in a timely and appropriate fashion.

Partnership Agreement

A key component of a formalized relationship between two organizations is the partnership agreement. It is important to address tough and potential problem areas as part of this agreement. Issues that are neglected at this stage might turn into insurmountable problems later on. The following guidelines can help in crafting a workable partnership agreement:

- The partnership should have a clear focus. There should be clearly laid out objectives, with measurable activities attached to each objective. The scope of the activities and the roles and responsibilities of each partner should be clearly delineated. The agreement should be specific on who will contribute what to the partnership and should also address security concerns if firm-specific proprietary knowledge is involved in the partnership.

- The partnership agreement should establish a structure for the relationship. This structure has to cover legal and management aspects of the partnership. The following concerns need to be addressed:

    o What business and legal structure suits the partnership (joint venture, strategic alliance, partnership)?

    o What are the tax and other financial implications of the structure?

    o What decisions will be made by whom?

    o How will conflicts be handled?

    o How will information be recorded and provided to various stakeholders in the partnership?

    o What will be the language used for communication?

- Financing and tax considerations need to be built into the agreement. Different business cultures will have different approaches to financial management and control issues that must be formally documented to build clear expectations.

- Measures that will be used to evaluate the performance of the partnership must be identified and documented. These can include both qualitative and quantitative measures such as return on investment and customer service. Processes, roles, and responsibilities for accurately capturing, reporting, and monitoring these measures must also be assigned to individuals within the partnership structure.

- The value of each partner's contribution to the relationship must be ascertained. This valuation should include accounting of tangible as well as intangible assets such as reputation and brand names. Especially important is the treatment of proprietary knowledge and intellectual property of the firms involved.

- The agreement must also include appropriate clauses so that future changes in the external and internal environment of the partnership can be accommodated. Such clauses facilitate change and help sustain and develop the relationship.
- Both partners must evaluate the possibility that things might not go well and a divorce might become necessary. Therefore suitable arrangements for a divorce settlement must be considered as part of the partnership agreement. However opt-out clauses should not be easy enough to encourage quick withdrawals based on minor issues.

Sensitivity Analysis

Once a partnership arrangement has been drawn up it might be helpful to test the limits of this business structure's response to internal and external shocks. Revenues, costs, government regulations, market demand, time periods, and other assumptions or facts can be varied to present a series of scenarios that will display the resilience of the partnership. These scenarios should be discussed and presented within both the organizations to clear expectations and provide broad guidelines for the future. The business relationship may fail for any of the following reasons:

- Lack of commitment from the partners
- Cultural differences
- Poor management
- Poor communications
- Lack of a dominant partner (shared management)
- Reliance on each other's skills changes over time
- Change in goals

A lack of commitment often stems from the realization that one partner is carrying an unequal burden of the partnership or is getting a less than fair share of the benefits from the collaborative arrangement. Vastly differing corporate cultures, poor management of the venture, and a lack of open and forthright communication can also doom a partnership to fail. In 1980 TRW signed an agreement with Fujitsu to sell some Fujitsu products, including point-of-sale terminals and automated teller machines. TRW hoped that with the partnership it could increase its profits from its U.S. distribution organization. However, the sales were far below expectations. TRW said it was the result of the Japanese partner's failure to rapidly adapt products to U.S. needs, while Fujitsu blamed its U.S. partner for not providing sufficient input on market decisions. In 1983, Fujitsu bought out TRW's interest and the alliance ended.

Typically partnerships with one strong, dominant partner last longer and do better than shared management ventures. As time goes on the skills that the partners possess and their relative differences begin to change. Such changes can contribute to the partners competing with each other or can cause a lack of interest in the future of the venture (Inkpen & Beamish, 1997). Partnerships formed in response to government fiat also do not last very long and are not very successful.

CHAPTER 6

Developing an Export Marketing Plan

Upon finishing this chapter you should be able to

- develop an export marketing plan that will be a practical aid to your company, not only in charting a course for business, including export, and keeping it under control, but also in dealing with banks and other agencies in the export sector;
- use frameworks for strategic analysis during the planning process.

Entering the export market for the first time is a significant commitment for most firms as it involves dealing with unfamiliar customers and markets that are often geographically distant. Therefore a good plan is essential for a good outcome. In addition to a substantial commitment, there are several other reasons why an export marketing plan is needed (Cavusgil, Knight, & Riesenberger, 2008; Czinkota & Ronkainen, 2002):

- It is part of a company's business plan. The marketing plan is an essential element in the overall business plan. It explains where the sales revenue will come from. It also states how much of each product produced can be exported. It is a vital factor in the production and financial planning process.
- It enables the company to react to change in market environments. Export markets are constantly evolving because of changes in technology, competition, imports, customer needs, and the general economic situation. These can be viewed as threats or opportunities. A good marketing plan specifies objectives and actions needed to resist threats and exploit opportunities emerging from the changing market environments.
- It assists in implementing changes in company strategy. Examples of these changes are expansion of exports in existing

markets and entry into new markets, launching of new products, and consolidation or contraction of the export effort.
- Above all, it helps control a firm's export activities by measuring and assessing its export performance.
- It makes communication and coordination within the firm and across export channel partners easy. It provides goals and directions to the organization and export partners.

A good marketing plan thus integrates a company's marketing activities into a coherent whole, protects the company from sudden market changes, establishes export targets, and acts as a focal point for management action relating to foreign markets (Czinkota & Ronkainen, 2002). However, it does not help in predicting business developments, preventing marketing mistakes, or providing guarantees of export success.

If an export marketing plan is for a foreign market in which the firm is already competing, the company will presumably already have much of the knowledge and experience required to draw up the plan. If, however, it is for a new market, outside advice will most likely be required to develop the plan. A firm that has never exported before should begin by documenting available information about the export market, using the following as a guide:

- Market size and trends
- Market structure
- Competitors
- Products
- Pricing
- Buyer behavior
- Marketing channels
- Marketing communications
- Barriers to market entry
- Possible competitive advantages

When Danisco, the Danish multinational food producer, went into China's market, it spent considerable time on feasibility studies, preparing market analyses, and marketing its brands. With 200 to 300 million Chinese people entering the middle class, the Chinese market for processed food was expected to grow to half the size of Europe's by the early 2000s. But the high degree of centralization erects entry barriers to foreign companies. As for the competition situation, there is no sign of careful protection for local companies. Local players are eager to improve efficiency and the quality of products, which would provide a potential market for Danisco's ingredient products. In addition to the market research, the ingredients team spent about 2 years on investigations, including identifying suitable sites, understanding the bureaucracy of permission, and identifying the customer base potential. Based on the overall situation in China's market, Danisco decided to expand business into China and plans on building a new $21 million ingredients factory near the southern industrial city of Kunshan.

The first step in drawing up an export plan is to determine the time span it is to cover. This could be 10 years (for a perspective plan), 5 years (a strategic plan), 1 year (an operational plan), or even 1 month (a control plan). No hard rules exist for choosing a particular length of time because it depends on the degree of uncertainty in the company's business environment. The higher the uncertainty, the shorter the plan period should be. Even if it is difficult to prepare strategic plans for a 2- to 5-year period, it is advisable to do so. The strategic plan can be broken down into annual operational plans and further subdivided into control charts for a monthly review.

The most important task in drawing up the export plan is to establish business objectives for the company. Company managers may already have an idea of the objectives that are feasible in the immediate future. However, these objectives can be improved in a systematic way, for example, by undertaking what is known as a Strengths, Weaknesses, Opportunities, and Threats (SWOT) analysis and by defining the scope of the company's business (Peter & Donnelly, 2007).

The next step is to decide on the activities needed to achieve the stated objectives. This means preparing a capital plan, a raw materials plan, a human resources plan, and a financing plan, along with the marketing plan. These plans are interrelated and must be complementary. Otherwise, a bad situation could occur; for example, while the capital plan is being carried out according to schedule, the raw materials plan may go out of control, the financing plan may become impractical, or the marketing plan may become irrelevant. It is important to understand that an export marketing plan is a subplan designed to achieve the firm's marketing objectives. The combination of this subplan with the other subplans will lead to an overall business plan for the company. There are a few steps necessary in preparing an export marketing plan:

1. Assess the past performance of the company.
2. Evaluate the competitors.
3. Study export markets to find opportunities and avoid pitfalls.
4. Decide on the export marketing objectives.
5. Determine how to achieve the desired strategy.

The first two steps reveal the company's strengths and weaknesses, and the third step assesses opportunities and threats. The last two provide the basis for the plan.

Assessing Competitors

Several forms can be used to identify a company's strong and weak points, and characteristics of the export market environment. These are aids in analyzing the company and its export marketing context and have been used by the authors in advising exporters. It may be useful for the company to ask outside people with some knowledge of the business to help complete the forms. While the emphasis in this analysis is only on marketing, other factors should not be forgotten, such as production skills and financial resources, which may be the firm's most obvious strengths and could lead to overall advantages in exporting (Cavusgil, 1993).

Form 1 lists some of the more important nonmarket factors to be considered in analyzing performance. The company can be assessed on each point. After the exercise is completed, efforts should be made to take advantage of the strengths or improve export performance as appropriate.

Form 2 deals with marketing strengths and weaknesses. As with Form 1, short answers should be given for each point. For example, for "knowledge of markets," a strength might be "know total market size" and a weakness might be "don't know breakdown by market segment."

Form 1: Nonmarketing strengths and weaknesses to evaluate

PRODUCTION RESOURCES	MANAGEMENT RESOURCES
Access to raw materials, components, and other inputs	Management experience
Possession of special equipment	Specialist management functions
Availability of specialized labor skills	Adequate organizational structure
Possession of patents or licenses	Coherent plans and strategies
Availability of quality packaging	Incentive options
Access to new production technology	Financial resources
	Access to additional financing
	Levels of profitability
	Availability of credit facilities

Form 2: Marketing strengths and weaknesses to evaluate

FACTOR	STRENGTHS	WEAKNESSES
Market knowledge		
Existence of a prior marketing plan		
Knowledge of markets (e.g., market size, segments, trends)		
Knowledge of customer's image of the company		
Knowledge of how the firm's buyers make purchasing decisions		
Availability of in-house information, such as sales analysis and advice of sales agents		
Access to external market information (e.g., trade magazines, information agencies)		
Dependence on		
A few key customers (1% of total sales to top 10 customers)		
A few key products		
A market covering a small geographic area		

FACTOR	STRENGTHS	WEAKNESSES
Promotion and selling		
Profile of customers		
Sales incentive system		
Brochures available		
Press material issued		
Experience in advertising		
Distribution system		
Number of outlets used out of total		
Incentive system for distributors		
Backup to distributors, such as displays, point-of-sale material		
Product		
Product development record, specifically the number of new products introduced last year		
Age of present products		
Use of brand name		
Quality and function of packaging		
Specific product benefits		
Customer service		
Credit facilities provided		
Rate of on-time delivery		

Form 3 is a checklist of ways to obtain information on competitors. This form can serve as a guide for assessing the competition. A separate form should be filled in for each market. The number of columns (A, B, C, etc.) can be increased, depending on the number of competitors in each market. A good knowledge of the competition is required to spot opportunities. Maximum advantage should be taken of the weaknesses of competitors and efforts should be made to offset their strengths.

Form 3: Competitor Assessment

NAMES OF COMPETITORS	COMPANY A	COMPANY B	COMPANY C
Equipment that they have including special machines			
Market segments in which they compete with the assessing firm			
Number of persons on their sales force			
Printed brochures and price lists that they issued			
Their experience in advertising			
Any publicity that they receive and where			
Their agents or distributors, including names			
Portion of the target market that they cover			
Their price levels compared to that of the assessing company			
Comparison of their terms with that of the assessing company			
How long their products have been on the market			
New products they have launched in the last 2 years			
Any special services they offer: installation, advice, guarantees, fast delivery			

Form 4 lists some sources of information for gathering information about your foreign competitors' business activities.

Form 4: Sources of Information on Foreign Competitors

GETTING INFORMATION ON COMPETITORS
1. Send for their brochures and price lists.
2. Collect copies of their advertisements and other publicity materials from newspapers and magazines.
3. Inquire about their delivery terms, credit terms, special capabilities, machinery, and special offers to large customers.
4. Place an order with them and examine their products and packaging.
5. Talk to their customers.
6. Visit their premises.

Opportunities and Threats

The preparation of an export marketing plan cannot be done in a vacuum. It should involve identifying outside factors that will have an impact on the business in the future, either by presenting opportunities or posing challenges. Therefore, before preparing an export plan, company managers should spend some time systematically examining the factors beyond the company's control that will affect the export business in the future, allowing the company to take advantage of or make allowances for these factors. The question is then, what factors should be monitored in the outside world and how will these factors affect the firm's export business? How can a company manager know what is likely to happen in the international business environment? The answer to the first question depends to some extent on the company's line of business and is discussed below. Finding the response to the second question involves keeping abreast of events and forecasts for the future and analyzing how these are likely to affect the firm.

Every business needs to study the following elements in the target country (Czinkota & Ronkainen, 2002):

- Economic situation
- Population trends
- Technological changes
- Environmental issues
- Regulations affecting your business
- Policy changes
- General changes in society

Within each of these broad categories, many factors will affect your business potential. But even a quick examination of the changes likely to happen in, say, the next 3 to 5 years will reveal both opportunities and threats to the company's export business. An export plan should help to prepare for these changes.

How do you identify such environmental factors? Reading daily newspapers and business magazines with an international outlook is advisable. They can help keep managers informed of the most significant events for international business as they occur. The possible implications of these events for the company can then be carefully studied.

Form 5 provides a possible framework for monitoring international events. It is designed to help determine how the international market-place is changing and how it will affect the company's business.

Form 5: **Framework for Monitoring International Events**

Outside influence on the company	IMPLICATIONS FOR THE COMPANY	
	Opportunity	Threat
A. Economic trends: List three trends that seem important to your company (e.g., growth in the service industry, lower inflation) and assess them		
1.	1.	1.
2.	2.	2.
3.	3.	3.
B. Trends in technology (e.g., increased applications of microchip technology)		
1.	1.	1.
2.	2.	2.
3.	3.	3.
C. Political and legislative developments (e.g., stricter laws on building materials)		
1.	1.	1.
2.	2.	2.
3.	3.	3.
D. Changes in society (e.g., rapid urbanization, more working wives)		
1.	1.	1.
2.	2.	2.
3.	3.	3.

Remember that even one good opportunity identified may be all that is needed. Action can then be planned to take advantage of it. Another way to identify export market opportunities is shown through the use of "opportunity boxes." With this technique, the evaluator can try to iden-tify new export opportunities. The best ideas are often the simplest, and yet good ideas are always elusive.

Export Objectives

Objectives are statements of what is expected to be achieved in the future. They are sometimes referred to as "goals" or "targets." Most company managers, if asked why they are in business, will probably say because they want to make money, because they want to be their own boss, or something similar. However, such statements are too vague to be useful in helping managers to decide on future courses of action. Objectives need to be written in such a way that they are useful for business managers. For a small company, it is sometimes difficult to distinguish personal objectives from business objectives. Therefore the first thing to do is to determine the differences between the two.

Personal Objectives

Personal objectives might concern what the company owner wants from his or her business (Miller, 1993b), including the following:

- A high annual income to permit the owner to achieve a good standard of living
- A business that will employ members of the family at a reasonable standard of living
- An initial low income with rapid growth prospects that will make it possible for the owner to sell the business in 3 years and start another one
- A fast growing business leading to an annual expansion of production, workforce, capital base, and profits in the foreseeable future, resulting in a major business position in the local community and social recognition of this fact

The points above are distinctly different objectives. The one that a business owner selects depends on his or her

- ability to manage a large workforce and cope with related problems;
- level of ambition;
- ability to raise more capital to expand the business;
- readiness to work long hours;
- desire for free time;
- health and physical stamina.

Before setting objectives for continued expansion, or market dominance, a business manager should consider the above points, as well as others that may be relevant.

Many owners of small business firms are satisfied when their parent company size ensures them an adequate standard of living; they do not wish to expand because of the problems that expansion could bring. In this situation, their business objectives should be geared to maintain their lifestyle. This may mean that sales should continue at least at their present levels for the foreseeable future. However, this does not necessarily mean no new products, new export markets, or new competition. Not wanting to grow does not mean not changing. Planning remains essential for business firms in ever-changing environments. However, ambitious managers may want to see their business develop and perhaps become a major force in their industry, expanding into new export markets and new export products.

Business Objectives

Export marketing objectives have to be set in the context of more general business objectives, such as the financial return expected on the overall investment (Miller, 1993b). For example, a company may want to have a 20% annual return on capital invested or to grow only to a certain size in terms of employees. Business objectives thus set boundaries for determining marketing objectives. Before a business manager can say what the specific export marketing objectives are, an analysis should be completed of

- the enterprise's strengths and weaknesses;
- the competitor's strengths and weaknesses;
- opportunities and threats in the export market.

Using the analysis of these items, the manager should look for the following:

- The market opportunity analysis may reveal a growing segment in a foreign market of which the company was unaware.
- The analysis of foreign competitors may show that they also missed this market segment but have become very price competitive in other areas.

- The analysis of strengths and weaknesses may show that the company's product quality is good, but that the sales literature does not highlight the product's positive points, that sales staff are untrained, or that the company is losing export orders because of late deliveries.

These findings would obviously point to what needs to be done by the company in the longer term (e.g., developing new market segments) and in the short term (e.g., preparing new sales literature, training staff, and improving delivery). Putting this in terms of objectives means making statements such as the following:

- Next year and for each succeeding year, this company wants to achieve an overall growth in its export sales and profitability of 10%.
- Next year the company will break into the following new export markets (defined geographically, by customer, or by market need).
- Next year the company will increase its share in export market by 2%.

Other examples could be used, but these give a basic idea of how to set objectives that will provide an overall direction for the firm, a measure of the change required, and a time span over which this change will be effected. Form 6 can be useful in setting down export marketing objectives.

Form 6: Setting Export Marketing Objectives

COMPANY OBJECTIVES	QUANTITY	WHEN TO BE ACHIEVED
1. Change in profit		
2. Change in export sales		
3. Change in export market share		
4. Introduction of new products		
5. Other objectives (state them)		

When the tasks of assessing the company, the competitors, and the export market have been completed and broad objectives have been set, the company manager should be well prepared to make decisions about what needs to be done to achieve these objectives. This involves looking at alternative strategies and deciding which one appears to be the best suited to the company's objectives.

For example, if the manager decides that the long-term (say, 5-year) objective is to export to markets A and B, while expanding the current domestic market base, the objectives for the next year might be as follows:

- Expand total sales by 10%
- Open up the market in country A and sell 1% of the company's products there

Alternative strategies for achieving the second objective could be:

- Conduct market research on the salability of the country's products in market A and carry out the necessary product changes
- Appoint a sales agent or distributor in country A
- Advertise in newspapers in country A and service customers from the home base

A useful framework for thinking about what is needed to put each strategy into action is the "marketing mix" concept, which consists of four areas (Peter & Donnelly, 2007):

- Product (and its presentation)
- Price
- Distribution (place)
- Promotion

These four "Ps" can help with the action plans. The example in the box shows how it is done. Parallel to completing the export marketing plan, the company manager has to develop other plans, especially production and finance plans. These various plans can then be combined into an overall business plan for the company. There is no definite pattern for a business plan; various forms are possible.

OVERALL OBJECTIVE: INCREASE SALES BY 10%	PRODUCT	PRICING	DISTRIBUTION AND SELLING	PROMOTION
Strategy 1: Expand sales to present buyers this year, as follows: Buyer A: +10% Buyer B: +20% Buyer C: +40%	Add a new line. Modify the present line. Improve packaging.	Offer a higher discount to the best buyers. Drop prices or raise prices.	Appoint an agent.	Develop a brochure.
Strategy 2: Find five new buyers in Country X: City A: 2 City B: 2 City C: 1	Meet new product requirements.	Offer them special introduction prices.	Appoint agents in Country X.	Exhibit in a trade fair in City B.
Strategy 3: Identify a new product line to complement existing ones and increase sales.	Find product ideas by: visiting a trade fair, contracting a chamber of commerce, examining competing products.	Develop a price strategy to penetrate the market segment.	Investigate distribution requirements.	Use public relations to introduce the product.

Example: Outline of a Business Plan

I. Introduction or summary of the business plan		
II. Brief background information on the company		
A. Current activity 1. Products 2. Capacity per annum 3. Annual sales 4. Number of employees	B. Marketing pattern 1. Domestic market (% of production) 2. Existing sales network 3. Export markets (% of production) 4. Export network	C. Other activities (if any)
III. Features of the planned or proposed activity		

| A. Product(s) to be manufactured
1. Product specification(s)
2. Annual capacity envisaged
3. Experience in the proposed activity | B. Markets to be served
1. Domestic markets (% of production)
2. Export markets (% of production) | C. Type of activities to be carried out
1. Obtain technology and marketing knowledge
2. Marketing
3. Training
4. Management
5. Obtain or generate capital
   a. Domestic markets
   b. Export markets | |

IV. Raw materials and components

| A. Available in domestic market and price | B. To be imported
Types required
Countries of origin
Import duty(ies)
Import license (if required) | |

V. Domestic production; market size and pattern (with respect to proposed activity)

| A. Local production | B. Market size and pattern | |

VI. Industrial costs

| A. Anticipated cost of local labor
• Unskilled worker (minimum wage)
• Semiskilled worker
• Skilled worker
• Highly skilled worker
• Supervisory worker
• Engineering worker
• Management worker
• Allowances
• Working time | B. Utilities | C. Cost structure of existing production (% of sales)
1. Materials
2. Direct labor
3. Overheads
4. Utilities
5. Other costs |

VII. Location, transport, and shipping

| A. Location
1. Land (square meters)
2. Buildings (square meters) | B. Nearest port and airport | |

VIII. Plant capacity

| A. Existing utilization | B. Installed machinery and equipment | |

IX. Estimated cost

| A. Land and buildings | B. Plant and machinery | C. Provision for contingency | D. Fees for technical knowledge |

X. Estimated revenue		
XI. Additional information on loan financing		
A. Sources	B. Name of national development bank	
XII. Printed material available		

The example can be adapted, for instance, by adding other subjects for coverage.

In the post-Uruguay Round era, firms will have greater opportunities to engage in global trade. However, as competition is likely to increase, they will need to sharpen their competitive edge. By developing practical and realistic business plans, as well as monitoring and revising them, small businesses should be in a better position to benefit from expanding trading opportunities.

The following boxes illustrate a method for organizing your thinking and strategically analyzing foreign market opportunities. Based on your choice of products and markets, the model explains four generic strategic approaches. These can be customized to suit your business needs.

Opportunity Boxes: The Concepts

	PRESENT PRODUCTS	NEW PRODUCTS
Present markets	1. Market penetration	3. Product development
New markets	2. Market development	4. Diversification

Box 1: Market penetration: This means marketing most of your current products to current customers or markets, or increasing penetration of the current market. Example: A shirt manufacturer has 5% of an export market and wants to expand sales by getting present consumers to buy more of the product and by encouraging consumers currently purchasing from the competition to switch to the firm's product.

Box 2: Market development: This concerns selling your present product in new markets. The new markets could be new country markets or new segments. Example: A small company producing men's clothing and currently supplying only the domestic market may want to develop an export market.

Box 3: Product development: This entails introducing new or adapted products to present markets. It involves developing new products or modifying existing products (e.g., by introducing quality or size variations). Example: A small engineering firm that makes locks for the construction market may want to sell building fittings to the same market.

Box 4: Diversification: This involves developing completely new products for new markets. Example: A small doors and windows manufacturer now wants to produce office furniture and sell in new markets.

Now try to answer these questions with respect to your company. Filling in these boxes will show you where opportunities exist and how they can be exploited effectively.

Opportunity Boxes: Exercise

1. MARKET PENETRATION	3. PRODUCT DEVELOPMENT
Ways of selling more to present export markets:	New products that could be sold to present export markets:
1. 2. 3.	1. 2. 3.
2. MARKET DEVELOPMENT	4. DIVERSIFICATION
New export markets or segments to which present products could be sold:	New products that could be developed for new export markets:
1. 2. 3.	1. 2. 3.

CHAPTER 7

Working With Facilitating and Support Firms

Upon completing this chapter you should be able to

- provide specific guidelines for selecting facilitating and support firms for export operations;
- describe the role and capabilities of support organizations, both government and private, which can aid you in developing international business;
- know the pros and cons of various partnering aspects;
- introduce computer-based information systems (CBISs) to help you make effective partnering decisions;
- utilize the links to government and private sources of information.

Exporting products for the first time is a major commitment for most firms and involves numerous facilitators and partners in the process. Such facilitators include your bank, freight forwarders, customs brokers, foreign distributors, and home and host governments, among others (Czinkota & Ronkainen, 2002; David, 2004).

Banks as Your Facilitator

Probably the most important facilitator of your export marketing is your bank. Your choice of banks or bankers is one of the keys to your success in exporting. Although many U.S. banks, and particularly regional ones, are not very excited about export financing, the same types of commercial loans available for domestic business, such as working capital loans and revolving lines of credit, may be available for short-term export financing. However, there is typically a demand for more collateral in the case of overseas sales. Longer term export financing is also available from some banks.

Find a Bank That Has the Appropriate Skills

Most likely you have your own bank with which you maintain a good relationship. Most regionally based banks do not have adequate experience or capacity to help you in your export activities. Therefore you have to assess their skills, scale of business, main line of products, and customer base to determine whether your bank has the ability to support your export activities. If not, you have to find the right bank for you. There are a few criteria in locating the right bank. First, consider banks that have international departments, or at least officers knowledgeable and skilled in international banking, even if they use one of the larger regional banks as a correspondent bank for documentary transactions and their international information network. If you have sufficient capital or an active domestic business, you might want to establish a second banking relationship to provide banking alternatives. If you are planning on a fair amount of need for transactional export financing, consider a bank that specializes in trade finance. Many of these are representative banks of large foreign banks and have considerable skills in trade finance. Many banks withdrew from trade finance, as well as foreign risk, in the 1980s, and it will require some patience on your part to find an interested banker with appropriate skills.

Your loan officer should be personally acquainted with international trade and trade finance. If your loan officer is part of a profit center in the bank, you may get more attention. If the bank of your choice is organized so that the international division is "staff" instead of its own profit center, be sure your loan officer is interested and eager to work both with you and the bank's international staff. Some loan officers clearly tend to avoid international trade and international staff altogether.

What Would Your Banks Like to See From You?

Your bank will help you succeed in export activities. However, you have to help your bank support your export activities. You can do a few things so your bank can support your business by arranging loans well in advance of when the money will be needed, paying down your general working capital loans, structuring your working capital loans, and developing several credit lines.

Arranging Loans Beforehand

If you can find a financial institution that suits you and your needs, it is important to get started on the right foot with them. When you request a loan, request something possible; do not expect the lender to take an equity position in your company. You must provide the basic equity and collateral to support your financial needs. The lender's job is to assist you with supplemental and peak funding needs. No bank is interested in venture capital; banks do not like risk, and it is quite true that banks prefer lending money to companies that do not need to borrow. Therefore it is axiomatic that you should always arrange for borrowing money before you need it. This is especially important in the case of transaction financing. Discuss the deal with your banker before, not after, signing the contract.

Pay Down Your General Working Capital Loans

It is important to recognize that banks do not like to see static conditions on general working capital loans. Banks want to see the loan paid down, even if in relatively small amounts, and despite the fact that you might borrow again in the near future, which is the nature of working capital. Working capital requirements change almost daily, therefore the bank does not expect to see a general working capital loan become a fixed, long-term loan. Also, expect that the bank will require that such a loan be paid off in full at least once a year, and possibly more often.

Structure Your Working Capital Loans

Most lenders and most borrowers prefer structured working capital loans, frequently based on accounts receivable. This usually removes some of the burden of periodically paying the loan off in full and provides both parties with a clear guideline based on a mutually agreed upon formula as to an acceptable maximum outstanding credit secured by a fluctuating asset value such as receivables. The open general assets working capital line is fine if you can get one, but you must have available substantial assets to support it. If you do have such a facility, handle this valuable credit line with care and save it for emergencies or unusual situations of short duration if possible.

Develop Several Credit Lines

If your bank has knowledge and interest in terms of international trade expertise, an accounts receivable loan based on insured foreign receivables might be the ideal working capital loan collateral for both you and your bank. If possible, develop several trade finance credit lines, divided among several specific purposes, as opposed to one overall credit line. An example would be a Foreign Credit Insurance Association (FCIA) insured accounts receivable line of credit or perhaps a smaller general working capital line of credit. The advantage is usually a larger total line, the disadvantage is in miscalculating your needs within each separate category.

If You Are a Third-Party Exporter, Find a Bank That Understands Your Business

If you are a third-party exporter, probably an export management company (EMC) or export trading company (ETC), it is important to find a bank that has other such customers and understands that an export company requires, and can support, more leverage in its lending facility than most businesses need or can justify. One reason for this is the lack of standing inventory that is not in danger of aging, and the lack of other tangible assets, such as capital equipment, that is not necessary in a business that consists of such a large service element.

The EMC/ETC business normally undertakes relatively large sales against fairly small margins or perhaps only commissions (Cho, 1987). This is possible because of the potential for substantial sales volume while employing a minimum amount of staff and equipment. Your biggest asset and borrowing leverage probably will be your receivables, which can be secured by letters of credit and accounts receivable insurance. A second opportunity for collateral borrowing is on inventory that is already clearly committed to export channels, over which your banker can exercise considerable fiscal control by means of liens, including the revenues arising from the sale of that inventory.

Establish a Good Relationship With Your Banks

It is important to note that banks are typically interested in developing an "overall relationship" and are most likely to provide export loans to firms with which they also do substantial amounts of domestic business. The bank will also expect to make a fair profit on export loans, which are often seen as being high risk.

Useful Guidelines Regarding Bank Relationships

- Select a bank that offers a full range of international trade finance capabilities. Be willing to establish the firm's main banking relationship with such a bank.
- Early on in the banking relationship, the exporter should discuss export and preexport borrowing requirements. This allows the banker to call on specialized resources to help determine the exporter's financial needs and the bank's ability to meet those needs.
- The bank is likely to demand more collateral for export financing and will be very concerned with the quality of export receivables. Common requirements will include

  - selling under letter of credit terms;
  - obtaining insurance for export receivables;
  - obtaining foreign bank guarantees of payment;
  - obtaining extensive credit data on the importer, including credit references and operating statements.

Do You Get Along Well With Important People in the Bank?

Talk at some length with your account or loan officer. Personal rapport is extremely important because of the judgment factor involved. That person, in many respects, is the "bank" as far as you are concerned. Do not wait for the banker to take you to lunch, take your banker to lunch. Your account officer and the other people in the bank who will be important to you—international department vice presidents, your documentary officers, perhaps the officer in charge of state and federal financing programs—all of these people can have an impact on the success and profitability of your export efforts.

Freight Forwarders as Your Facilitator

Firms exporting to or doing business in a relatively few foreign countries may have substantial logistics problems due to the expansion of geography and time required to support those markets. Transportation costs increase substantially with the distance to market. Furthermore, international transportation can be very complex. Shipments of single, identical contents to the same overseas destination can be routinely handled in-house. However, in-house shipping decisions can be costly.

One solution to the problem of logistics complexity is to develop a close working relationship with a third party that specializes in international freight forwarding (Czinkota & Ronkainen, 2002). Just as in hiring accountants and consultants, hiring forwarders has many potential benefits. A freight forwarder (FF) is an agent intermediary who arranges for carrier and commercial documentation; insurance; licensing requirements; visas; customs clearance; and ocean, air, or surface transportation. In the mid-1990s, Case Corporation, a leading company in the agricultural and construction equipment business, selling products in more than 150 countries, established a 5-year partnership with Fritz Companies, a global freight forwarder. As a premium specialist in global logistics, transportation, and related information services, Fritz has more than 350 offices in major international cities and enjoys a reputation of commitment to clients. Its innovative information systems can link with Case's other alliance members and provides Case with an integrated logistics program. Under the agreement, Fritz will act as the lead integrator to manage all air, ocean, and ground shipments in cooperation with alliance members Schneider Logistics and GATX Logistics. Case is confident that the freight forwarding partnership with Fritz will significantly improve its logistics process and inventory management. When the right freight forwarder joins a firm's export marketing, it can substantially enhance the firm's international logistics.

The evaluation and selection of an international freight forwarder is a critical strategic decision for managers involved in international operations. Freight forwarders should be evaluated on their expertise, specialization, communication and information capabilities, responsiveness and attention, financial strength, and efficiency and reliability.

Expertise

The expertise and experience of forwarders in various markets with different types of products, shipping methods, and terms constitute the most important factors in evaluating and selecting a freight forwarder. The expertise of the forwarder can be critical even in "routine" shipments that require special export documentation, customs clearance, and tracking. The forwarder must be knowledgeable about customs requirements and must be able to track your business continuously. A freight forwarder's expertise can be assessed by posing the following questions:

- How knowledgeable is the freight forwarder with the import rules and regulations of your destination country?
- How knowledgeable is the forwarder in various methods of shipping, such as free on board (FOB), cost and freight (C&F), and cost insurance and freight (CIF), and various trade services?
- How knowledgeable is the freight forwarder in U.S. government export regulations?
- How dependable are the freight forwarder's quotations of freight costs, port charges, consular fees, and handling fees?
- How capable is the forwarder of making recommendations concerning the type of packaging, warehousing, and insurance to use for shipping?
- Can the freight forwarder arrange for warehousing facilities if your shipment needs port warehousing?

- How experienced is the freight forwarder in handling high security?
- What is the extent of the freight forwarder's working experience with other clients?
- How long has the freight forwarder been in business?

Specialization

Many freight forwarders specialize in very specific areas—fine art, agricultural products, hazardous products—while others will handle almost anything. Consider the nature of your own product. If it requires specialized handling, equipment, or expertise, a specialized forwarder becomes important.

Another source of specialization is geographic. Forwarders who specialize in specific regions or countries have valuable international shipping and handling expertise. The number of forwarders providing an on-site presence at destination ports is also increasing.

Product/Service Specialization

In recent years, the scope of services provided by freight forwarders has broadened significantly. In an effort to provide "one-stop" services, some forwarders specialize in dealing with particular products and services. Some forwarders specialize in very specific areas such as fine art, agricultural products, or hazardous goods, while others specialize in various transportation or port services. Ideally your freight forwarder should have specialization in the product category you are interested in. The following questions will help you assess the forwarder's product specialization:

- How specialized is the freight forwarder in handling your type of merchandise?
- Does the forwarder have specialized equipment (e.g., hydrostatic suspension [air ride]) to handle your type of merchandise safely?
- How specialized is the freight forwarder in port operations?
- How specialized is the freight forwarder in arranging shipment for your type of product?

- How specialized is the freight forwarder in consolidating cargo (making full loads by grouping small shipments)?
- How specialized is the freight forwarder in handling customs formalities for shipments requiring complicated transactions?
- How specialized is the freight forwarder in multimodal transportation (bringing together road carriers and shippers)?

Geographical Specialization

Some forwarders, usually called regional forwarders, specialize in serving certain geographical regions or markets. Specialized knowledge in customs clearance and carrier/commercial documentation specific to a region is a major strength of geographically specialized forwarders. Depending on the market or country, additional documentation such as consular invoices or chamber of commerce certification may be required. Forwarders specializing in particular markets or regions usually have branches or offices in those markets or regions. Furthermore, you need to make sure that the freight forwarder can arrange for port services at the specific port of entry you wish to use. The port of entry is the port at which foreign goods are admitted into the receiving country. Port authorities at the port of entry control various airports and ocean cargo pier facilities, transit sheds, and warehouses. These authorities have the power to levy dockage charges and landing fees. Also, some shipments may require emergency diversion services, for example, diverting part of an ocean shipment to air shipment. Hence the services of a forwarder at the port of import can be critical, particularly when dealing with countries where little previous experience exists.

Communication and Information

In an era when national markets are becoming increasingly interrelated and interdependent, an extensive communication and information network is highly desirable. Communication between all parties involved in the forwarding process, particularly between the exporter and forwarder, is crucial. The forwarder must understand the exporter's needs, and the exporter must direct the forwarder to respond to the exporter's or client's needs. Many forwarders are adopting new technologies to respond to the information needs of their clients. Automation and computerization are efficient methods used in tracking and tracing shipments. They also enable a forwarder to uncover and solve problems at any point in a shipment's transit. For effective communication and information exchange with the freight forwarder, the following questions should be answered:

- Is the freight forwarder located conveniently to your office?
- How would you evaluate the communication network of the freight forwarder with port operators, custom brokers, and carriers?
- How do you evaluate the forwarder's capability to instantly track and trace shipments worldwide?
- Does the forwarder use electronic data interchange (EDI) or similar systems involving shippers, carriers, and customs brokers?

Some types of supply chain systems (e.g., EDI) can enhance the forwarder's ability to receive a shipper's instructions online and to transmit them to the carriers for booking and bill of lading information in a timely manner. Thus using such systems not only accelerates communication, but saves money and time, and reduces errors.

Responsiveness and Attention

Along with communication and information exchange, a freight forwarder's responsiveness and attention to your business is critical in determining the success of your business. Responsiveness and attention can be important, particularly if your export business is small in volume and infrequent. Performance can be enhanced by assigning a highly competent person to handle your transactions, thus securing high-quality, continuous trade services, transportation services, and value-added services; competent decision making in case of an emergency or crisis; timely responses to your inquiries; and customization of forwarding services to your particular needs.

Distributors as Your Facilitator

Selecting a distributor is one of the most important decisions a manufacturer will make in exporting (Bello & Williamson, 1985). Foreign distributors or agents are responsible for marketing the manufacturer's product and servicing customers in the local market. The characteristics that contribute to making successful distributors are numerous, making it imperative for manufacturers to employ a systematic approach to selection. There are five major dimensions that influence the selection of a foreign distributor: commitment level, financial and company strength, marketing skills, product factors, and facilitating factors.

Commitment

As discussed in Chapter 4, your distributor's overall commitment to the relationship is the most important factor in evaluating a foreign distributor. A distributor who is highly committed will devote more energy to making the sale of your product a success in that particular country. The commitment level of your potential foreign distributor can be predicted by assessing the following areas (Cavusgil, 1993; Miller, 1993a).

What Is the Degree of Volatility That the Distributor's
Product Mix Has Shown Over Time?

Be careful in choosing a distributor whose product mix exhibits extreme volatility over time. You should, instead, consider distributors who have stable product portfolios. This stability suggests that the distributor has long-term commitments to its product lines, that is, it has grown by focusing its efforts on just a few product lines at a time.

What Percentage of the Distributor's Sales
Is Accounted for by a Single Supplier?

Although you should look for a distributor who is financially strong and capable, you should be wary if a large percentage of the distributor's sales are from a single supplier. This often means that the distributor is already committed to the product lines of this supplier and may not give you the necessary attention that your product deserves.

Is the Distributor Willing to Maintain a Satisfactory Level of Inventory?

If your distributor is willing to stock your products, this means it is willing to commit some attention to the marketing of your product. If your potential distributor is willing to maintain only a minimum level of inventory it may mean it is not serious about the relationship. However, keep in mind that the level of acceptable inventory that the distributor is expected to carry varies quite substantially across industries.

Is the Distributor Willing to Commit an Adequate Sum of Money Toward Advertising and Promotional Efforts?

This factor may be important if your product is the type that needs to be advertised or promoted to end users. If your product needs upfront advertising to create awareness among targeted customers, it is wise to find a distributor who is willing to share some of the advertising and promotional expenditures. Again, the more your potential distributor is willing to spend its financial resources on advertising and promotions, the higher the level of commitment of your potential distributor.

Does the Distributor Participate in Major Trade Fairs?

Some products, because of their characteristics, are difficult to sell unless the potential buyer has an opportunity to examine them first hand. In this instance, trade fairs and shows are most useful for bringing buyers and sellers together. A distributor who participates frequently in trade shows reveals a commitment to its business and may increase distribution opportunities for your business. If your products require such sales promotions, you should ask the distributor for a list of trade fairs they have previously participated in and their plans for the coming year.

Will the Distributor Provide a Sufficient Number of Experienced Sales and Support Personnel to Your Product?

The distributor must assign an appropriate number of experienced individuals to your product. Only then can you be assured that your product will get the necessary attention for it to become established in a foreign marketplace. You should be careful with distributors who seem reluctant to dedicate personnel to your product, as this is likely to indicate a low level of commitment to your product. Determine the quality and size of the sales force that will be dedicated to your product. Another factor you need to consider is the sales and technical training and compensation your potential distributor is willing to provide to the sales force dedicated to your product.

Will the Distributor Commit to Achieving Minimum Sales Targets?

It is important for potential distributors to have a clear understanding of your objectives and expectations from the outset. One of these objectives should be the target sales volume of the distributor for your product. If the distributor is willing to work with you toward achieving this sales objective, it shows some commitment on its part. Ask the distributor if it is willing to accept minimum sales level provisions in the contract to evaluate the level of its commitment.

Overall, How Do You Assess the Willingness of the Distributor to Cooperate With You?

While it may not be realistic to expect any distributor to be cooperative on all issues (e.g., promotion, advertising, warranties, etc.), you should judge each distributor (intuitively) on how willing it is to cooperate with you in the long run. Can you have a long-term relationship with this distributor? Can you work effectively with him? Does it share similar business goals with you? These are some of the questions that you should ask when considering a long-term relationship with a foreign distributor, which cannot simply be answered by examining balance sheet statements.

How Is the Financial Strength of the Company?

The financial standing of the distributor is the second most important criterion next to its commitment level (Czinkota & Ronkainen, 2002). First, it shows the ability of the distributor to make money. Second, it indicates the ability of the distributor to perform some marketing functions such as extension of credit to customers and risk absorption. Remember, if the distributor is not financially capable of performing these and many other marketing activities, it becomes your burden. Furthermore, it is important for you to understand that your potential distributor's financial strength can determine its business potential as well as his commitment to the sales and marketing of your products. Your potential distributor's financial strength can be evaluated by looking at its financial record, including balance sheets and income statements. However, along with such record, or in case such record is not available, you will find that answering the following questions will help you understand the overall financial strength of your potential distributor:

- Does the distributor have the ability to finance initial levels of imports and subsequent growth?
- Does the distributor have the ability to formulate and implement 2- to 3-year marketing plans?
- Does the distributor have the ability to secure additional local funding to support your business when it becomes necessary?
- Is the distributor a recognized member in key industry trade associations and other business groups?
- To what extent does the distributor have a critical mass of organizational capabilities to meet your needs?
- Does the distributor have the financial resources for technical support of your product?
- Does the distributor have the financial capability to maintain a satisfactory level of inventory?
- Does the distributor have the ability to provide an adequate level of financial resources for advertising and promotional efforts?

Marketing Skills

Although a high level of motivation and commitment are necessary factors to consider in the distribution evaluation, they are not sufficient. The extent of geographical coverage of the distributor and its knowledge of the target markets segments are also equally important. Very often distributors who are knowledgeable about their markets are also the ones who are familiar with customer requirements. The quality of management, size of the distributor, and experience of its sales force also bear directly on the marketing ability of the distributor.

The Experience and Expertise of the Distributor
With Your Product and Markets

Seek distributors who are knowledgeable about your product and your customer segments. Often such knowledge indicates that the distributor is familiar with the needs of the market and will be able to provide the most suitable forms of marketing support for your product. You should consider the number of years and level of experience of the distributor. You might ask the distributor to provide a list of its customers. You should also check to see if it has the necessary expertise and connections with industry leaders, retailers, final customers, and consumers. Using an inexperienced distributor may be costly, both financially and timewise.

The Extent of Geographic Coverage of
Your Target Market by the Distributor

Nearly all distributors will claim that they cover their entire national territory, and if this is not true, you may run the risk of using a distributor who cannot reach all your potential customers. Certain benchmarks to look for include the distributor's physical facilities, the size and training of the sales force, and the number of sales outlets. Try to determine the particular market segments the distributor services and the extent of market share in each. This can be the basis for awarding several exclusive distributorships in one country, each for a specific market segment. Evaluate the distributor's geographic coverage in terms of principal market areas.

The Experience of the Distributor's Sales Force to Be Dedicated to Your Product

The extent of market coverage of a distributor and how well these markets are served are often good indicators of an experienced sales force. In addition to these factors, there are more precise ways to judge the experience of the distributor's sales personnel. First, you should look at the number of customers visited by the sales force on a regular basis. Second, you should consider the average size of customers' orders. These indicators suggest a high-quality experienced sales force. In doing these assessments, it is helpful to use the industry average as a reference point.

The Distributor's Combined Domestic Market Share

Market share is often an indicator of marketing performance. High market share has also been shown to be correlated with high profitability. Therefore distributors with high market shares frequently have strong marketing skills and may also have stronger financial resources vis-à-vis other distributors with smaller market shares. Distributors with more experience often tend to have higher market shares than newer distributors. Therefore it is a good idea to examine the distributor's share over a number of years in the market segments in which it competes.

The "Trainability" of the Distributor's Sales Force

If you need to train the distributor's sales force to handle your product, an important factor to consider is the ability of the sales force to absorb training in your product line. Besides evaluating qualitative factors such as the level of motivation, you should also consider whether their prior experience and level of education will facilitate them in the training program. It is the willingness and capability of the sales force to absorb training that you need to assess. If the distributor's sales force has limited capabilities to absorb training, you might have to send your own sales force to the local marketplace, thereby incurring additional setup costs.

The Distributor's Ability to Directly Support
Your Advertising and Promotional Efforts

If the distributor is capable of providing direct support for your advertising and promotional efforts, that is a valuable marketing skill that will be very helpful. This capability is derived from its experience, skills, or connections in the local market. In particular, the distributor's access to local media placement and scheduling is of great importance for your advertisement campaign. The distributor may also support your efforts by preparing promotional materials (e.g., brochures, handouts, etc.) himself. However, make sure that you ask for samples of promotional materials it has previously produced. Do not let the distributor handle the production of promotional materials unless you are satisfied with the quality, design, and appearance of the materials you have seen.

The Distributor's Ability to Provide On-Time and Complete Delivery

You should consider distributors who have the capability to provide deliveries that are both on time and complete. These capabilities often reflect the quality of the distributor's logistics management. The ability to provide timely and complete deliveries can lead to higher customer satisfaction and, consequently, higher sales. You should ask for evidence of on-time shipment when making an assessment.

The Distributor's Ability to Handle Customer
Requests, Complaints, and Concerns

A customer-oriented distributor attends to customer requests, complaints, and concerns as quickly as possible. If the distributor is able to handle these within 24 hours, this indicates attentiveness to its customers. This is an important indicator of the customer service capabilities of the distributor.

Internal Sales Training, Meetings, and
Communications Among Salespeople

The point this question addresses is whether the distributor has a disciplined way of training and communicating with its sales force. The details of the actual process are not as important as its existence, acknowledgment, and regularity. The appropriate frequency of formal face-to-face meetings, for instance, can be very different for different industries, and even for specific distributors within the same industry. What you need to make sure is that the distributor has an established and effective sales training and communication structure.

The Reputation of the Distributor Among Its Customers

You should obtain all the information you can about the distributor's reputation and effective performance in the industry. It is wise to talk with customers such as retailers and other end users who have dealt directly with this distributor. They are a good source of information concerning the work ethic of the distributor, its financial standing in the marketplace, and its general reputation in the business community. However, this information is only available by visiting these key people, so it is often worthwhile to make a trip to the overseas market to meet with these people and get their views on the distributor. You may also ask the distributor for a list of references, and you should contact each one on the list. You should also seek additional information from U.S. Department of Commerce officers in that country. In addition, check with the banks of the distributor; they are a good source of information about the distributor's credit and financial standing. Consulting previous and current suppliers who have been represented by the distributor will also help you gain some insight into the overall capability of the distributor.

The Distributor's Senior Management Team

The way the distributorship is managed is another critical factor to consider. The quality of senior management can be assessed through objective measures as evidenced by their experience level, strong performance measures, or through objective evaluation methods such as the motivation level of employees, the care and attention given to the distributor's workplace, and so on. You should check to see whether the distributor has competent people who will carry out the mission. You can ask for the curricula vitae (CVs) of the top management team to get a better sense of their qualifications and the length of time they have been with this distributor. Moreover, try to get a sense of the managers' share in ownership of the company as well as bonus/compensation plans of the distributor. Again, an overseas trip and visiting and talking to the distributor's employees will help you form a better opinion of the distributor's quality of management.

Product Factors

Product-related factors primarily concern the distributor's knowledge about of product and characteristics of its existing product lines. Check the number of product lines carried by the distributor. It may be spread too thinly, concentrating only on those products that provide the best compensation. Avoid distributors who are handling direct competitors' products. Instead, concentrate on distributors who handle complementary product lines and who have already achieved some degree of specialization in sales and service. When assessing the product factors of a potential distributor, focus on the areas discussed below.

Familiarity of the Distributor With Your Product Line

Here, product line refers to the collection of your products that the distributor will be handling. If the distributor has a high level of familiarity with and knowledge about your product, this will increase its awareness of product applications, customer requirements, before- and after-sales service needs, as well as special inventory, packaging, and delivery arrangements, and so forth. In addition, having a distributor with knowledge about your product is helpful, as it may also be familiar with the marketing aspects of your product.

Complementarity of Your Product
Line to the Existing Product Portfolio

You will sometimes find that the best distributors are already handling competitive products and are therefore unavailable. In this case you should look for other equally qualified distributors who handle related products or who have the same level of technical expertise. You might check to see if the distributor is serving a particular industry or segment only. Or it might be interested in handling a wider product line representing a number of industries or segments.

The Quality Level of the Existing Product Lines

The quality match for products is important for product-positioning reasons: a high-quality product may suffer from a bad distributor reputation. At the same time, you have to find a match between the quality of your product and the quality of the product lines carried by the distributor. This can affect the types of retailers who will want to sell your product. It is important to realize that quality is very hard to assess; however, a few guidelines can help you make a better assessment. If the distributor is a manufacturer, you might use ISO 9000 quality standards. Some questions you should ask include the following:

- Has the distributor received any quality awards from customers or business buyers?
- Have any favorable articles been written about the distributor?
- Does the distributor have good name recognition in the sector?

You should also ask for literature about the products the distributor is currently handling.

Technical Sophistication Level of the Existing Product Lines

If your product is nontechnical in nature, you can ignore this criterion. Otherwise, you should determine whether the distributor has any experience in carrying technically sophisticated products. If you have a technically sophisticated product, it is highly likely that it will need special handling, training for after-sales service, and so on. A distributor that has experience handling similarly sophisticated products will be a better choice for you.

Protection of Your Patent, Copyright, or Trademark

If your product is not covered by a patent, copyright, or trademark, this criterion can be ignored. Violation of intellectual property rights by foreign business partners is an increasing problem in many countries that do not provide stringent intellectual property protection by law or impose strict sanctions against violators. Beware of distributors who will provide merely adequate protection for your product overseas. Specifically, consider distributors who are willing to invest money in ensuring this protection. Note, however, that in certain countries the distributor's hands may be tied and it may be unable to bring about effective enforcement. At a minimum, the following four issues should be carefully examined:

1. The existence of an intellectual property protection law
2. The efficacy of the law
3. Enforcement of the law
4. The ability of the distributor to protect your intellectual property regardless of regulations and enforcement (check with other suppliers on this)

Competing Product Lines in the Existing
Product Portfolio of the Distributor

You will sometimes find that the best distributors are already handling competitive products and are therefore unavailable. In this case you should look for other well-qualified distributors. If the distributor is willing to drop competitive product lines for your product, this suggests that it may have a very favorable opinion of your product, hence the distributor is likely to invest significant time and effort on your product.

Facilitating Factors

This last factor does not have a major influence in the decision-making process, but it is helpful in facilitating a smoother relationship between you and the foreign distributor. This is particularly so in certain countries. Things to consider include the distributor's English speaking and writing skills, prior experience with U.S. exporters and local government contacts, and overall reputation.

Connection of the Distributor With Government Officials, Trade Associations, and Other Key Influential Groups

It is important to choose distributors that have political clout in countries that have a lot of political red tape. For example, an executive who was trying to establish a market in Indonesia stated that, "We lost part of our business in Indonesia when one of our distributors was unable to persuade the government to lift some discriminatory regulations." A distributor with good local connections may be able to offer much better business capabilities than what is apparent.

The Distributor's Experience With Other U.S. Exporters

Conducting business overseas is easier with a distributor who has considerable experience with other U.S. exporters. This familiarity can translate into more manageable business negotiations and relationships. But again, make sure the profile of the exporters who have been served by the distributor are similar to your company (i.e., in terms of size, export volume, etc.). This will allow you to make a comparison of the performance of the distributor across other U.S. exporters. Make sure that you ask the distributor for a list of references of its other U.S. suppliers.

Familiarity of the Distributor With U.S. Accounting Methods and Business Practices

It is easier to work with a foreign distributor who is knowledgeable about U.S. accounting methods and business practices, especially if the methods and practices are substantially different from those of the distributor's country. Seek distributors who have a strong working knowledge in these two areas.

Distributor's Ability to Communicate In English

Having a distributor with a good command of the English language can be an advantage, as this minimizes the need for translators or back-translators of spoken and written communication. Both you and the distributor will know exactly what the other person is trying to say, minimizing the possibility of miscommunication due to language problems. Make sure that you have a clear idea about the extent of their understanding of English. Talk with them over the phone and use these phone conversations as a test. Use technical terms and expressions relevant to your business or product to determine if the other person understands what you are talking about.

The Distributor's Previous Work Relationship With Foreign Suppliers

While an earlier section addressed the extent to which the distributorship has working experience with U.S. suppliers, this question is more general and asks whether the distributor has represented foreign suppliers on a long-term basis. If a distributor has represented a large number of suppliers for a long period of time, this suggests that the distributor is committed to its business and works very hard at maintaining relationships with its foreign suppliers.

Governments as Your Facilitator

The U.S. government provides a number of programs to help exporters do business in foreign countries. Although room for improvement exists in these government programs, they are valuable resources for exporters (Kotabe & Czinkota, 1992). Some of the more important ones include the following: Export-Import Bank (Eximbank), Foreign Credit Insurance Association (FCIA), Overseas Private Investment Corporation (OPIC), U.S. Department of Commerce (DOC), and U.S. Department of Agriculture (USDA).

The Export-Import Bank (Eximbank)

The Export-Import Bank, or Eximbank, is the primary U.S. agency charged with providing support for American exports through credit risk protection and lending programs. It has no involvement with imports, despite of its name. Its role in support of export financing and credit should grow as banks become increasingly averse to trade finance in general, and country risk in particular. Eximbank joins in cofinancing large projects with other U.S. government financial agencies, the World Bank, and regional multilateral development banks (MDBs), as well as private-sector financial institutions.

Eximbank's mission is to assume most of the risk inherent in financing the production and sale of exports, provide financing to foreign buyers of American goods and services when not available from the private sector, and help American exporters meet officially supported or subsidized foreign credit competition. These roles fit into three functional categories: the working capital guarantee program, foreign credit risk protection programs, and direct loans and loans to intermediary lenders.

Working Capital Guarantee Program

The working capital guarantee program is a relatively minor part of Eximbank's lending program, but it is growing rapidly and is the keystone of the bank's response to congressional mandates to provide better service to small businesses. The program is unique in that it addresses the needs of businesses for working capital to undertake an export commitment or expansion; other programs are meant to finance exports after shipment or performance and pending payment. Exporters can approach Eximbank through their bank or directly for a working capital guarantee.

Foreign Credit Risk Protection Programs

Foreign credit risk protection comprises the second Eximbank function, covering two areas: short- and medium-term foreign buyer and country risk insurance protection through FCIA, and Eximbank medium- and long-term loan guarantees that cover the risks of nonpayment by the foreign buyer or country due to political or economic problems. These guarantee programs have been among Eximbank's most active programs in recent years.

Direct Loans and Loans to Intermediary Lenders

Direct loans and loans to intermediary lenders comprise the third Eximbank function. The direct loan program used to be Eximbank's major activity, but in recent years this program has declined significantly in importance and availability. The loans are at fixed rates and come in two forms: direct loans by Eximbank to the foreign buyer, and loans to responsible intermediaries. For the loans to intermediaries, there is no Eximbank guarantee covering payment by the foreign buyer. A separate Eximbank guarantee or FCIA insurance coverage must be obtained if protection is desired for that risk.

Foreign Credit Insurance Association

Although Eximbank is by far the largest of the government agencies discussed, most likely your first need will be for the services of the Foreign Credit Insurance Association (FCIA). FCIA is a quasi-governmental insurance organization that has a number of products to protect the foreign contracts and accounts receivables of American exporters. FCIA is developing new policies to enable new and smaller exporters to make better use of their insurance and to provide coverage for the special needs of all exporters. It is considered a quasi-governmental organization because it was originally started by Eximbank in cooperation with a consortium of private insurance companies.

If you decide to deal with an insurance broker for an FCIA policy, it is best if you find one that specializes to some degree in FCIA policies, as well as international insurance in general. Alternatively, you might contact an FCIA regional office, and the staff will work with you directly to obtain your policy or give you the names of appropriate brokers. The cost is the same in either case. FCIA must determine that you are creditworthy before it will issue a policy. While the requirements for acceptance of your firm are modest, your export experience, customer list and target countries, transaction size, past credit losses, and proposed annual insurable volume all will affect your eligibility, as well as the type of policy and its premium rate.

Overseas Private Investment Corporation

The Overseas Private Investment Corporation (OPIC) can be very useful when dealing with developing countries. Organized as a self-sustaining corporation, OPIC received only startup funding, which has been repaid. Its purpose is to promote economic growth in developing countries by encouraging American private investment in those nations. Its primary functions are project-related medium- to long-term political financing and political risk insurance. OPIC also has a special small business orientation and engages in educational and informational undertakings notably through its investment missions. The Omnibus Trade Bill of 1988 increased its overall guarantee ceilings and loan funds.

Because of OPIC's unique characteristics, it can be difficult to clearly determine its programs, which might shift at times as a result of budgetary restrictions and congressional mandates. The same is true to an extent of the countries in which OPIC can operate. Some countries might emerge from developing-nation status, while others become so destabilized that it is impossible for OPIC to accept risks any longer. Since OPIC is always attempting to add developing countries to its list of eligible nations, it is best to check with OPIC if you are uncertain about the status of a program or country. A nation must permit OPIC operations through a government-to-government agreement. Those programs offered by OPIC are discussed below.

Investment Insurance Program

The largest OPIC program is its investment insurance program that covers against the risks of inconvertibility of currency, expropriation, and political violence. OPIC primarily insures new medium- and long-term investments (3 years or longer), or in some cases, expansion of an existing investment. OPIC also has special insurance programs to encourage exploration for and development of minerals, oil, and gas, as well as international leases and institutional loans.

Investment Financing Program

The Overseas Private Investment Corporation provides medium- to long-term loan guarantees and even direct loans to ventures that involve significant equity and management participation by American business. The loans are available principally for project financing, and OPIC's participation is based primarily on the economic, technical, marketing, and financial soundness inherent in the project.

International Leasing Program

The international leasing program is actually a twin program, comprised of both insurance and financial assistance. The insurance portion is tailored along OPIC's typical insurance approach to cover losses of the insured leaser because of currency inconvertibility, expropriation, or political violence. It can be applied to cross-border operation or capital lease transactions. It also can cover equity investments in offshore leasing companies, management and maintenance agreements, and consigned inventory.

Contractors and Exporters Insurance Program

The contractors and exporters insurance program is a specialized coverage insurance program to help protect American contractors and exporters from wrongful action by government agencies, and to a lesser degree private buyers, in the developing world. The program represents an exception to OPIC's usual emphasis on medium- to long-term commitments, and coverage can be acquired for a minimum of 6 months.

Small Contractor Guarantee Program

If the contractor is qualified as a small contractor (not among the "Fortune 1,000"), the small contractor guarantee program addresses a bane of small business, getting a guarantee for the bank to support a standby letter of credit to be used as a performance bond. In some cases this might permit utilization of at least part of the down payment for working capital purposes instead of being held as collateral for the standby letter of credit, so often necessary to validate the underlying contract.

Opportunity Bank and Investor Information Services

The opportunity bank is a computerized database maintained by OPIC to match American investors with developing country projects. It currently has more than 1,000 overseas projects and 4,000 potential American investors on file. Most investors are firms interested in joint ventures to increase their potential worldwide sales territory or improve their efficiency and competitiveness domestically and abroad, perhaps even to secure a necessary component or raw material for their U.S. production.

The U.S. Department of Commerce

The U.S. Department of Commerce (DOC) addresses both the domestic and international commercial activities of the United States and is a very large and complex organization. It offers several useful programs for firms with limited experience and resources: International Trade Administration (ITA), Census Bureau, and National Technical Information Service (NTIS).

International Trade Administration

The International Trade Administration (ITA) is responsible for the bulk of international commerce support except for agriculture. The ITA is a vital instrument of the federal government. As an exporter, your primary focus in terms of government affairs as they apply directly to your business should be on the ITA, whose policies are developed and governed by the Under Secretary for International Trade. ITA arranges for programs to assist your export promotion efforts, develops information and statistics that make your own market research possible, determines the availability and effectiveness of our domestic trade specialists and overseas officers, and participates in formulating and implementing part of our foreign trade and economic policies in cooperation with the U.S. Trade Representative (USTR). However, there are no financing or financial assistance programs offered by ITA.

Census Bureau

The census is one of the major functions of the DOC and is the principal gatherer of statistics, including all import and export statistics. Most of their statistics that apply to exporting are utilized for trade analysis by the ITA. The office of key importance to the exporter within the Census Bureau is the Center for International Research (CIR). This organization gathers useful data for international marketing purposes on overseas demographic trends. The categories for these data are numerous and include such statistics as infant mortality, migrations, marital status and family planning, literacy, and housing indicators.

National Technical Information Service

Also part of the DOC, but under a different administrative division than the Census Bureau, the National Technical Information Service (NTIS) is a government research clearinghouse. It gathers information and publishes market share reports and country market surveys. The NTIS is responsible for coordinating the publishing of as many as 70 to 80 useful publications and country-specific newsletters.

U.S. Department of Agriculture

The U.S. Department of Agriculture (USDA) has an aggressive export program. The Foreign Agricultural Service (FAS), a major unit of the USDA, administers export affairs for the USDA and has a worldwide network of attachés and counselors who gather and access information on world agriculture production and trade. The FAS offers marketing assistance through the Agricultural Information and Marketing Service (AIMS). AIMS functions as a liaison between American companies and foreign buyers seeking food and agricultural products, and assists in introducing American products to foreign markets, as well as expanding present overseas markets. The four primary services of the USDA to assist food and agricultural exporters are trade leads, product publicity, foreign importer listings, and the buyer alert program.

CHAPTER 8

Budgeting for Exporting

Upon completing this chapter you should be able to

- understand the effects of foreign exchange rates on budgeting;
- understand how to control budgets in exporting.

Budgets for Export Activities

Budgeting systems are part of the firm's accounting system and are very useful as administrative planning mechanisms. A budget can be defined as a forecast of revenues and expenses expected to occur within a future time period. One of the problems that exporters often face in foreign markets is that the lack of internal control mechanisms. Thus managers use budgets to compare actual results with planned results as a means of controlling their foreign market activities. However, budgets also assist in decision making by assembling knowledge and disseminating it to managers.

Budget Development

Budgets are developed by using key planning assumptions about the business, such as product prices, foreign currency exchange rates, external prices of inputs, and unit sales (please refer to the spreadsheet). Each key planning assumption must be forecast using past experience, field estimates, and statistical analysis (e.g., regression analysis).

Budgetary Control

While controlling foreign market activities is challenging, exporters should prepare budgets to control the company's export performance internally (Miller, 1993b). Here, control is a process of ensuring that an enterprise's activities conform to what has been planned to happen as indicated in the budget. Therefore no control is feasible without objectives and plans developed in advance. Some of the critical components of budgetary control are variance analysis, budget choice, and sales estimation.

Variance Analysis

Variance is the difference between budgeted and actual costs, or standard costs and actual costs. The variance may relate to price or quantity for labor, materials, and overhead. However, in export activities, such variance can result from unanticipated movement of exchange rates between multiple currencies. Hence the key to control process in an exporting firm is the provision of accurate up-to-date information on actual results compared with budgeted results.

Budget Choice

There are different types of budget categories; for example, short-term versus long-term budgets, static versus flexible budgets, lapsing versus nonlapsing budgets, and incremental versus zero-based budgets (Hirsch, 1994). However, in our context, we will discuss the first two categories.

Short-Term Versus Long-Term Budgets

Budgets that project only 1 year at a time are called short-term budgets. Starting in the first year, firms develop detailed plans for the next year of how many units of each product they expect to sell at which prices, the estimated costs of such sales, and the financing necessary for operations. A good example is the annual budget. Most firms also make projections for 2, 5, and even 10 years. These types of budgets are called long-term budgets. Long-term budgets are highly tied to the firm's strategic planning and management mechanisms. Strategic planning and management refers to the process whereby managers determine corporate and business strategies and allocate resources based on the goals and tactics outlined in these strategies. One important difference between the long-term and short-term budgets is that the former is not and should not be used for annual performance control because the key parameters used in it incorporate a longer planning horizon for the firm's activities.

For an exporter, both of these budgets are necessary. Whereas short-term budgets help in performance evaluation, long-term budgets help the firm assess the profit potential of the export business and deploying resources among export markets and the domestic market.

Static Versus Flexible Budgets

Static budgets do not vary with volume, where each line item is a fixed amount. Flexible budgets are stated as a function of some volume mea-sure and are adjusted for changes in volume. Thus they can be used to evaluate performance after controlling for volume effects. Flexible bud-gets take into account the fact that some costs (fixed and variable) vary with changes in the activity level. Static budgets are not recommended unless export managers have control over the volume of sales.

Let us illustrate the difference between these two budgets with a sim-ple numerical example. The management of Company IBC is curious about the performance of the firm in its export markets over the previous year. While some executives want to evaluate the performance of export managers using their traditional static budget, some propose a flexible budget for a more realistic comparison. The claim of the latter is that export managers do not have direct control over export sales and there-fore should not be judged based on a predetermined volume. Finally, they decide to use both types of the budgets.

ACTUAL VOLUME = 6,000 UNITS	ACTUAL	FLEXIBLE	STATIC
Revenues	$35,000	$36,000	$31,000
Costs	20,000	21,800	19,000
SG&A expenses	4,000	4,000	4,000
Operating income	11,000	10,200	8,000

For the static budget, the figures are fixed and predetermined during the budgeting period. These figures reflect the management's estimate of revenues and related costs for the next year and are independent of unit sales. The flexible budget, however, reflects changes in volume. While revenues and costs are functions of volume, selling, general, and adminis-trative (SG&A) expenses are independent of the unit of actual sales:

$$\text{Revenue(V)} = 18,000 + 3.0V$$
$$\text{Costs(V)} = 11,000 + 1.8V,$$

where coefficients in the linear functions are determined through a simple linear regression.

Sales Estimation

As was shown in the previous section, an important part of budget setting is sales estimation. This is especially important when a firm uses a static budget for evaluation. In order to estimate sales in the foreign market, as well as in the domestic market, both the microenvironment (market structure) and the macroenvironment (international/national economy, government regulations, social organizations, etc.) should be taken into consideration. Since control of the macro factors is difficult, management should base their estimations on the constituents of the microenvironment without neglecting the possible impact of changes in the macroenvironment.

One way to estimate sales is to do a "feature-based competitive analysis." Use of feature-based competitive analysis can help a manager in identifying the relevant competitors and therefore come up with a realistic price.

Standard Costs and Export Control

Another way to control a firm's export activities is to rely on standard costs that can be compared with actual costs. Standard costs represent the expected future cost of a product or process (Cavusgil, 1988). Once standards are set, managers can judge performance by comparing actual results against the standards. The amount by which actual and standard costs differ is the standard cost variance. Standard costs arise from the budgeting process. In setting the budget for the next year, managers determine expected production volumes, per-unit costs of goods, and prices to charge for the output. For an illustration of the concept of standard costing, take the following example:

Company IBC produces only three products (X, Y, and Z). Product X, Product Y, and Product Z require $20, $30, and $40 per unit of production costs, respectively. The firm plans to produce 10 units of Product X, 50 units of Product Y, and 30 units of Product Z this year. In this example, per-unit costs of production (materials, labor, and overhead are included in these costs) are standard costs and are used in the operating budget. As a result, the total operating budget is equal to

($20 × 10) + ($30 × 50) + ($40 × 30) = $200 + $1500+ $1200 = $2900.

This will be the operating cost of the firm for the coming year based on standard costs and estimated units of production.

Types of Standard Costs

Standard Labor Cost

To estimate the standard labor cost, one should make a detailed study of the time required to produce a unit of the product. These times can be obtained by conducting a time and motion study, which determines the most efficient production method. For each operation, a standard minute value or standard hours can be established. These times then have to be multiplied by a standard direct labor rate, which is the rate planned for over the period for which the standard cost will be effective.

Material Standard Cost

In this process, the amount of raw materials required in the product is multiplied by a standard price, the planned purchase price for a period of time, to give the total standard costs of materials.

Overhead Standards

Overhead standard costs can be calculated using the following formulas (assuming full absorption of costs):

$$OHR = [FOH/BV + VOH],$$

where FOH and VOH are the estimated fixed and variable overheads, respectively, and BV is the budgeted volume, the amount of production expected to occur during the year, usually stated in terms of a common input measure such as direct labor hours.

Use of Standard Costing

Standard costs are useful for both decision making and decision control. Some advantages of standard costing include the following:

- *Budget setting.* During the calculation of standard costs, detailed production specifications such as labor times, materials content, and standard prices need to be gathered. These specifications allow for more accurate budgets.
- *Provision of control information.* The use of a standard cost resembles the use of a budget. By comparing actual costs incurred over a period with standard costs, variances can be calculated in total and by materials, labor, and overhead. By monitoring these variances, effective corrective action can be taken if there are any deviations from the planned performance.
- *Determination of best methods.* The fact that an enterprise has to identify the various operations, times, and appropriate materials to calculate standard costs can help focus attention on the most efficient use of resources.
- *Enhancing motivation.* Standard costs can become targets for individuals at work. For example, standard labor times can be used as a basis for payment of workers. However, this type of reward system should be approached with caution.
- *Aid in price determination.* Perhaps the main advantage of standard costing for the exporter is the use of standard costs to provide the basis for export quotes. However, exporters should always review the standard cost variances to avoid unrealistic price quotes, because basing quotes on a standard cost estimated some months ago may misrepresent current costs (see Chapter 13).

Foreign Exposures

As a firm engages in export activities, it faces various unwanted foreign exposures and risks, which are mostly uncontrollable factors to the firm. Foreign currency exchange rates, interest rates, and inflation are three external factors that affect international operations of a firm through various exposures (Cavusgil, Knight, & Riesenberger, 2008; Hill, 1997). Foreign exchange rates, in particular, have the most significant effect on the budgeting process because interest rate and inflation differentials affect the future movement of the spot exchange rate. That is, foreign exchange rate fluctuations may affect the operations of an exporter through translation exposure, transaction exposure, and economic exposure. Each of these exposures has a different impact on the profit planning and control process and will be discussed below.

Translation Exposure

Translation exposure is also referred to as "accounting risk." Companies incur gains and losses resulting from translation to their home currency (throughout this section we are assuming that the firm has two budgets for control: one for export activities and the other for selling in the domestic market). Usually firms choose an anticipated exchange rate when preparing the budget. However, the actual exchange rate will likely vary from the anticipated rate throughout the budgeting period.

One way to remove the direct (but not the indirect) effects of exchange rate fluctuations is to use the same exchange rate existing at the time the budget was developed to evaluate performance at the end of the budget period. A more comprehensive way of removing the effects of exchange rate variations would be to use a different exchange rate for each revenue and expense category being reviewed (Hill, 1997).

Transaction Exposure

Transaction exposure results from unhedged contracted cash flows that characterize international transactions. For example, if the exporter is paid with a currency other than its own national currency, a depreciation in that foreign currency (against its own domestic currency) will adversely affect the exporter's profitability. Thus an exporter should hedge its export-related cash flows. In addition to the hedging methods discussed in Chapter 12, the exporter can reduce its transaction risk by diversifying over many export markets.

Hedging involves additional transactions and expenses that must be recognized in the budgeting process. The exporter should develop a hedging policy to identify the minimum amount of cash flow to be hedged, the hedging methods used, and the conditions for hedging. Managers involved in planning cash flows should identify transactions requiring hedging during the budget process.

Economic Exposure

Economic exposure actually involves uncontracted future cash flows generated from operations of a multinational company. However, market-related policies of the budgeting process equally apply to exporters. Some of these market-related policies include the following:

- Selecting and segmenting export markets that minimize the effects of foreign currency fluctuations while maximizing long-term profits
- Establishing a pricing strategy that is based on either market shares for products with a high price elasticity or on profit margin for those with a low price elasticity
- Adjusting promotional budgets to take advantage of improved price positioning in the event of a currency devaluation
- Developing sales mix strategies for both currency devaluations and revaluations

These market-related policies will dictate the manner in which the sales budget will vary with respect to changes in the exchange rate. Once established, the policies will be part of the profit planning process while also being used to evaluate the actual performance of foreign operations that are subject to exchange rate fluctuations.

Flexible budgeting is useful for budget control in exporting where a large degree of uncertainty exists. For example, an increase in the taxes imposed on imported goods or a sudden devaluation of the importing country's currency against the exporter's currency will adversely affect the exporting process. However, many of the uncontrollable influences of the international environment can be isolated to provide a better picture of the exporter's actual performance. Flexible budgeting allows management to forecast the effects of a variety of scenarios so that strategies can be prepared and implemented if necessary.

Exporting companies face various external factors that influence budget policies, composition, and control. Budgeting in a global business environment calls for an enhanced level of coordination and communication throughout the company because of the variety of components that impact organizational performance.

CHAPTER 9

Analyzing the Legal Environment of Exporting

Upon completing this chapter you should be able to

- understand what key legal issues are relevant in exporting;
- recognize the basic types of contracts involved in international transactions;
- comprehend the background and current state of key U.S. laws and treaties regarding exporting;
- describe the major restrictions on exporting;
- be familiar with resources containing important information.

Understanding Legal Implications for Export Activities

The law enters every facet of business relationships, and exporting is no exception. There are a few key legal issues that companies beginning to export always face. These include contracts, customs benefits, and barriers to trade (Cavusgil, Deligonul, & Zhang, 2004; Deligonul, Kim, Roath, & Cavusgil, 2006; Jain, 1989). In addition, with changes in the international climate over the past decade, several other legal issues have become more important. Such concepts as intellectual property rights, antitrust, and the practices of foreign countries must now be considered (Jain, 1996). This chapter attempts to provide you with the basic information you need to avoid legal problems in the future by taking the correct steps at the beginning of your export process.

Keeping this in mind, it is essential to consult an experienced lawyer when beginning export operations. The documentation involved in exporting is complex, and small mistakes in documentation can lead to enormous difficulties. After completing this chapter you will be aware enough of the legal issues involved in exporting to understand why your lawyer requests certain information and be able to provide the necessary

Figure 9.1. Legal considerations in exporting.

information, having prepared it in advance. You will also be able to identify legal questions specific to your company's export operations, which will need to be addressed by your corporate counsel.

U.S. Policy Regarding Exports

In general, the government of the United States attempts to encourage U.S. businesses to export because of the obvious economic gains achieved by doing so. The Export Administration Act of 1979 (50 U.S.C. 2401 et seq.) sets forth the official policy of the U.S. on exports. A few important restrictions included in this act are as follows:

- Exported products must be "consistent with the economic, security, and foreign policy objectives of the United States."
- Exports of goods or technology that may make a significant contribution to the military potential of other countries may affect U.S. national security and are therefore stringently regulated.
- Agricultural exports are strongly encouraged, due to their "critical importance to the maintenance of a sound agricultural sector...positive contribution to the balance of payments, to reducing the level of Federal expenditures for agricultural support programs, and to United States cooperation in efforts to eliminate malnutrition and world hunger."
- Goods that are "hazardous to the public health and the environment which are banned or severely restricted for use in the United States" are tightly controlled because of concern for health and for the "international reputation of the United States as a responsible trading partner."

The Commerce Control List (CCL) from the Bureau of Industry and Security (BIS) identifies specific goods and technologies as well as destinations that are subject to Export Administration Regulations (EAR). The current U.S. commodities control list and destination restrictions can be found at the EAR Web site (http://www.access.gpo.gov/bis/ear/ear_data.html).

For most products, an export license is not required. However, whether an export license is required can be only determined by the product, the destination, the buyer, and the use of the product. Those products not controlled by the U.S. government are labeled as EAR99. Only a selected list of products and destinations, or non-EAR99 items, require an export license (ITA, 2008). Even if the product doesn't require an export license, the exporter should also consider the current U.S. regulations on export destinations. The level of restrictions vary from country to country. Therefore the product and country have to be considered to determine whether the destination is one of the allowed countries for the product. However, countries like Cuba, Iran, North Korea, Sudan, and Syria, which are currently on the U.S. sanction list, are most restricted and therefore an export license is most likely required. Even if a destination is not on the restricted destination list, the exporter is expected to determine if the product is on any of the following lists the BIS maintains: Entity List, Treasury Department Specially Designated Nationals and Blocked Persons List, Unverified List, and Denied Persons List. These lists are all available on the BIS Web site (http://www.bis.doc.gov). Finally, after the product, destination, and buyer are all cleared, the U.S. government likes to make sure that the end use of the product is not contrary to U.S. interests and security. For instance, nuclear and biological products have to go through further scrutiny to ensure that such products are not used for the production of weapons of mass destruction; that is, the end use should not be prohibited by U.S. regulations.

If a product is allowed to export to a destination for the use purpose of the buyer, the exporter is not required to obtain an export license; this is also called a general license. Exporters can simply indicate NLR (No License Required) on the Shipper's Export Declaration. If an export license is required to export the product, the exporter can apply to BIS for an Individually Verified License (IVL). BIS currently accepts applications for export licenses online through its Web site (http://www.bis.doc.gov).

Figure 9.2. Determining whether export license is required.

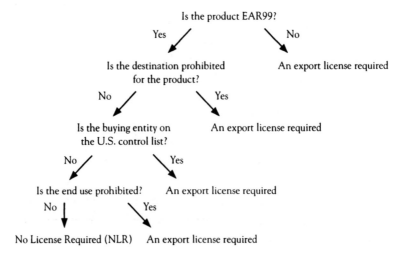

Export Contracts

An export contract contains the specifics on every possible aspect of a transaction. Since it involves legal obligations and commitments, exporters need to assess the implications of the specifics before signing. There are several key questions that must be answered before the contract can be written:

- Who will be involved in the agreement (distributors, sales representatives, manufacturers)?
- When will the contract terms take effect and how long will they be in effect?
- How will the companies involved comply with government regulations?
- How and where will disputes regarding the contract be settled?
- What are the terms of payment?
- Under what circumstances may the contract be changed or terminated and by whom?
- What are the prices specified in the contract and how long will they be good?
- How will training of the foreign company's personnel be handled, and who will pay for it?
- What information is considered confidential?
- Who will have responsibility for obtaining customs clearance?
- What information will the foreign company supply to the exporter (sales reports, names of active prospects, government regulations dealing with imports, etc.)?
- What responsibilities are involved regarding claims and warranties?
- What products or services are covered by the agreement?
- Is agreement exclusive?
- What is the sales or distribution territory covered by the agreement?

After these questions are answered, an experienced lawyer should draft a formal contract. The lawyer will probably request more information at that time, depending on the nature of the transaction, the parties involved, and the country targeted for export.

The following sections explain the three types of contracts and the key issues involved in creating such contracts. The three types of contracts are sales contracts, distributor/agency/representative contracts, and technology transfer/licensing contracts.

Sales Contracts

International sales contracts are similar in form and function to domestic sales contracts: they constitute an agreement between a seller and a buyer to exchange a set amount of goods or services, within a set time frame, for a set price. Since 1988, international sales contracts of U.S.-based firms have been governed by the rules of the United Nations Convention on Contracts for the International Sale of Goods (CISG). This agreement applies to international sales contracts in much the same way that the Uniform Commercial Code applies to domestic sales contracts.

The CISG automatically applies to any international sales contract between signatory countries (called "contracting states"). For a list of signatory countries, see the exhibit at the end of this chapter. One provision in the CISG allows the parties to opt out of conforming to the CISG regulations entirely, but this must be expressly stated in the contract.

The CISG regulates the contract formation process and several specific elements of the contract, such as the rights and obligations of each party and the method for resolving disputes (usually arbitration). An experienced lawyer who specializes in international business can help your company understand the implications of the CISG and create a contract that conforms to the CISG to protect both contracting parties.

Distribution/Agency/Representative Contracts

An overseas agent is the equivalent of a manufacturer's representative here in the United States. The agent uses the firm's product literature and samples to present the product to potential buyers. The agent usually works on a commission basis, assumes no responsibilities or risks, and is under contract for a definite period of time. Agents as a type of business relationship give the exporter the advantage of greater control over performance, resale, pricing, and so on.

A foreign distributor is a merchant who purchases goods from U.S. exporters and resells them at a profit (Bello & Lohtia, 1995). Distributors will normally handle noncompetitive but complementary product lines. Generally the distributor carries an inventory of products and a sufficient supply of spare parts at facilities staffed by trained personnel to provide normal servicing. Payment terms and length of association, as with the agent, are established by contract.

Many companies that are new to exporting prefer distributors who allow them to minimize their economic and management involvement. A distributor provides the exporter with a local sales force and office, the ability to import into the distributor's country, and a knowledge of local customs and business practices (Cavusgil, Knight, & Riesenberger, 2008). The exporter reduces his risk because the distributor buys for his account and resells.

One of the most important issues in creating a contract with a distributor or agent is that of exclusivity: Will the representative have exclusive rights to a certain territory? Some countries require that all contracts with importing companies include an exclusivity clause. This presents risks and advantages to the U.S. exporter in the same way that contracting with only one supplier for parts does. The agent or distributor is likely to offer lower prices, feel more loyal, and establish a long-term relationship if an exclusive contract is offered. However, if the distributor or agent fails to perform the duties expressed in the contract, the exporting company is likely to lose sales and incur a financial loss.

Technology Transfer/Licensing Contracts

Technology transfer involves offering technological know-how or other intellectual property to a foreign business in exchange for some type of compensation (Cavusgil et al., 2008). Generally the exporting firm engages a foreign party to manufacture or merchandise a technology-oriented product. Technology transfers can be accomplished through licensing agreements, or a U.S. firm can use a transfer of technology as part or all of its contribution to a joint venture abroad. The joint venture uses the technology to manufacture and market the product or component, and the U.S. firm's return is a percentage ownership in the joint venture.

Some U.S. companies prefer technology transfer agreements for several reasons, including lack of capacity in domestic manufacturing facilities, a weak research and development department, or inadequate marketing capability abroad. Technology transfer arrangements are a method of gaining access to foreign markets without raising additional capital. However, many countries place restrictions on technology transfer agreements so that licensees in those countries have more rights. When investigating the possibility of creating a technology transfer agreement, it is necessary to look into country-specific restrictions. Technology transfers often include the following key elements discussed below.

Rights to Use and Conditions of Use

The licensor often agrees to provide various services to facilitate the anticipated activities, such as assistance in setting up an assembly line, training, or technical support. Common restrictions on the licensee's use of the technology include geographic limitations on manufacturing or marketing activities and field of use limitations, which restrict the applications for which the licensee may employ the technology.

Competitive Circumstances

Licensees sometimes seek to protect their investments in manufacturing or marketing resources by requesting exclusive rights to the technology within a specified geographic area. The licensor may not want to comply with this request because of the risks involved, including a licensee's lack of commitment, inability to secure financing, or ineffective marketing. One way a licensor can protect itself in such a situation is to grant rights to two or more licensees who are willing to compete to develop the target market.

Confidentiality

Licensors usually require the licensee to keep the licensed technology confidential so that third parties cannot exploit the technology. The length of time that confidentiality is required is often a bargaining point for both the licensor and the licensee.

Intellectual Property Rights Considerations

The United States provides a wide range of protections for intellectual property, including patents, trademarks, service marks, copyrights, trade secrets, and semiconductor mask works. Many businesses—particularly high-technology firms, the publishing industry, chemical and pharmaceutical firms, the recording industry, and computer software companies —depend heavily on the protections afforded their creative products and processes.

The rights granted under U.S. patent, trademark, and copyright laws can be enforced only in the United States, its territories, and its possessions; they confer no protection in a foreign country (Jain, 1996). The protection available in each country depends on that country's national laws, administrative practices, and treaty obligations. A country's business environment can be further affected by the customs in that country regarding protecting such intellectual properties (Jain, 1996). International treaties set certain minimum standards for protection, but exporters should remember that individual country laws differ significantly and that it is ultimately the exporter's responsibility to protect its intellectual properties outside the United States.

Patents and Trademarks

To secure patent and trademark rights outside the United States, a company must apply for a patent or register a trademark on a country-by-country basis. However, U.S. individuals and corporations are entitled to a "right of priority" and to "national treatment" in the 100 countries that, along with the United States, are parties to the Paris Convention for the Protection of Industrial Property. National treatment means that a member country will not discriminate against foreigners in granting patent or trademark protection. The rights conferred may be greater or less than those provided under U.S. law, but they must be the same as the country provides its own nationals. However, it is important to note that many countries still discriminate against foreign corporations.

Copyright

The level and scope of copyright protection available within a country also depends on that country's domestic laws and treaty obligations. In most countries, the place of first publication is an important criterion for determining whether foreign works are available for copyright protection.

The Berne Convention for the Protection of Literary and Artistic Works provides for the automatic protection, in more than 80 countries, of works first published in the United States on or after March 1, 1989 (Wikipedia, 2008). The United States also maintains copyright relations with a number of countries under a second international agreement called the Universal Copyright Convention.

Responsibilities of Exporters

Intellectual property rights owners should be aware that after valuable intellectual property rights have been secured in foreign markets, enforcement must be accomplished through local law. Practically speaking, intellectual property rights are private rights to be enforced by the rights owner. Enforcement varies substantially from country to country and depends on such factors as the attitude of local officials, substantive requirements of the law, and court procedures. In summary, U.S. exporters with intellectual property concerns should consider the following:

- Obtain protection under all applicable U.S. laws for inventions, trademarks, service marks, copyrights, and semiconductor mask works.
- Research the intellectual property laws of countries where they may conduct business. The United States and Foreign Commercial Service (US&FCS) has information about intellectual property laws and practices in particular countries, although it does not provide legal advice. Further information can be obtained by contacting the U.S. Commercial Service at 1-800-872-8723 or by visiting its Web site at http://www.export.gov/eac/index.asp.
- Secure the services of competent local counsel to file appropriate patent, trademark, or copyright applications within priority periods.

- Adequately protect trade secrets through appropriate confidentiality provisions in employment, licensing, marketing, distribution, and joint venture agreements.

Dispute Resolution Mechanism

When creating a contract for an international transaction, consider including a clause specifying arbitration as the dispute resolution mechanism. Arbitration is a procedure in which two disagreeing parties present their arguments to a neutral, third-party arbitrator and agree to be bound by the arbitrator's decision. There are several reasons to use arbitration (Hill, 1997):

- The choice of law to be applied to an arbitration proceeding is specified in the contract, which facilitates familiarity with the applicable law for both parties.
- Costs are more predictable.
- Procedures are more flexible than those of courts.
- Arbitrators are more expert and experienced than judges in national courts.
- Arbitration decisions are efficiently enforced in the courts of countries that are signatories to the United Nations Convention on the Recognition and Enforcement of Foreign Arbitral Awards (more than 60 countries).

When designing a contract to include arbitration, consider the choice of location for proceedings, the choice of language, the number of arbitrators and manner of their appointment, and whether arbitrators can act as amicable intermediaries (i.e., apply equitable doctrines).

The International Chamber of Commerce (ICC) often acts as an arbitration agency. To request arbitration, send a written request to the Secretariat of the Court of Arbitration through its National Committee. The contact information for the ICC Court of Arbitration is as follows:

ICC Dispute Board Centre
International Chamber of Commerce
38 cours Albert 1er
75008 Paris, France

More information can be found on their Web site at http://www.iccwbo .org/court/dispute_boards/id4346/index.html. When contacting the Court of Arbitration, make sure you include the following information:

- Names in full of the parties and their addresses
- Circumstances of the case
- Reason for the request
- All original documents or copies proving the existence of the arbitration agreement
- Wishes of the party concerning the number of arbitrators

The request may be written in English or French.

Antitrust laws exist in the United States and other countries to encourage competition and provide consumers with competitive products. U.S. antitrust laws may also apply to business conducted outside the United States, and U.S. companies must abide by the antitrust laws of host countries. The Effects Doctrine developed by Judge Learned Hand provides for U.S. courts to assume jurisdiction when the conduct of a U.S. company outside of the United States has a "direct, substantial, and foreseeable effect" on U.S. commerce. Furthermore, the Sovereign Compliance Doctrine allows a U.S. firm to defend its actions on the grounds that its actions were compelled by a foreign state (i.e., the foreign government). However, the action must be proven to have been compulsory rather than encouraged or suggested.

Tax Laws

There are several categories of tax- or import duty-related laws that extend special treatment and tax exemptions to foreign entities or buyers from outside the country.

Drawback Tax Relief

Drawback is a form of tax refund in which a lawfully collected customs duty is refunded or remitted in whole or in part because of the particular use made of the commodity on which the duty was collected. This practice encourages U.S. exporters by permitting them to compete in foreign markets without the handicap of including in their sales prices the duties paid on imported components. To obtain drawback, the U.S. firm must file a proposal with a regional commissioner of customs or with the Entry Rulings Branch, U.S. Customs Headquarters (http://www.customs.treas .gov/impoexpo/impoexpo.htm). These offices may also provide a model drawback proposal for U.S. companies. A regional commissioner of customs regarding drawback can be contacted at one of the following U.S. drawback center locations:

Chicago
U.S. Customs and Border Protection
9915 Bryn Mawr Ave.
3rd Floor
Rosemont, IL 60018
Drawback Chief: 847-928-6077

Houston
U.S. Customs and Border Protection
2350 N. Sam Houston Parkway East
Suite 1000
Houston, TX 77032
Drawback Chief: 281-985-6890

Los Angeles/Long Beach
U.S. Customs and Border Protection
Port of Los Angeles—Seaport
301 E. Ocean Boulevard
Long Beach, CA 90802
Drawback Chief: 562-366-5706

New York/Newark
U.S. Customs and Border Protection
1100 Raymond Boulevard
Room 310
Newark, NJ 07102
Drawback Chief: 973-368-6708

San Francisco
U.S. Customs and Border Protection
555 Battery Street
Room 109
San Francisco, CA 94111
Drawback Chief: 415-782-9245

U.S. Foreign Trade Zones

Exporters should also consider the customs privileges of U.S. foreign trade zones. These zones are domestic U.S. sites that are considered outside U.S. customs territory for tariff purposes and are available for activities that might otherwise be carried on overseas for customs reasons. For export operations, the zones provide accelerated export status for the purposes of excise tax rebates and customs drawback.

There are now 250 general purpose foreign trade zones throughout the United States. Associated with these projects are some 450 subzones. These facilities are available for operations involving storage, repacking, inspection, exhibition, assembly, manufacturing, and other processing. Information about the zones, including a full list of current free trade zones in the United States, is available on the International Trade Administration's Web site (http://ia.ita.doc.gov/ftzpage).

Foreign Free Port and Free Trade Zones

To encourage and facilitate international trade, more than 3,000 free ports, free trade zones, or similar customs-privileged facilities are now in operation in some 116 foreign countries, usually in or near seaports or airports. Many U.S. manufacturers and their distributors use free ports or free trade zones to receive shipments of goods that are reshipped in smaller lots to customers throughout the surrounding areas.

Bonded Warehouses

Bonded warehouses are government-approved duty free buildings or areas that can be found in many locations. In a bonded warehouse, imported goods can be stored and processed without duties being assessed. Once goods are released, they are subject to import duties.

Import Barriers

Tariffs

The most common type of trade barrier is a tariff, which is a tax imposed by a government on goods entering its country. A tariff can also be constructed in the form of an import or export duty. However, export tariffs are not common. Governments use tariffs to raise revenues or to discourage the importation or exportation of certain goods. The current tariff schedules across countries can be found on the International Trade Administration's Web site (http://www.export.gov/logistics/country_tariff _info.asp).

Nontariff Barriers

In addition to tariffs, governments can place numerous restrictions on imports through the use of nontariff barriers. Some examples of nontariff barriers include the following:

- Quotas—limitations on the amount of a certain type of good imported into a country
- Monetary barriers—refusal to allow importers to exchange national currency for their own currency or creating differential exchange rates for less desirable categories of goods
- Standards—regulations regarding product quality or safety
- Approvals and processes—excessive approvals or processes required for importing certain merchandise

Political Export Controls

Occasionally an exporting country will restrict its own exports from being shipped to certain countries for political reasons. The export policies of the United States with regard to China illustrate this: China's alleged human rights violations have led to severe trade restrictions in recent years.

The U.S. Foreign Corrupt Practices Act

The Foreign Corrupt Practices Act (FCPA) was enacted by the U.S. Congress in 1977. The FCPA makes it unlawful for any American citizen or U.S. firm to offer, pay, or promise to pay money or anything of value to any foreign official for the purpose of obtaining or retaining business. Furthermore, as a U.S. business manager, it is also unlawful to make a payment to any person while knowing that all or a portion of the payment will be given to any foreign official for the purposes of assisting the person or firm in obtaining or retaining business.

The FCPA also contains provisions applicable to publicly held companies concerning financial record keeping and internal accounting controls. The Department of Justice and the Securities and Exchange Commission are responsible for enforcing the FCPA. The Department of Commerce supplies general information to U.S. exporters who have questions about the FCPA and about international developments concerning the FCPA.

Other Sources of Government Assistance

There are several other sources of U.S. government assistance that exporters are likely to find helpful. These include foreign sales corporations and Eximbank, among others.

Foreign Sales Corporations

One of the most important steps a U.S. exporter can take to reduce federal income tax on export-related income is to set up a foreign sales corporation (FSC; IRS, 2008). The tax incentive provided by the FSC legislation is in the form of a permanent exemption from federal income tax for a portion of the export income attributable to the offshore activities of FSCs (26 U.S.C., § 921–927).

An FSC is a corporation set up in certain foreign countries or in U.S. possessions (other than Puerto Rico) to obtain a corporate tax exemption on a portion of its earning generated by the sale or lease of export property and the performance of some services. An FSC must meet basic formation tests and several foreign management tests throughout the year.

An FSC can be formed by manufacturers, nonmanufacturers, or groups of exporters, such as export trading companies. An FSC can function as a principal, buying and selling for its own account, or as a commission agent. It can be related to a manufacturing parent or it can be an independent merchant or broker. However, taxes paid by an FSC to a foreign country do not qualify for the foreign U.S. tax credit. States, regional authorities, trade associations, and private businesses can sponsor a shared FSC for their state's companies, their association's members, or their business clients or customers, or for U.S. companies in general.

Small FSCs are designed to give export incentives to smaller businesses. A small FSC is generally the same as an FSC, except that a small FSC must file an election with the IRS designating itself as a small FSC, which means it does not have to meet foreign management or foreign economic process requirements.

For more information about FSCs, U.S. companies may contact the Office of the Chief Counsel for International Commerce or a local IRS office:

Office of the Chief Counsel for International Commerce
U.S. Department of Commerce
14th St. and Constitution Ave., N.W., Room 5624
Washington, DC 20230
Tel: 202-482-0937
Fax: 202-482-4076

Eximbank

As discussed in Chapter 6, the Export-Import Bank of the United States (Eximbank) is an independent U.S. government agency that helps finance the overseas sales of U.S. goods and services (Eximbank, 2008). Its mission is to create jobs through exports. Through various loan guarantees and credit insurance, Eximbank helps provide a level playing field for U.S. exporters by countering the export credit subsidies of other governments. It also provides financing to creditworthy foreign buyers when private financing is unavailable. To qualify for Eximbank support, the product or service must have at least 50% U.S. content and must not adversely affect the U.S. economy.

Eximbank supports the sale of U.S. exports worldwide. In recent years its focus has shifted to emerging nations, whose economies are growing at twice the rate of the industrial nations. Eximbank will finance the export of any type of good or service, including commodities, as long as they are not military related (certain exceptions exist). Two of the bank's major goals in this area are to increase the export of environmental goods and services, which are in strong demand among the developing nations, and to expand the number of U.S. small businesses using Eximbank programs. While Eximbank is not a foreign aid or development agency, its programs often help U.S. exporters participate in development projects.

In addition to these government programs, a number of local government, industry-specific, and regional agencies provide assistance for export programs.

Exhibit: Sales and Distributorship Agreement for an International Distributorship

Date: September 15, 1997

MEMORANDUM OF AGREEMENT between Electra International Corporation, hereinafter called Electra, and

Appliance Distribution International
1325 Osaka Highway
Osaka, Japan

hereinafter called Distributor.

THE PARTIES AGREE as follows in consideration of their mutual promises herein contained:

Purpose of This Agreement

(1) The purpose of this agreement is to set forth the relations of Electra and Distributor in the sale of the following Electra Products:

Electra series 901 and 902 washers and dryers.

Distributor agrees to represent Electra and to promote vigorously the sale of all Electra products covered by this agreement in the area herein designated as its primary responsibility. Electra agrees to supply Distributor with sufficient products to enable Distributor to promote the sale of such products in its area. The sale by Electra of any products covered by this agreement to any official governmental agency within the territory of this agreement, including agencies of the government of the United States of America, is not within the scope of this agreement, and Electra shall have the sole discretion regarding any compensation that may be made to the Distributor for any of the Distributor's efforts relative to such sales.

Geographical Area

(2) The geographical area covered by this agreement is Japan. The Distributor shall be primarily responsible for representing Electra and vigorously promoting the sale of all Electra products mentioned herein in this geographical area.

Distributor Price

(3) On all sales of Electra products mentioned above which may be made by Electra to Distributor, the price and terms of sale shall be the standard Electra distributor price and terms of sale, as established from time to time by Electra. Distributor shall resell said products at prices fixed by it and Electra retains no control over such resale prices.

Sales Promotion

(4) Distributor will employ and maintain an adequate sales force to sell the Electra products mentioned above in its area and will participate in and cooperate with Electra in such promotional plans as are devised to stimulate sales of Electra products. Distributor consents to the inclusion in such plans of provisions rewarding Distributor's employees and salesmen for their efforts. Electra will make available to Distributor sales assistance, merchandising advice, advertising materials, and promotion campaigns. Electra will assist Distributor in the marketing of Electra products by scheduling advertising in international media as it deems appropriate.

Dealers

(5) Distributor will endeavor to sell Electra products to aggressive and well-financed dealers with adequate service facilities in all trading centers of importance throughout its area and shall keep Electra informed of any changes in its list of dealers. Electra will make available, from time to time, training aids and promotional material for Distributor to use with its dealers.

Sales Performance

(6) Distributor will maintain a level of sales that shall be reasonably satisfactory to Electra. In evaluating the sales performance of Distributor, Electra shall consider the nature and extent of Distributor's competition as well as the level of sales in similar markets in which Electra has had experience.

Monthly Report

(7) Distributor shall send each month to Electra a report detailing sales made since the preceding report and its stock on hand by types.

Shipments

(8) Electra will endeavor to ship products specified in any accepted order, but will not be liable for failure to ship any such products because of strikes, differences with workmen, accidents, fires, or shutdowns of its manufacturing plant(s) supplying it, by order or requirements of the U.S. government, embargoes, inability to secure transportation facilities, or other contingencies beyond the control of Electra, including those arising out of or due to national defense activities or emergency conditions. Distributor will not be liable for any failure to accept shipments of products ordered from Electra when such failure is due to strikes in Distributor's establishment or any other cause beyond its control and through no fault or negligence on Distributor's part.

Allotment of Production

(9) Electra will endeavor to make products available as ordered to meet Distributor's reasonable requirements but reserves the right to allot its

production as it deems best. Distributor agrees that any failure to supply such amounts that may be agreed upon from time to time, or making only part shipment or no shipment at all against any order of Distributor, shall not make Electra liable or responsible to Distributor to any extent.

Advertising

(10) (a) Distributor agrees that in cooperation with its dealers it will spend in advertising the Electra products covered hereby at least five (5) percent of Distributor's total selling price to dealers. Such expenditure will be in accordance with the standard cooperative advertising policy and procedure specified in writing by Electra from time to time. In addition, Distributor will also be responsible for seeing that its dealers will match this amount by spending, themselves, at least an equal amount in approved cooperative advertising of the products covered hereby.

(b) Electra will contribute to a cooperative advertising fund two (2) percent of the billing price to Distributor of all products sold under this agreement or such similar percentage as Electra may from time to time designate for certain models, except upon the sale of parts and kits of unassembled Electra trademarked products, and any other products specified in writing by Electra from time to time. Distributor is not entitled to any credit whatsoever against the said fund until the Distributor submits to Electra tear sheets or other evidence of the aggregate amount spent in advertising by Distributor and its dealers. Upon verification of such amount, Electra will reimburse Distributor from the fund for one-fourth of this combined Distributor and dealer expenditure, provided, however, that this reimbursement shall not exceed the two (2) percent contribution made to the advertising fund by Electra as a result of Distributor's purchases. Reimbursements will be issued by Electra only for approved advertising covered by tear sheets or other evidence satisfactory to Electra and received by Electra from Distributor within sixty (60) days after the date on which the advertising expenditure was made by Distributor.

(c) In the event that Distributor is engaged in both wholesaling and retailing, it agrees to assume both the wholesaler's and retailer's shares of the advertising expenditures as stated above, and the reimbursement to Distributor by Electra will be made in accordance with the above provisions.

(d) Electra reserves the right, with respect to the above advertising fund created by Electra, to withdraw from the advertising fund any unused portion of the fund at the end of each calendar year or upon the termination of this agreement for any reason whatsoever, with the understanding that Distributor may have a grace period of sixty (60) days thereafter to deliver to Electra's office all tear sheets or other evidence of advertising for which Distributor claims reimbursement under this agreement.

Service

(11) Distributor will be responsible for consistently high-quality service for Electra products. Distributor agrees to maintain, at its place of business, permanent training facilities for dealers and independent servicemen, including shop and service clinics. Distributor shall also maintain a stock of parts adequate to supply the needs of its dealers and shall see that its dealers provide expert service on Electra products through service departments organized and maintained by qualified technical personnel or through contractual arrangements with reliable service organizations that will render such service for them. Electra will maintain facilities to which Distributor may send appropriate employees for service information and instruction.

Warranty Policy

(12) A standard printed warranty is issued to the original purchaser of the above-listed products bearing the trademark Electra. Electra's obligation under the standard warranty does not include any labor cost incident to the replacement of defective parts, and the Distributor agrees to include in the retail agreements with its dealers appropriate provisions under which the retail dealer is to assume any such costs. In the event that the retail dealer fails to discharge properly his responsibilities in connection with the standard warranty to the original purchaser, Distributor shall assume the dealer's unfulfilled responsibilities. If any product listed above bearing the trademark Electra is not sold at retail within twelve (12) months after the date of purchase by Distributor, then Distributor shall relieve Electra from all obligations of the standard warranty to the original purchaser. Distributor agrees to cooperate fully

with Electra in carrying out the general warranty policy upon the above products in accordance with the standard procedure specified in writing by Electra from time to time.

Financial Statement and Responsibility

(13) Upon execution of this agreement and at such times thereafter as may be requested by Electra, Distributor agrees to furnish Electra duly certified balance sheets and such other statements in sufficient detail as may be reasonably required by Electra to establish to the satisfaction of Electra the financial responsibility of the Distributor as provided herein. Distributor agrees that it will provide, maintain, and reserve, out of its total financial resources, working capital funds in the amount deemed by Electra from time to time to be adequate in light of all attendant circumstances to properly finance the purchase of Electra products when due and to ensure the orderly and effective merchandising, sale, and dealer financing of such products.

Credit Terms and Payments

(14) This agreement does not entitle Distributor to any special credit or terms and all payments shall be made in accordance with the terms established from time to time by Electra, in default of which shipments may be suspended at Electra's discretion.

Quarterly Operating Statement

(15) Distributor shall send to Electra a quarterly operating statement in such form as Electra suggests, not later than the twenty-fifth (25th) of the month following the end of each quarter. In the preparation of these operating statements, Distributor will follow all reasonable requests for information made by Electra.

Notice of Internal Change

(16) The parties hereto agree that, due to the close relationship involved in a distributorship arrangement, Electra must necessarily rely on Distributor's business experience and good reputation to ensure the protection of

Electra's trademarks and goodwill. Therefore Distributor agrees to give Electra immediate notice in writing of (a) any transaction affecting the ownership of its capital stock, if a corporation; (b) any change in the respective interests of the partners, if a partnership; and (c) any transaction affecting the ownership of any part of the business, if an individual. Distributor also agrees that during the term of this agreement, it will not make nor suffer to be made a change of more than fifty (50) percent of the ownership of Distributor without first obtaining the written consent of Electra.

Use of Name

(17) Distributor will not use the name or trademark Electra as part of its firm, corporate, or business name, and shall not use the name or trademark Electra in any way except to designate the product purchased from Electra in accordance with this agreement. Distributor shall exercise reasonable vigilance to detect and shall report to Electra any instances coming to the Distributor's attention of infringement by any party of the name or trademark Electra.

Liabilities

(18) Electra agrees to protect Distributor and hold it harmless from any loss or claim arising out of inherent defects in any Electra product existing at the time such product is sold by Electra to Distributor, provided that Distributor gives Electra immediate notice of any such loss or claim and cooperates fully with Electra in the handling thereof. Distributor agrees to protect Electra and hold it harmless from any other kind of loss or claim arising out of the installation or use of any of the products sold hereunder, including any loss or injury to the property or person of the purchaser thereof or the purchaser's representatives or employees or any other person.

Relationship of Parties

(19) During the term hereof the relationship between Electra and Distributor is that of vendor and vendee. Distributor, its agents, and employees shall, under no circumstances, be deemed agents or representatives of

Electra. Distributor will not modify any Electra products without specific written permission from Electra. Neither Distributor nor Electra shall have any right to enter into any contracts or commitments in the name of, or on behalf of, the other, to bind the other in any respect whatsoever.

Duration of This Agreement

(20) The term of this agreement shall be from the date hereof, for an original period ending on September 15, 1998, and for yearly automatic renewal periods of one calendar year; provided, however, that either party may, by written notice to the other given not less than thirty (30) days prior to the expiration of the current period, whether original or renewal, specify the end of such period as the date of termination, and on such date this agreement shall terminate. This agreement may be terminated only at the end of the term as provided above or by either party upon a failure of the other party to comply with any of the provisions of this agreement. In the event of the failure of either party to comply with any of the provisions of this agreement, the other party may terminate this agreement as a result of such failure by giving written notice to the other party not less than thirty (30) days before such termination.

Effect of Termination

(21) In the event of termination (or at the end of the stated term of this agreement if it is not terminated sooner), Electra shall thereafter stand wholly freed and discharged, and Distributor hereby expressly releases and discharges Electra of and from any and all obligations or liability whatsoever, whether arising hereunder or from, or in connection with, any matter or thing relating to, or in any manner connected with, the subject matter of this agreement. The foregoing right of termination and the additional right on nonrenewal at the end of the stated term are absolute, and neither Electra nor Distributor shall be liable to the other because of the termination or nonrenewal hereof (whether with or without cause) for compensation, reimbursement, or damages on account of the loss of prospective profits on anticipated sales or on account of expenditures, investments, leases, or commitments in connection with the business or

goodwill of Electra or Distributor, or for any other reason whatsoever. Wherever herein reference is made to the termination of this agreement, it shall be construed as referring to termination either by the expiration of the stated term, or sooner by the act of either party, in accordance with any of the provisions hereof. Distributor shall not be relieved, however, of any obligations for any unpaid balances for goods shipped hereunder prior to termination or for special goods ordered by Distributor that are in the process of manufacture.

Termination Cancels Orders Not Shipped

(22) The termination of this agreement will operate as a cancellation, as of the date thereof, of all orders that have not been shipped, and neither party shall thereafter be under any obligation to the other with respect to orders so canceled.

Other Distributor Contracts

(23) If any other contract existing between Distributor and Electra shall, during the term hereof, be terminated other than by expiration of its stated term, Electra may, at its discretion, terminate this contract forthwith, anything herein contained to the contrary notwithstanding.

Repurchase

(24) Distributor understands that at any time during the term of this agreement or of any renewal thereof or after termination, Electra has the right to repurchase from Distributor and Distributor will resell and deliver to Electra, upon demand, such Electra products or Electra material in Distributor's stock as Electra shall elect to repurchase. The repurchase price to Electra for new and unused Electra products, except for obsolete inventory, shall be the net price paid by Distributor, less any price reductions actually received by Distributor for Electra products delivered to Distributor's premises. In the case of obsolete inventory (any products or materials not in the current line shall be considered obsolete), the repurchase price to Electra shall be such price as Electra

and Distributor may agree upon at the time Electra elects to exercise its right to repurchase obsolete inventory, if Electra so desires.

Use of Trademark Prohibited After Termination

(25) Upon termination of this agreement, Distributor will remove and not thereafter use any signs containing the name and trademark Electra, and unless Electra exercises the right to repurchase with respect to such material granted to it by paragraph (24) immediately destroy all stationery, advertising matter, and other printed matter in its possession or under its control containing the word Electra. Distributor will not at any time after such termination use or permit the word "Electra" to be used in any manner in connection with any business conducted by it or in which it may have an interest, or otherwise whatsoever as descriptive of or referring to anything other than Electra merchandise or products. Irrespective of the cause of termination, Distributor will immediately take all appropriate steps to remove and cancel its listings in telephone books, other directories, and public records, or elsewhere, which contain the name Electra. If Distributor fails to obtain such removals or cancellations promptly, Electra may make application for such removals or cancellations on behalf of Distributor and in Distributor's name, and, in such event, Distributor will render every assistance.

No Other Agreement

(26) This agreement contains the full agreement between the parties relating to the matters contained herein, and Distributor and Electra declare and agree that there are no other terms or conditions, representations, or understandings except those set forth in this agreement. The parties further agree that no other agreement or understanding hereafter in any way modifying or supplementing this agreement, nor any promises made by representatives of Electra, shall be binding on Electra unless confirmed in writing and signed by a duly authorized officer of Electra.

Notices

(27) Notices to the parties under this agreement shall be sufficiently served if mailed by Distributor to Electra at 1325 Coolidge Highway,

Royal Oak, Michigan, or if mailed by Electra to Distributor at the address herein before set forth. Such notices shall take effect as of the date of mailing.

Construction

(28) This agreement is nonassignable and nontransferable by Distributor. This agreement is executed at Royal Oak, in the State of Michigan, and both parties hereto agree that this agreement, and every matter or thing arising therefrom or incident thereto, shall be construed in accordance with the laws of the State of Michigan. In like manner, the parties hereto agree that all sales that shall be made by Electra to Distributor during the term of this agreement will be made, if made, by the acceptance by Electra of the orders of Distributor at Royal Oak, and that all such sales shall be construed in accordance with the laws of the State of Michigan, notwithstanding the fact that deliveries pursuant to such sales may be made outside of the State of Michigan. The paragraph headings in this agreement do not form a part of it but are for convenience only, and shall not limit or affect in any way the meaning of the paragraphs. The failure of either party to enforce at any time or for any period of time the provisions hereof shall not be construed to be a waiver of such provisions or of the right of such party thereafter to enforce each such provision. The parties hereto declare it is their intention to be legally bound hereby. IN WITNESS WHEREOF, the parties hereto have caused this agreement to be executed by their duly authorized officers.

ATTEST: ELECTRA INTERNATIONAL CORPORATION

By Ellen Lefevre
TITLE: President
ATTEST: APPLIANCE DISTRIBUTION INTERNATIONAL
By Noritoshi Doi
TITLE: President

CHAPTER 10

Managing Logistics and Supply Chain in Exporting

Upon completing this chapter you should

- understand the concept of the supply chain;
- understand how each function within the supply chain impacts the entire chain;
- understand how and why information can be used to improve supply chain performance;
- understand the systems concept as it applies to supply chain management;
- be familiar with the two main modes of transportation utilized for international shipping.

The concept of the supply chain is a relatively new development. The supply chain concept encourages firms to view their entire flow of information and materials as one process. The supply chain includes both internal functions, such as procurement, manufacturing, and physical distribution, as well as external parties, such as suppliers, wholesalers, retailers, and consumers (Kim, Cavusgil, & Calantone, 2006; Mentzer et al., 2001). The external parties play a vital role in the supply chain by providing feedback information to the internal parties. Figure 10.1 illustrates the supply chain concept using Sears as an example.

Figure 10.1. Supply chain of Sears.

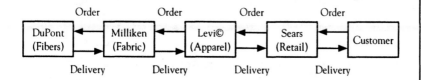

The supply chain is also sometimes called the "integrated enterprise," because it integrates information from the firm's external suppliers and customers into the firm's internal functions. This integration is important because it guides improvements in the firm's internal functions and processes. Information from external parties is critical in determining what a firm should produce; what aspects of procurement, production, and distribution add value for customers; and how much of each product will be necessary. In addition, suppliers and customers can be excellent sources of ideas for innovative products and product modifications (Kim et al., 2006).

The performance cycle of any firm links together the locations where the firm stores information and inventory. The performance cycle of most firms can be broken down into the following stages (although not always in this exact sequence):

- Order transmission: the company receives an order via phone, fax, mail, or e-mail
- Order processing: the order is entered into the company's information system and assigned an order number, scheduled delivery date, total price, and so on.
- Order selection: the products ordered are either manufactured or are selected from inventory, then are packaged and prepared for shipping
- Order transportation: the products ordered are transported, often to a warehouse or distribution center
- Customer delivery: the products are delivered to the customer's home or office, or to a prespecified pickup location

The goal of performance cycle management is to be consistent. The processes used in each step, as well as the time required for each step, should be the same for all customers. Once consistency is achieved in a performance cycle, the next goal is often to reduce the duration of the performance cycle in terms of total time. The performance cycles of most firms are similar, so the performance cycle is considered the basic unit of measurement and evaluation in logistics and supply chain management. Because of the similarities across firms, comparisons are possible (David, 2004).

Within the performance cycle, logistics management "includes the design and administration of systems to control the flow of material, work-in-process, and finished inventory to support business unit strategy" (Bowersox & Closs, 1996). The material, work-in-process, and finished inventory must be positioned geographically where it is required (by customers) and at the lowest total cost possible. Some attributes of good logistics systems include high product availability, consistency, speed, flexibility, and accuracy. Recently performance cycle measurements have focused on shortening lead times, that is, the time each individual step takes. For example, delivery lead time can be shortened by having products available when people order and by using fast modes of transportation, such as truck or air. The most challenging aspect of performance cycle analysis is balancing the costs involved in improving the performance cycle with the benefits to be obtained.

The supply chain includes several functional areas, including inventory, transportation, manufacturing, packaging, procurement, and information systems (Bowersox, Closs, & Cooper, 2002; Bowersox, Closs, & Stank, 1999). Inventory, transportation, and information systems are covered in depth in this chapter. Manufacturing, packaging, and procurement (via supplier relationships) are covered in other chapters.

Inventory

Inventory management is a key element of the logistics process. Inventory strategy must support the firm's overall strategy. The costs of holding inventory can be extremely high: up to 40% of a firm's expenditures. The costs associated with holding inventory include the following:

- Interest: the interest your firm would have earned by investing its money in something other than inventory (such as securities or loans to other companies). Interest might also include the interest your firm pays on a loan taken out to cover the expense of holding inventory

- Storage costs: buying or renting warehouses, providing electricity and other utilities in warehouses
- Obsolescence/pilferage/damage: the cost of inventory deteriorating, spoiling, being stolen, or otherwise being damaged
- Maintenance: the cost of providing the correct environment for the inventory, such as refrigeration
- Insurance
- Taxes

Understanding the high costs associated with holding inventory, why would any firm hold inventory? The answer lies in the costs associated with not holding inventory. Many times, if inventory is not available to fill a customer's order, the customer will buy the product elsewhere. Once a firm has lost a customer, it is very difficult to get that customer to return. This is especially true in exporting: each individual customer is extremely valuable, and it is risky to maintain low inventories with the possibility of frequently being out of stock.

There are several reasons a company might hold inventory, but the most important one concerns holding inventory as a buffer against stockouts. This type of inventory is sometimes called safety stock. Physio-Control Corp., a manufacturer of medical equipment, is the undisputed leader in its line of business. One important strategy of Physio-Control is related to its inventory management. That is, it requires its printed circuit board (PCB) suppliers to keep at least 2 weeks' worth of inventory on consignment in the Redmond plant. With this safety stock, the company can deal with unexpected demand and satisfy its customers. In exporting, because of the long transportation times involved, exporting firms often hold high levels of safety stock.

Transportation

The primary purpose of transportation is to move physical products from one location to another. Transportation purchases can result in both economies of scale and economies of distance. In economies of scale, shipping larger volumes of product results in a lower cost per product than shipping smaller volumes. In economies of distance, the further a product is shipped from its origination point, the lower the shipping cost per mile (or per kilometer). A business whose primary function is to provide transportation services for other businesses is called a carrier. The different types of transportation (rail, highway, boat, pipeline, and air) are called modes.

In most countries, carriers are subject to economic regulations and price restrictions. Some carriers face restrictions concerning what types of materials they are permitted to transport and where they may pick up or deliver materials. When selecting a carrier within a foreign country, it is important to know the restrictions placed on different carriers. For international transportation, the two most frequently used modes of transportation are ocean (vessel) shipping and air shipping (David, 2004).

Ocean Shipping

Three types of vessels operating in ocean shipping can be distinguished by their type of service: liner service, bulk service, and tramp or charter service. Liner service offers regularly scheduled passage on established routes. Bulk service mainly provides contractual services for individual voyages or for prolonged periods of time. Tramp service is available for irregular routes and is scheduled only on demand.

There are three basic types of cargo a vessel can carry. Conventional vessels are the most common type, and are useful for large or unusual cargoes. Container ships carry standardized containers, which facilitates the loading and unloading of cargo, as well as transfers of product to other modes of transportation. Roll-on/roll-off vessels are much like ferries: trucks can drive onto built-in ramps and roll off at the destination. When deciding on a type of vessel and a type of service, investigate the target country's restrictions regarding ports. In many countries, especially developing countries, the ports cannot accommodate container ships (David, 2004).

Because carriers are often used for large and bulky shipments, you should reserve space on a carrier well before the actual shipment date. Always consider the cost of shipment, delivery schedule, and accessibility to the shipped product in selecting the method of international shipping.

For small package shipments (say, less than 90 pounds), a general rule of thumb is that air shipments are faster, safer, and more cost effective.

Air Shipping

Air shipping is available in most countries. Airfreight has shown the fastest growth rate for freight transportation, even though it accounts for only a fraction of total international shipments. Air shipping is typically used for high-value items that would be susceptible to breakage or pilferage if shipped via ocean carriers. Other candidates for air shipment are perishable products or products that are needed urgently in the target country (e.g., medical supplies or certain industrial equipment). Air shipping is more predictable in terms of scheduling than ocean freight. It is also more expensive: two to five times the cost of ocean shipping. Almost all commercial airlines provide cargo space for exporters.

Choosing a Mode of Transportation

Before selecting a mode of international shipment, an exporter should calculate the direct and indirect costs of air versus ocean freight. Although air carriers are more expensive, their cost may be offset by lower domestic shipping costs (less distance from the manufacturer to an airport and from the foreign airport to the distributor or warehouse). Direct costs can be directly compared by considering the differences between

- air and sea insurance;
- inland transportation to port or airport;
- freight forwarder's fees;
- wharfage or airport terminal charges;
- freight cost of ocean or air transportation;
- loading and unloading charges;
- customs duties;
- inland transportation to the buyer.

Indirect costs are more difficult to calculate but are equally important to consider in developing profit projections. Consider the following:

- Ocean freight is slow and less reliable than airfreight.
- Each day cargo is in transit, the exporter has carrying charges on inventory.
- Distributors dislike carrying the huge inventories necessary because of ocean freight transit time.

Always double-check the mode of transportation and the actual destination of the goods with the foreign buyer. Often the buyer may wish the goods to be shipped to a free trade zone (for information, refer to Chapter 8) or a free port, which allows exemption from import duties while the goods are in the zone.

In some countries, the government owns or subsidizes national carriers. The government may exert strong pressure on you to use the national carrier, even when it is not the most economical choice. In such situations, it is generally wise to comply with the government's demands in order to facilitate cooperation at other stages in the export process.

Freight forwarders are businesses that specialize in arranging for transportation services for other businesses. Freight forwarders achieve economies of scale by booking large shipments made up of the products of several companies. Because freight forwarders are experienced and clearly understand the transportation industry, their choices of modes and carriers is highly reliable and provides consistency for their clients. Some freight forwarders also offer local delivery in the target country. Freight forwarders are discussed in detail in Chapter 6.

Information in Supply Chain Management

Information has recently gained importance in supply chain management. Managers have begun to see that accurate and timely information can be substituted for inventory, lead to significant cost savings, and improve performance cycle consistency and speed (Kim et al., 2006). Information can substitute for high levels of safety stock in inventory. If demand for a product can be accurately forecasted using information systems, only the actual amount of the product demanded needs to be shipped. The information system can reduce demand uncertainty by increasing the accuracy of forecasts and by accurately accounting for current inventories and products on order. In some production environments, production is delayed until an order is transmitted via an electronic network, eliminating the need for inventories. With decreased inventories, companies can allocate their assets to other resources, resulting in cost savings and increased return on investment. In addition, the effective utilization of information can focus the company on its most profitable customers or products, creating strategic implications for the use of information.

It is important to note that in exporting, the time-based advantages provided by traditional logistics information systems are not fully realized. Because of the long transit times involved in exporting, most exporters carry significant levels of safety stock rather than relying on information systems to warn management in time to prevent an out-of-stock situation.

Supply Chain as a System

It is commonly thought that the performance of any system relies on the performance of each individual part. Therefore the logical implication would be that each part of a system must be strong and efficient. However, recent studies of many business systems have found that this is not the case. Businesses work best, in fact, when all of the parts function with one common, specific goal in mind, and each area adapts to meet that goal.

The realization that systems are more important than components has led businesses to increasingly utilize cross-functional teams, encouraging communication throughout the company at all stages of system development. For example, it would be useless for a transportation manager to reserve an entire fleet of delivery trucks for a week in an attempt to improve customer service if the manufacturing plant can only produce enough products to fill one truck in that time. This concept applies to exporters as well. It is important to consider the goals of the company as a whole in choosing export logistics systems and other components of the manufacturing, distribution, and marketing process.

CHAPTER 11

Understanding Foreign Cultures

This chapter will help you

- develop an appreciation for differences in cultures and societies across the globe;
- identify the impact of culture on business strategy and its implementation;
- introduce research-based frameworks that classify global cultural dimensions;
- become familiar with some of the dimensions of cultural differences;
- develop and recommend some practical guidelines for doing business in a foreign cultural setting;
- learn about resources that can provide information on various national cultures.

Culture is one of the least understood aspects of doing business abroad. Culture manifests itself in many forms and is present in all interactions within a society (Calantone, Kim, Schmidt, & Cavusgil, 2006; Kim & Cavusgil, 2006; Nakata & Sivakumar, 1996, 2001; Steenkamp, ter Hofstede, & Wedel, 1999). Three elements can be used to define culture:

- A culture is learned by people.
- A culture is shared by all members of a society.
- One element of a culture affects other elements of the culture.

The first element, that a culture is learned by people, means that culture is not a hereditary trait, such as hair color. Rather, culture is a framework through which people evaluate their environment and make decisions. The second element, that culture is shared by all members of society, is what makes the framework into a culture rather than a personal preference or personality. It should be noted, however, that the society in question must be strictly defined when discussing culture. For example, in the United States, there is a general national culture that can be described as individualistic, but there are subcultures, such as African American, that can be described as collectivist. In other words, a national culture has its own subcultures at different levels, such as regional or organizational subcultures. The third element, that one element of a culture affects other elements of the culture, relates each element of a culture to the other elements. For example, a person's social status within a culture will affect the vocabulary that person uses.

At the broadest level, a country has a national culture that reflects nationally consistent attitudes, behaviors, and norms. Within this, different classes of professionals have their own professional culture that is based on the training and the requirements of their profession; for example, lawyers, doctors, and engineers might have certain attitudes that are more reflective of their professional training rather than broad-based national cultural considerations. A third dimension of culture is organizational culture. Organizational culture reflects the work ethic and the patterns of inter- and intraorganizational interaction between employees. Such work ethics and interaction patterns vary significantly from one organization to another.

Business executives who hope to profit from their travel have to learn about the history, culture, and customs of the countries they visit. Business manners and methods, religious customs, dietary practices, humor, and acceptable dress vary widely from country to country. Understanding and heeding cultural norms is critical to success in international business. A lack of familiarity with the business practices, social customs, and etiquette of a country could weaken a company's position in the market, prevent it from accomplishing its objectives, and ultimately lead to failure (Calantone et al., 2006).

Therefore, before entering a new market, it is important to understand how culture can potentially affect you and your business. For instance, in Muslim countries, social norms require that people not drink alcoholic beverages. However, in actuality, alcoholic beverages are popular in some areas.

Raju (1995) created a model that illustrates several levels at which culture can affect business transactions. Three of these levels are discussed below.

- Buying behavior: This has to do with the perceptions people of a culture hold regarding imported products, the value of brand equity in a society, the existence and strength of brand loyalty, and the impact of social norms on buying behavior.
- Consumption characteristics: Issues in consumption include the product versus service consumption in the culture, social class and reference group influences, and urban versus rural consumption patterns. An example of this would be food consumption in Brazil. In urban areas, Brazilians are beginning to eat on the run, favoring snacks and quick meals. In rural areas, however, the traditional large, sit-down meal is still predominant.
- Disposal: Resale, recycling, and remanufacturing considerations constitute the disposal level. In addition, some cultures are strongly influenced by social responsibility and the environmental implications of product disposal.

How well prepared are you to conduct business in cultures other than your own? Are you familiar with the cultural factors that play a fundamental role in international business transactions? You need to appreciate that different cultures require different behavior patterns by exporters. Products, strategies, and technologies that are appropriate in one culture might be dismal failures in another.

One of the primary challenges of international business is the ability to operate effectively in foreign cultural settings. The challenge for business managers is to remove the blinders imposed by home cultures, a somewhat difficult but essential task if operations in foreign cultures are to succeed. It is important to understand that cultural differences will have an effect on the way you do business overseas. The greater the involvement of your firm abroad, the greater will be your reliance on an understanding of foreign cultures for your firm's growth and survival.

Roles of Culture in Export Marketing

Operating in a foreign culture impacts your export marketing activities in two key areas: demand side impact and management impact. On the demand side, you are now dealing with customers who have different behavioral patterns than those you are accustomed to. Customers vary in many dimensions, including purchase behavior, communication aspects, and product preferences. Understanding such differences is critical in creating values for customers across countries. In addition, in a foreign culture the management of your business operations becomes quite different from what it is at home. Negotiating skills, levels of initial trust, and the control of middlemen become harder to determine when you operate in a different environment, and the implementation aspects of business strategy become substantially different.

Furthermore, personal interactions pose the most risk in terms of cultural influences on business success. For example, in Japan, a manager's smile accompanied by the words "I don't think so" carries the same meaning as an American manager's "Absolutely not!" That's because in a collective society, people try to avoid saying "No" to prevent other people from losing face. In Egypt, a training exercise that required the managers to stand on a blanket and turn the blanket around without stepping off had to be canceled. The reason? One of the managers was a woman, and the men in Egypt were forbidden to touch her. Because each culture is different, it is best to research each individual culture as part of your market research effort.

An understanding of interactions in different cultures is often a fundamental prerequisite to marketing products or services abroad. There are two aspects that managers need to address:

1. Gain a more than superficial understanding of people and their behavior.
2. Make sure that your message is getting across.

Every culture has its own subtle relationships between words and actions. Getting people to understand what one means and wants is one of the primary tasks of management. Such communication is not only necessary but also an important means of furthering incentive-based plans and productivity. Moreover, sensitivity to daily habits, such as the importance of 4-hour lunch breaks in some societies, or the physical distance between people engaged in conversation, can be among the most vital aspects of the business relationship in export marketing.

Understanding Cultures

Many psychologists and cultural anthropologists have defined factors that provide dimensions for comparing cultures. Some of the commonly used approaches are the six questions approach, the four dimensions approach, and the Hofstede model.

The Six Questions Approach

Florence Kluckholn and Fred Strodtbeck (1961) developed a set of six questions that compare cultures across six dimensions:

1. What do members of a society assume about other people? That is, are other people good, bad, or a combination?
2. What do members of a society assume about the relationship between a person and nature? In other words, do they believe in establishing a harmonious relationship with nature or are they willing to turn nature to their advantage?
3. How do people act in a society? Are they individualistic or do they perform tasks in groups?
4. How are plans formulated and accomplished in a society? Is the status quo accepted or is it challenged? Are plans formed and implemented according to preestablished schedules?
5. What is the conception of space in a society? How close do people stand to each other when communicating? What are the differences in terms of public and private space?
6. What is the dominant temporal orientation of a society? Is it past, present, or future?

The Four Dimensions Approach

Another classification scheme was developed by Edward T. Hall (1990). His work emphasizes four dimensions along which cultures can be compared:

1. The amount of information that needs to be transferred if a message is to be stated
2. The concept of space
3. The importance assigned to time and schedules
4. The speed of information flow between individuals and organizations

The Hofstede Model

The third major conceptual approach to viewing cultures was developed by Geert Hofstede (1980), an IBM employee, who surveyed IBM employees across 40 countries to define cultural dimensions. He developed and presented a framework that had four main factors:

1. Power distance: This denotes the degree to which individuals in a society automatically accept hierarchical or power differences among individuals.
2. Uncertainty avoidance: This attribute measures the degree to which individuals in a society are comfortable in working within uncertain circumstances. It also examines their relative degree of comfort in working with long-term acquaintances rather than strangers.
3. Individualism versus collectivism: Individualistic cultures stress individual performance and achievement, whereas collectivist cultures tend to view work, performance, and achievement as group processes and outcomes. This aspect especially impacts organizational culture.
4. Masculinity versus femininity: Masculine cultures tend to be aggressive and favor the acquisition of material wealth. On the other hand, feminine cultures are comparatively subdued.

Applications of Cultural Understanding in Business

Culture can be viewed using different conceptual aspects. However, there are some practical, readily usable ways that will help you understand foreign cultures. Some important attributes that differ across cultures include the following:

- Deal focused versus relationship focused
- Rigid time and scheduling (monochronic) versus fluid time (polychronic)
- Informal business culture versus formal business culture
- Low context versus high context
- Expressive/verbal communication versus reserved/nonverbal communication

Deal Focused Versus Relationship Focused

Deal-focused cultures tend to be very task oriented. There is an urgency to get to business without too many preliminaries. Small talk is usually not necessary before a business conversation. Agreements in such a culture tend to be very specific and legal. Contracts are a standard form of business agreement. In case of disputes there is an impersonal, legalistic, and contract-based approach to dispute settlement. Typically disputes are resolved through litigation.

In relationship-focused cultures, personal trust and relationships are very important. There needs to be personal rapport and understanding before business conversations can begin. In some cases, managers make international trips only to cultivate the relationship, and avoid discussing business at all. The real business is often taken care of over the phone after the trip.

Rigid Time Versus Fluid Time

Depending on how people in a society use time, the culture in the society is considered either monochronic or polychronic. In monochronic cultures, punctuality is very important. The clock is worshipped and schedules are set accordingly. Agendas for business meetings are usually preestablished and meetings are rarely interrupted. In fluid time (polychronic) cultures, there is less of an emphasis on punctuality. Scheduling is loose, and in some cultures to keep someone waiting signals authority and superiority and may be deliberate.

Informal Business Culture Versus Formal Business Culture

Some cultures stress an informal mode of interaction between people. These cultures are more egalitarian compared to other more hierarchy-oriented cultures. In formal cultures, people are addressed using suffixes and a strong code of etiquette is followed. For instance, in Japan, a very formal society, employees commonly wear dark suites and workplace uniforms are very common. Using suffixes or addressing others by their titles in front of the last name is routinely expected in Japan. Western managers, even after years in a business relationship, often do not remember the first names of Japanese managers, as they rarely use them.

Low Context Versus High Context

Introduced by Edward Hall, the contexts of cultures are used heavily to understand the communication orientation of foreign partners. In low-context cultures, people tend to emphasize direct, explicit, and frank communication. The meaning of words is clear and straightforward. The context of the communication is rarely interpreted as a meaningful element of communication.

However, in high-context cultures, "saving face" is crucial. Communication tends to be indirect, polite, and vague. Much of the meaning of what is said is implicit. Meaning is found more in the context surrounding the words, rather than the words themselves. This mode of communication stems from the desire to maintain smooth and harmonious relationships.

East Asians mask negative emotions by remaining expressionless or by putting a smile on their face. Showing impatience, frustration, irritation, or anger disrupts harmony and is considered rude, offensive, and therefore unacceptable. High-context cultures can be found in some Latin American countries (Mexico and Venezuela) and in some newly industrializing countries (Korea and Thailand). Low-context cultures are found in North America and the Scandinavian countries.

Expressive Communication Versus Reserved Communication

In cultures that place importance on expressive communication, primarily words and the meanings of words convey the message. People tend to be loud in their communication, and facial expressions are also used to convey meaning. On the other hand, reserved communication stresses body language, listening, and pauses. People tend to be soft-spoken and maintain a certain distance when communicating. Sometimes touch behavior like shoulder patting, elbow grabbing, back slapping, or holding hands is used to convey a important message.

Common Cultural Differences

There are numerous cultural elements, and some show more apparent difference than others. The following dimensions represent areas of major differences across cultures:

- Linguistic differences
- Concept of space
- The meanings associated with different aspects of body language
- The value and significance attached to material possessions
- The importance assigned to trust in relationships
- The form of agreements

Linguistic Differences

In exporting it is quite possible to do well without learning or understanding a foreign language. Most international business people speak some English and therefore have a common language to facilitate transactions. However, words and expressions sometimes convey different meanings across countries. Even if they convey correct meanings, the communications can be slow enough to make some impact on the transactions. Therefore it is important for exporters to understand that it is possible that a similar language may be spoken in two countries, but the interpretation of certain words or expressions is very culture specific.

The Concept of Space

The physical distance that people prefer to keep from each other is also a very interesting dimension of culture, as it varies quite significantly across cultures. In the Middle East and Latin America, you may feel crowded, people stand very close to each other and may lay their hands on you. If you back away from someone who stands too close, you may be perceived as cold, unfriendly, or distrustful. In Scandinavian countries and West Germany, on the other hand, the conversation distance between people is greater, thus giving the impression that they are a little cold and distant. In Asian countries like Korea, Japan, and China, it is not uncommon to observe someone whispering in the ear of another person.

Body Language

Body gestures and eye contact signal different behavior patterns and feelings that are often unique to certain cultures. For example, the habit of people of the same sex holding hands is shunned in the U.S. or Canada, although it is a very common practice in Africa, Asia, and the Middle East, especially among females.

Hand gestures such as the OK sign (thumb and forefinger), which is also the symbol for "Made in America," may have a vulgar, indecent connotation in Latin America or the Middle East. (Interestingly, such a sign can mean money and change from a payment in Korea.) Instead, one should beckon to a person be extending the arm and hand, holding the hand out palm down, and closing it repeatedly. Also, diet conscious Americans may feel complimented if you tell them that they are slim. In other countries, however, heaviness is a sign of health, wealth, and status. Such a statement would not be a compliment.

Not all cultures regard eye contact as acceptable behavior. Eye avoidance is accepted as normal in some oriental countries such as Japan and Korea, and in many instances it is used to indicate superiority. In some African countries, prolonged eye contact may be regarded as disrespectful.

The Significance of Material Possessions

Americans are often characterized as being materialistic and gadget crazy. Lacking a fixed class system and having a very mobile population, Americans have become highly sensitive to how others make use of material possessions. We use everything from clothes to houses as a complex means of ascertaining each other's status.

In the Middle East, on the other hand, status is determined through other indicators such as family, connections, friendship, and education. The desire for technology and modernization is not shared by all. Modern gadgets may not always be sought after; in certain cultures, social graces are more important than material things. However, in some countries, such as Japan, Korea, and Turkey, high-technology items are in great demand. The Japanese often take great pride in expensive items and tasteful arrangements in their homes that are used to produce the proper environment.

The Importance of Trust in Relationships

Some societies encourage the formation of loose friendships. Friends come and go in a highly mobile society. Lifetime friendship is extremely rare. There are few well-defined rules governing our obligations to friends, consequently we move to a very personal level very quickly when we engage in conversation. We use first names and prefer informality. We feel comfortable about teasing and criticizing each other in public, with little regard for the target person's face. However, such behaviors are frowned on in many other countries. Particularly in collective societies, saving "face" is very important. Latin Americans and Arabs are slow to make friends, but are very loyal to the people they do consider friends. The Chinese prefer to do business with people they know. Such a business network among Chinese businessmen in Asia is called *Guanxi*.

Approaches to Agreements

As mentioned above, in Southeast Asia and China, "face saving" is very important and seems to play a quite crucial role in business relationships. It is wise to avoid embarrassing or confrontational behavior in these societies. In one case where a Swedish firm was negotiating for a project in Thailand, the chief negotiator from the Thai side insisted on better terms of payment, although his arguments were based on incorrect information. The Swedish negotiator, knowing this, promised to look into the matter. Later, when they were alone, the Swedish negotiator told him that his information was incorrect; the Swedish negotiator did not say this earlier to avoid embarrassment. The Thai negotiator appreciated this gesture and became very helpful in future negotiations.

Not only saving face, but also different timelines in negotiations with business partners from different parts of the world play a role. Many exporters have found that their Asian counterparts often take a much longer timeline in finalizing an agreement. It is important to be patient with the pace of negotiations to avoid any misinterpretation of intentions.

There are few different types of rules for negotiating agreements:

- Rules that are spelled out as regulations or laws
- Mutually agreed upon moral practices, taught to the young as principles
- Informal customs to which everyone conforms without being able to state the exact rules

All societies favor one of these or another. In the North American culture, businesspeople tend to rely on written contracts or agreements. To Americans, signing a contract means negotiations have been completed. In the Arab world, a manager's word is just as binding as a written contract. In fact, a written contract may violate a Muslim's sensitivities and reflect on his honor. Therefore understanding which types of rules the society emphasizes helps in interpreting the true meanings and implications of an agreement with a foreign partner.

Self-Referencing

The typical reaction of a person to a foreign culture is called self-referencing. This is a process in which we form judgments about other people by evaluating them against our own past experiences and cultural programming. We tend to see others through our own colored lenses. This behavior can lead to serious misperceptions and a lack of understanding, potentially resulting in export failure. Successful negotiators have the ability to process information from three different perspectives during negotiations:

- Monitoring your own words and actions
- Understanding the meanings the other side gives to those words

- Monitoring and understanding the words and actions of the other side

Culture has a strong bearing on how business negotiations are conducted and concluded. It is important to ascertain the following:

- Determine the background, status, and expected negotiating approach of your foreign partners
- Make sure that whatever is said is communicated clearly and is understood as such
- Understand issues of timing associated with talking
- Say whatever is appropriate at the right time

It also important to understand the organizational culture and the risk-taking tendencies of individuals, as these have a strong bearing on the outcomes associated with negotiations. There are major differences in negotiating styles between Americans and most other cultures, especially East Asian countries. Therefore it is important to develop an appreciation for the negotiating approaches of these people before attempting to conclude a deal.

Navigating the Cultural Differences

Your international business counterpart will realize that you are a foreigner, make some allowances for your behavior and lack of knowledge, and will forgive any inadvertent cultural faux pas. Of course, he will be more impressed by the knowledge you have acquired prior to entering his country. Always remember that your personal image will be linked to the company.

If you consider something morally objectionable, culturally insensitive, or socially outrageous in a foreign country, it may be a good idea to try and understand why a foreign culture acts as it does before passing judgment. The golden rule of business etiquette is to be open-minded, nonjudgmental, patient, and flexible.

Try to be more formal and polite with foreigners. Being conservative in formality and politeness will always help. Show respect for your hosts by making formal introductions with full names and titles. Never call an individual by his first name until invited to do so. Also, remember that in some countries, to call a business partner by his first name is unacceptable. And it will never hurt to try to learn the correct pronunciation of their names.

There are different ways of shaking hands and acknowledging the other person. Bowing your head slightly or a nod might be customary in many countries (e.g., in Japan and Korea). The French prefer a quick handshake, the Chinese pump the hand, and the Arabs offer a limp hand. There are numerous others you may want to be familiar with before going on a business trip to a foreign country. Here are several more suggestions.

Socializing

If you are invited to a social affair, accept the invitation as a sign of respect for your hosts. In some countries it is considered rude not to accept an offer of hospitality. Many cultures use social occasions as a means to get to know you, your company, and your country. Business is usually not discussed during these social events, but you never know. For instance, Korean businessmen may discuss and decide some business matters at such informal social events.

Business Cards

You should have business cards with your information printed in the local language on the reverse side; this is very common practice among export managers, even in the United States. In some countries business cards are treated quite reverently, as indicators of status. Do not bend, write on, or put away the business card while in the company of the presenter. Try to glance at the information on the business card as you receive it and talk about it briefly. This will be appreciated by the presenter.

Gifts

Presenting business gifts may be unusual in the United States, but in many countries gifts are not only accepted but are expected. Flowers are a must when visiting a French home for dinner. Chrysanthemums, which represent mourning, should be avoided. Do not buy perfume for a woman in Europe unless she or her husband requested that you purchase a certain type for her.

Brand name gift items are appreciated, particularly in Japan and Korea. Always bring a gift when visiting a home in Japan. Bringing several extra gifts is a great idea if you are going to Japan. Wrap nonlogo gifts and avoid bold colors, dark grey, and black-and-white combinations. The black-and-white gift wrapping combination is reserved for funerals in many parts of Asia. The color red is appreciated, as it is associated with healing and good health.

In the Arab world it is good idea to give something with intellectual value, such as a book. This complements the Arab's concept of an educated self.

Adapting the Container and Package Size

An exporter who is aware of foreign cultural sensitivities, tradition, and heritage increases its chances for success abroad. Such knowledge is especially beneficial when designing containers and packaging for export. In Japan, product packages are generally smaller than those in Western countries. For instance, consider the package size for detergent. In Japan, the best-selling package size of detergent is less than one-quarter of what is popular in the United States. Also, you will have a really hard time finding mouthwash in the typical size found in the United States. The typical size of mouthwash packages in Japan is about one-third the size of those in the United States. So is the package size for fruit juices. Why are they small in Japan? It is probably because most Japanese people either hand carry the items or use a bicycle and thus cannot carry products in a large package size.

The typical family size would be another fact to consider in determining the size of the package. In the United States, families have an average of less than four members. However, it goes up substantially in numerous emerging markets. This means a family pack of product should have more units in those countries than in the United States.

In India, inexpensive, reusable containers must be used. In fact, many countries stipulate that a products packaging or container must be reusable. In the Ivory Coast, for instance, cylinders are used as measuring cans, and packages with plastic lids become salt and pepper shakers.

The Significance of Numbers and Colors

Certain numbers, colors, shapes, or phrases can be important when marketing in another country. In many cultures, different numbers can have either positive or negative connotations; for example, the number 7. The number 13 is associated with bad luck throughout Western societies. Different numbers have different meanings for different cultures, and to disregard or ignore their meaning could hurt your sales prospects in those markets. A leading U.S. golf ball manufacturer targeted Japan as an important new market by virtue of the expanding popularity of golf in that country. Special packaging in sets of four was developed for export. The company's sales were well below their anticipated volume. Research eventually targeted packaging in fours as a primary factor for lagging sales; four is the number of death not only in Japan but also in some other Asian countries, including Korea.

Cultural preferences should also be considered with regard to color. Some cultures prefer bold colors, some more subtle ones. For instance, most African countries prefer bold coloring, and they especially favor the colors of their flag. In Korea, red is strictly avoided in writing a person's name, as they relate the color to bloodshed and thus is seen as life threatening, although it is generally well accepted for other purposes. West Germans dislike red because of its association with Communism, while the Danes and Czechs like red. An exporter who is aware of these cultural preferences can color his packaging appropriately.

Shapes That Matter

The shape and size of a package is also susceptible to cultural overtones. In Colombia and Romania, triangular and circular packages attract customers. Circular and square shapes are preferred in Taiwan, because they represent completeness and correctness, while a triangle represents complications. Although most shapes are quite neutral to U.S. exporters, it is important to understand that shape can affect how well your product sells in other countries.

Consumer Purchasing Behavior

In the United States, men buy diamond rings for their fiancées, however, in Germany, for example, young women tend to buy diamond rings for themselves. Advertising campaigns must consider such cultural traits. In many countries, including Western ones, wives are involved in the purchasing decisions of major items. However, the role of wives in purchasing decisions is much less significant in Arab countries.

Cultural Attitudes That Work

As a businessperson interacting with other cultures, you cannot afford to be insensitive to the existence of cultural differences. Differences do exist, and to ignore this fact is to invite embarrassment, if not disaster. The following points should help you cope more effectively with cultural differences.

Avoid Cultural Bias

We tend to view other cultures through the lens of our own culture. We accept our own culture as the norm and view everything else as strange. Our acceptance of our own culture tends to condition how we react to different behavior, values, and systems. Consequently we must be conscious about such "built-in" bias.

Develop Empathy and Sensitivity for Foreign Cultures

We need to develop empathy for other points of view. We must avoid ethnocentrism and appreciate the differences in cultural patterns and traits. Try to understand where the other person is coming from and why such different cultures prevail in their countries. Remember, you can only criticize those who eat dog meat in Asia when you are ready to be criticized by Hindus for eating beef.

The Importance of Experiential Knowledge

The key to successfully doing business in a foreign culture is using common sense derived from experience. It is advisable to begin exporting to relatively similar markets and then move into culturally dissimilar markets over time. Employees can be briefed beforehand on the norms of a foreign culture, but still it is important to realize that direct experience will be very important as well. Sometimes anthropological models can provide help in dealing with cross-cultural business situations. However, acquiring factual and interpretive knowledge about other people and cultures will certainly help.

Watch Out for Overgeneralizations

Sometimes, given your understanding of the cultural dimensions of various cultures, you might tend to stereotype a certain group or individual that might be different from the larger cultural grouping as a whole. Such overgeneralizations can stem from misidentifying social and ethnic groups within societies. Be wary of such generalization.

Learning Local Language

All in all, cultures are closely intertwined with language. Therefore learning the local language is the most effective way to begin navigating a foreign culture. This will expedite the cultural learning process, reducing the time required to understand a foreign culture.

If you are interested in obtaining some hands-on information on the culture in a country, you should visit the following Web sites:

- http://www.buyusa.gov/home/export.html
- http://www.fita.org
- http://www.executiveplanet.com

A good collection of country-specific books is offered at http://www.worldbiz.com.

Successful export marketing is a learning process. Learning about people's attitudes, preferences, ways of living, and ways of doing business can help exporters to navigate foreign cultures. In doing so, just remember that learning a foreign culture involves a significant level of individual adaptation, tolerance, flexibility, curiosity, and knowledge. When such cultural maturity is translated into a product adapted to locally prevailing requirements, an exporter can move on to the next level of business.

CHAPTER 12

Product Adaptation

Upon completing this chapter you should be able to

- understand the primary arguments against adapting products for export markets;
- identify the three main forces that lead to product adaptation;
- recognize the types of adaptations that are made in exported products;
- use three strategies for managing product adaptation;
- comprehend the arguments presented in current debates about product adaptation.

Product adaptation includes two types: mandatory adaptation and discretionary adaptation. While mandatory product adaptation is done to modify the product according to local legal regulations, economic reality, and religious and social requirements so that the product is acceptable in the export market (Cavusgil, Zou, & Naidu, 1993; Farley & Lehmann, 1994; Hill & Still, 1984), discretionary product adaptation is done by export managers in order to make the product more appealing to export customers and to gain a competitive advantage in the export market. Product adaptation for export markets has traditionally been a controversial topic. Many factors play into the decision of whether to standardize products across all markets or to adapt them. In fact, the product adaptation decision is not of an "either/or" nature. A company may decide to standardize products globally, with one product offered to all markets. Alternatively, a company may decide to offer a few products to suit the needs of all markets: for example, one product for Europe, one for the Far East, and one for North America. Finally, the company may adapt its products so that each one is suited to a particular country: one product each for France, Spain, Germany, Japan, Taiwan, the United States, and Mexico. The firm must also make a decision on when to adapt its products: upon market entry or after entry. When product adaptations are made, they generally fall into one or more of the following categories:

- How the product is used or operated
- Labeling
- Quality
- Packaging
- Styling

Typically the cost of product adaptations is relatively minor in relation to other product costs. One study noted that 90% of the adaptations surveyed cost less than 10% of the selling price. This minor investment can sometimes be critical in gaining product acceptance in overseas markets. For example, through an understanding of consumer tastes and adaptation of its products to foreign markets, Top Green, TCBY's master franchisee, has hit the sweet spot in China's growing appetite for frozen desserts. To satisfy their customers' concerns for health, the company deliberately avoids the word "yogurt" in its Chinese name and markets its products as low-sugar, low-fat desserts. Eight flavors—chocolate, mint chocolate, coffee, lemon, lime, peach, strawberry, and vanilla—are served to meet various taste requirements. Also, a few different packages are available. Hard-pack products are generally sold in supermarkets for consumption at home, while traditional soft-serve products, sold in cones or cups at TCBY stores and kiosks, lend themselves to eating on the go. In March 1996, the company planned to add a frozen yogurt minicup, a small, hard-pack product, to meet increasing demand.

Some companies choose to alter their promotional strategies (both the message and the media) in lieu of adapting their products. This can be a viable solution, but it will not work in every situation. For more information on promotion adaptation, see Chapter 14.

Standardization Motivations

Given that product adaptation incurs only small costs and can be a benefit to exporting companies, why would a company choose not to adapt its products? A number of reasons prompt companies to use standard products in export markets, including lower research and development (R&D) costs, predictable product life cycles, production economies of scale, preempting the competition from introducing substitute products, and product development and market penetration.

All product adaptations incur R&D costs. By using a standard (pre-existing) product, the firm can avoid incremental R&D costs from product adaptations. In some industries where the price is the selling point, there are likely tremendous cost reduction pressures to remain competitive. Under such circumstances, even incremental R&D costs may affect a company's competitive position in the market (Szymanski, Bharadwaj, & Varadarajan, 1993).

Using a standard product, a firm may be able to predict the product's life cycle in a new market better than using an adapted product. The firm can use its experience and data from the original product launch to forecast the product's life cycle in the new market. However, some external factors within the export market may alter the product's life cycle: for example, if you try to sell streetlights in a country with very little road infrastructure, the introduction stage of the product life cycle will be very long. Once the country develops an extensive road system, the product will enter the next stages of the product life cycle.

Another obvious benefit of standardizing products in export markets is production economies of scale. When products are adapted, the production process requires new tooling, training, and possibly increased personnel. These costs are not typically incurred when a firm begins exporting a standard product.

The first-mover advantage should not be underestimated. By introducing standard products into export markets, a firm can speed up its entry into those markets, preempting the competition from introducing substitute products. The process of introducing a standard product is faster because it does not require time for product development, R&D, or production line changes. Thus, by launching a standard product, the firm can enter a market first and grab a greater market share. This puts the firm in a good position to maintain that market share later on by introducing new products.

Adaptation Factors

According to research by Cavusgil and Zou (1994), three main factors can affect the decision of whether to adapt products (or promotion). These factors are company characteristics, product/industry characteristics, and export market characteristics. Within each of these categories, many variables exist. A more complete model dissects these general categories into more specific areas.

The following discussion elaborates on the components of each of the three categories.

Product and Industry

Each of the components of the product and industry has the potential to influence a product adaptation decision. First, the technology orientation of the industry can determine the necessity to adapt the product. If the industry is highly technical, such as aircraft manufacturing, it is likely to be similar across markets and therefore will not require adaptation. On the other hand, in a very nontechnical industry, such as clothing, adaptation is more likely to occur.

Figure 12.1. Framework for product adaptation.

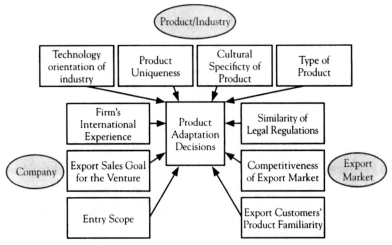

Second, the product's uniqueness may relate to the adaptation decision. If a product is designed to meet universal needs, it is likely to be standardized across markets. If the product meets only unique needs, greater adaptation will be required to meet export customers' product use conditions and to educate export customers in using and maintaining the product. Many firms that market unique products choose to adapt the promotion (positioning, packaging, labeling, advertising) of the product rather than adapt the actual product.

Similarly, cultural specificity may influence the product adaptation decision. Cultural specificity, or the degree to which the product caters to the needs of a specific culture or subculture, most often influences adaptations in promotion rather than the product. Occasionally it prompts product changes as well. For example, when Unarco Commercial Products, of Oklahoma City, Oklahoma, decided to export its products, it found that its shopping carts should sell in counties that are beginning to move into U.S.-style mass merchandising. Unarco found that in the Pacific rim countries, traditional merchandising was done by lots of little service stores, where salesclerks would take products off the shelves and bring them to the customer. Now those countries are coming out with major self-service stores similar to those in the United States. However, they are not as large and Unarco has to adjust their products by making smaller shopping carts.

In addition, the type of product under consideration affects the product adaptation decision. Generally, durable goods are less likely to be adapted than nondurables. Consumer goods are developed to meet the lifestyle and functionality needs of a particular market segment and consequently need to be adapted to suit new markets.

The Export Market

The most influential factor in product adaptation in the export market category is the similarity of legal regulations (Calantone, Kim, Schmidt, & Cavusgil, 2006). Obviously, if the regulations concerning technology, packaging, or safety are significantly different in the export market, these must be addressed through adaptation. For instance, exporters who want to sell floricultural products in Europe must be familiar with the packaging regulations there. According to the regulations in force, floricultural products should be packed in a manner that ensures their protection. Packaging materials, and especially the paper used inside the pack, should be new, clean, and of a material that cannot cause any alteration, either external or internal, of the product.

The competitiveness of the export market can encourage product adaptation (Zou & Cavusgil, 1996). In a highly competitive market, competitive pressures may necessitate customization to gain an advantage over rivals by matching local conditions more precisely. In contrast, in a captive market where the product already enjoys a leadership position, a high degree of standardization may be desirable.

Product familiarity of export customers can facilitate the use of a standardized product (Zou & Cavusgil, 1996). Products that already have high levels of awareness, knowledge, and familiarity are likely to be received with more favorable attitudes and greater acceptance. A lesser known product, on the other hand, may require adaptation to enhance customer reception.

The Company

The company's export sales goal for the venture may necessitate adaptation (Szymanski et al., 1993). The adaptation usually occurs in the promotional efforts of the company, not in the product itself. If the company has an ambitious goal for the venture (e.g., to gain 50% of the market share), it will need to penetrate the market more deeply than if it has a limited goal. In order to gain this type of market share, the firm will need to adapt its promotion to meet the specific desires of the export market's consumers. Future research may show that export sales goals also affect the decision to adapt the product itself.

The firm's international experience can also positively correlate to the decision to adapt a product. Firms with more international experience are more likely to be aware of consumers' needs in different markets and may therefore experience more success when they adapt products and promotions to meet those needs. On the other hand, an inexperienced firm seeks the closest match between its current offerings and overseas market conditions so that a minimal adaptation of product or promotion is required.

The last factor within the company that affects product adaptation decisions is the scope of entry. A firm with a large scope of entry is one that exports products simultaneously into multiple export markets. A small scope of entry indicates that the firm exports to only a single market or a relatively few markets. Firms that enter multiple markets are likely to need economies of scale, which prevents them from adapting products for each individual market. For them, the costs of product adaptation may simply be too high. However, firms that export to only one market are more likely to be able to afford to invest in product adaptation.

Timing Product Adaptations

When the issue is product adaptation, cultural specificity of the product and technology orientation are relevant considerations both upon and after entry (Cavusgil & Zou, 1994). Beyond this, however, there are differences. Initial adaptation of the product appears to be prompted by the legal regulations of the export market (e.g., health, safety, and technical requirements that are often mandatory) and the cultural specificity of the product. In contrast, product adaptation subsequent to entry is governed primarily by considerations such as management's international experience, the competitive intensity of the export market, the technology orientation of the industry, and the export customers' familiarity with the product.

Over time, exporters will begin to face competition from firms native to the target market. Those firms will experience a period of learning but will ultimately have lower costs than the export firms because of their proximity to the market (low transportation costs and no tariffs). This puts the domestic firms in a position to gain market share and take significant profit opportunities away from the exporters. Exporting companies should consider the potential for domestic competition when deciding on product or promotion adaptations. If domestic firms in the target market are very close to being capable of producing and distributing a similar item, it may not be wise to enter the market.

A Word of Caution

Although the factors discussed above are helpful in considering product adaptation decisions, even the most thorough framework does not always yield the "right" answer. Consider the literature on adaptation of industrial goods: industrial goods are thought to be prime candidates for standardization across all markets. However, Robert Buzzell (1968) noted in his article, "Can You Standardize Multinational Marketing?" that even industrial goods must sometimes be adapted: "A U.S. producer of farm equipment found that one of his pieces of machinery could not be moved through the narrow, crooked streets of French and Belgian farm villages."

Each product adaptation decision must be considered carefully and in the full context of the dimensions of the target market.

Product Adaptation Approaches

Peter Walters (1986) has identified two distinct approaches to product adaptation: the modular approach and the core-product approach. The modular approach involves developing a standard range of components usable worldwide and that can be assembled in a variety of configurations. This allows moderate flexibility to meet the needs of the buyer, while achieving substantial economies of scale for the producer.

The core-product approach requires the design of a uniform "core" product that can accept a variety of standard attachments, parts, and components. Depending on the nature of the attachments to the core, product performance characteristics can be substantially modified to meet specific customer needs and conditions of product use. At the same time, the standard nature of the core product and the range of attachments allows the firm to enjoy most of the advantages of product standardization.

An alternate approach would be to enter a single market or a small number of markets with specially adapted products for each. This enables the firm to accurately meet the demands of each market, but it requires a great deal of financial commitment.

Product adaptation is a hot topic for current research. There is a great deal of debate about the future of product adaptation in an increasingly global economy (Szymanski et al., 1993). Theodore Levitt, one of the

Figure 12.2. Levitt's standardization strategy.

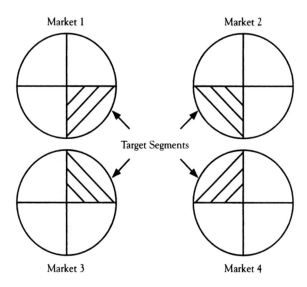

pioneers of marketing theory, believes that companies need to market to homogeneous segments around the world, even if those segments are made up of customers with differing demographics: "[The best global exporters should] compete on the basis of appropriate value—the best combinations of price, quality, reliability, and delivery for products that are globally identical with respect to design, function, and even fashion" (Levitt, 1983, p. 94). "The global competitor...will never assume that the customer is a king who knows his own wishes" (Levitt, 1983, p. 96). However, other studies have found that as people around the world become better educated and more affluent, their tastes actually diverge.

J. J. Boddewyn and his colleagues wrote an article in reaction to Levitt's assertion that standardization should become the norm in international marketing. Their (Boddewyn, Soehl, & Picard, 1986, p. 74) response was that "Regardless of what the best global competitors should do, many marketers of industrial goods (those which should be most standardized) are 'anticipating moving toward greater product adaptation to national markets.' Similarly, branding and particularly advertising are not moving toward greater standardization." This debate is likely to continue long into the future.

CHAPTER 13

Advertising and Promotion in Export

Upon completing this chapter you should

- recognize the role of promotion in an export program;
- understand how to develop a promotional campaign;
- understand what information market research should provide;
- be able to choose the right medium for promotion;
- understand the typical cultural and language barriers to effective promotional communications;
- be able to select the right type of promotional communications for your company or product.

Business schools typically teach promotion within the context of the marketing mix, which consists of four elements necessary for the successful marketing of any product: product, price, place, and promotion. Of these, promotion is the element most directly tied to the marketing department in American businesses. Promotion can have several purposes:

- To inform potential buyers that a product exists
- To educate potential buyers about the product and its uses
- To convince buyers that they want or need the product
- To convince buyers to purchase the product

In some cases, fulfilling these purposes can be easy because the products are in demand and the buyers are easily identified. In other cases, the task is not so for the following reasons:

- The seller may not know whom to contact.
- There may be too many buyers to contact directly.
- Buyers may not be interested in learning about the product.

- Buyers may prefer to buy from other suppliers who they know and trust.
- The product may be unknown so that no buyers are interested in it.
- Buyers may base their decisions on the wants of their customers (e.g., the exporter's indirect customers).

The purpose of an individual promotional campaign depends largely on the product's stage in the product life cycle in that market (Cavusgil & Zou, 1994). For example, a promotional campaign in Canada for a fax machine would aim to influence customers to buy that brand of fax machine based on the machine's speed, memory capacity, price, and so on. Canadian customers are already highly familiar with fax machines, and fax machines are well into the growth stage of the product life cycle in that market. A promotional campaign for the same product in Ethiopia would need to focus on educating customers about what a fax machine does and how it can save time for businesspeople. This is because in Ethiopia the fax machine is in the introduction stage of the product life cycle.

The creation and implementation of a successful promotional campaign relies on a great deal of preliminary research:

- Export opportunity assessment tells you how receptive a market is likely to be and gives you general background information about the market's size, growth rate, economic data, and so on (Hite & Fraser, 1988).
- Partnering strategies give you methods for choosing partners for key functions, including promotion.
- Legal considerations in exporting present contracts and trade barriers, as well as local regulations on promotional activities, which can influence promotional efforts (Farley & Lehmann, 1994; Zou & Cavusgil, 1996).
- Understanding foreign cultures can help your company overcome communication and resource barriers in product promotions (Donnelly, 1970; Fatt, 1967).

- Product adaptation and compliance with regulations introduces market-specific requirements for product design and market-specific promotional needs (Zou & Cavusgil, 1996).

A few explanatory notes are necessary before proceeding to instruction on the development of a promotional campaign. First, we focus primarily on the needs of exporters, as opposed to multinational corporations (MNCs) or local firms. MNCs and local firms have different resources available for promotional campaigns, and they often use different promotional strategies than exporters do. In addition, the goals of MNCs and local firms in creating promotional campaigns often differ from the goals of an exporter. Also, we make a distinction between customers and consumers. Customers are the individuals or companies to whom you sell your product directly. They may be distributors, wholesalers, retailers, or end users. Consumers are the end users of the product. For some exporters, customers and consumers may be the same, but usually exporters sell products to an intermediary (a customer) who then funnels the products to end users (consumers).

Creating Promotional Campaigns

The following six steps are critical in creating and maintaining effective promotional campaigns:

1. View of the market: In your opinion, based on initial research, how does this product fit into this market?
2. Validate your view: Is your initial view correct? Conduct market research to find out.
3. Create the message and goals: What is the purpose of your promotional campaign, and what information is critical to disseminate? What is your goal for this promotion (i.e., to sell 50 products in the first year, to sign a contract with a distributor)?
4. Investigate tools: How can you reach the target customers and communicate your message?
5. Select tools: Pretest the tools you believe will work the best. Also, evaluate your competitors' methods of reaching their customers.

6. Implement and evaluate: Use the tools you select to convey your message to customers; provide a mechanism for continuous improvement.

Validating Your View With Additional Data

Step 1 can be completed based on your export opportunity assessment. You may have developed a preliminary picture of what market conditions are like in your target market. However, in order to successfully penetrate the market, you will need more specific information. What information do you need in order to successfully introduce your product to a new market? You will need to collect information on the following items through market research.

- The target audience for your promotions: import agencies, retailers, end users
- The media available to reach your target audience
- The most effective media to reach your target audience
- The characteristics of the target users of your product
- Trade fairs for information or connections in this market
- Relevant local customs and rules of business etiquette
- Local costing and pricing methods
- Competing suppliers' capabilities, activities, brands, market shares, customers, promotional techniques, plans, and so on.
- Consumption trends in the market

Many countries have a government-run trade information service that can provide much of the necessary information. The U.S. Trade Information Center (1-800-872-8723) was established as a comprehensive source for U.S. companies seeking information on federal programs and activities that support U.S. exports, including information on overseas markets and industry trends. The center maintains a computerized calendar of U.S. government-sponsored domestic and overseas trade events. The National Trade Data Bank is another useful resource. Many country-specific sources also exist.

You may, at some point, need to conduct field research. Field research is distinct from desk research in that it requires interaction with members of the target market to obtain specific information not available in printed sources. Desk research can often answer questions such as "How much?" or "How many?" Field research is often necessary to answer such questions as "What kind?"; "What size?"; "What color?"; and "What flavor?" Exporters can particularly benefit from field research involving intermediary firms: retailers, wholesalers, and other middlemen.

Obtaining information through field research is expensive and time-consuming. The effort must be related to the value of the information in improving marketing decisions; it is not worth spending $10,000 to get information that will enable you to make sales of $5,000. Field research should be conducted in the following way:

1. Decide on the objectives of the field research
2. Decide what kind of people will be surveyed and where they live
3. Decide on the questions to be answered
4. Decide on the form of the questionnaire
5. Decide how it will be used: by mail or by personal visit
6. Tabulate the results
7. Draw the conclusions

It is necessary to prepare the questions very carefully before starting field research to make sure you get the information you really need. It is very helpful to try out the questionnaire beforehand on a small sample. Too much information is as bad as not enough information. Questions must be limited to provide only the specific facts needed in the easiest way.

Creating a Promotional Message

Once you have gathered valid market research about your target customers, consumers, and country, you can begin to develop a specific plan. The first step is to create a message that is appropriate and effective for your target market. Who the target audience is will affect the content of the promotion—the "message"—and the way it is presented. If you are promoting a food product, for example, your publicity aimed at consumers might stress its exotic taste, while your publicity aimed at trade customers might stress more technical factors such as quality control procedures, ease of storage, packing, and the quantities available.

You may wish to focus your efforts on only one target, for example, distributors of imported foods. Or you may want to publicize your product to each level of the buying chain. Your market research can tell you who influences buying decisions and, consequently, who should be the focus of your promotional campaign.

In conjunction with creating a message, it is necessary to specify your goals (Cavusgil, Zou, & Naidu, 1993). Do you hope to sell 50 products in the first year or to sign a contract with a distributor? Your goals will influence both the message and the media you select.

Reaching Your Customers With the Right Tools

How can you reach your target customers and communicate your message? Most markets have a variety of tools available, which are discussed below.

Personal Selling

One of the most common tools is personal selling, where a representative from your company visits a few key decision makers in the target market. These decision makers may be import agencies, government buyers, or influential distributors or retailers. Personal selling is generally seen by buyers as a sincere effort to develop a relationship. It is also a way for your company to gain critical information about the buyers and the market, since you will be in direct contact. In addition, your company is assured of having a knowledgeable person in contact with the buyers rather than relying on an intermediary who might not be as familiar with the product. This is especially important for technology-based products.

Trade Fairs/Shows

Another common communication tool is the trade fair. Trade fairs are events where individuals, companies, associations, governments, or anyone else display their products and services. Trade fairs promote the exchange of many commercial services. Buying and selling often takes place at trade fairs, although this may not be the immediate purpose of all

exhibitors. Trade fairs can be used for at least four major export marketing purposes:

1. Sales promotion: supporting the sales efforts of existing agents or
   importers by promoting the products to the trade and end users and
   by uncovering new sales prospects for them to follow up
2. Market penetration: establishing contact with importers of agents
   and promoting the handling of your products
3. Selling: actually selling to the trade or the public, with or without
   the participation of local representatives
4. Testing: presenting products in order to get the reaction of a large
   cross section of the trade or public as a guide for product adaptation
   and marketing strategy

The main advantages of trade fairs are concentration of contacts,
product displays, and exporter and importer participation. For example,
Sun Metal Products, Inc., of Warsaw, Indiana, is a manufacturer of wire
spoke wheels and alloy and steel rims for bicycles. The company took full
advantage of overseas trade shows in testing the export potential of products. The company participated in IFMA, a major bicycle trade show, on
a quite regular basis. Benefiting from these trade shows, it made sales to
numerous European markets and other parts of the world.

Trade fairs are highly effective. According to the U.S. Department of
Commerce's International Trade Administration, in 1993, U.S. companies, surveyed at 50 high-profile fairs, received a total of $86.5 million in
off-the-floor sales. They also reported 309 representative contracts completed, 35 licensing agreements, 54 joint ventures, and 45,532 opportunities through business leads. Private-sector organized trade shows were
reported to have been equally profitable for participating U.S. companies.

To receive the most benefit from a trade show, first decide what the
objective of trade show participation is for the company (see the four
examples of purposes above). The most accessible shows are probably
U.S. Department of Commerce-sponsored shows. These government
shows have excellent pavilion space for exhibiting and are cost effective.
Government shows have many support services for first-time exhibitors,
including information on how to exhibit and how to conduct meetings
with potential buyers, travel arrangements, cultural differences to expect,

and which shows will provide the greatest success rate for your product. Contacting the trade show liaison office at the U.S. Department of Commerce is the best way to become a trade show participant. Local branch offices of the Department of Commerce can also provide valuable insight (to obtain the local branch office contact information, check the International Trade Administration [ITA] list at http://www.buyusa.gov/home/ us.html or call 1-800-872-8723). The following are some steps you will need to take if you decide to participate in a trade show:

- Create a list of all the shows in which the company is interested in participating. A list can be generated using the ITA database at http://www.export.gov/eac/trade_events.asp.
- Write to the show director or the government agency sponsoring the show to determine if that show is a valuable use of your time and resources.
- Prioritize the list, establish a budget, and schedule the personnel who should attend (if any).
- Make travel arrangements as far in advance as possible and check customs clearance requirements.
- Design the program and demonstration booth, keeping in mind the targeted audience.
- Have price quotes ready.

An enormous amount of information about trade shows is available via the Internet. One excellent resource to consider is GlobalEDGE (http://globaledge.msu.edu). Information on international trade shows, seminars, and business events can be found at http://globaledge.msu .edu/resourceDesk/showsAndEvents.asp. This listing is updated regularly. Another excellent starting point is the U.S. International Trade Administration Web site at http://www.export.gov or http://www.trade.gov.

Numerous print materials are also available that provide information about trade shows. One of the good printed directories is *Trade Shows Worldwide*, published by Gale Research. It is an annual publication covering major trade shows.

Trade Press

Trade publications focus on subjects of interest to particular trades, industries, professions, or vocations. Business journals can also be considered in this category, or at least in a category distinct from the mass media. The trade press can be one of your most important communication tools. The number of readers is often small, so their advertising charges are relatively low. At the same time, the readership is so specialized that they can provide an efficient way of reaching the people you want to reach. For example, in some industrialized countries there are not only trade magazines that are read by people in the food business but separate magazines for people at different levels of the food business—processing, wholesaling, and retailing. If you have correctly analyzed your marketing communications needs and have identified your target audience, you may find the trade press is the best way to reach your audience at the lowest cost.

Mass Media

A number of mass media types are available to promote new products in almost any market. Mass media reach large numbers of the general public. Because advertising rates are based in part on the number of people who are reached by a medium, mass media advertising is usually expensive. Mass media should only be used when your target audience is the general public. Even then, you should identify the particular segment you want to reach (middle-class women, people who like to travel, etc.) and then choose the mass medium that reaches this segment most efficiently. Selecting an appropriate mass medium is a highly refined skill and is best left to advertising agencies or media consultants. However, a listing of potential mass media is included here for illustrative purposes:

- Newspapers
- Consumer magazines
- Television (programs and commercials)
- Radio
- Cinema
- Posters/billboards

TCBY's venture in China illustrates how a firm can use mass media. When TCBY's franchise Top Green started business in China, it recruited Leo Burnett Co., Inc., an international advertising agency, to plan and implement a public relations campaign in this market. In 1994 Top Green launched a $4 million advertising campaign, sponsoring the World Volleyball Grand Prix in 1994. In addition, a television game show, "Love in Five Rounds," was created in its first target city, Shanghai. Following the evening news, the show was broadcast on Shanghai Oriental TV each Saturday night for 10 weeks. During the game show, the audience wore TCBY shirts. Five families with children were invited to participate in a competition to make the most attractive TCBY yogurt. Each program also included three "yogurt information" breaks in which company spokespeople explained frozen yogurt's nutritious attributes.

Media Selection

Based on your research and knowledge of the media available, you must now choose which media will be most effective in reaching your target audience. A very critical element of selecting a medium is pretesting, in which your company tries out its promotional campaign on a few volunteer customers. Typically a company will create a print advertisement or a radio or television spot and then pay a few volunteers a small fee to view the ad and provide structured feedback. This can provide a great deal of insight into the mindset of your target audience and can save your company a great deal of money in the long run.

There can be a number of cultural and language barriers to effective promotional communications (Fatt, 1967). International marketers must be careful not to advocate an action inconsistent with the local culture (Cavusgil et al., 1993). Consider the following example with Nike. In 1996 Nike exported 38,000 basketball shoes to Arab countries, but found only intense protests from Muslims. Why? The problem was the flame-design logo printed on the shoes. The logo resembled the word for Allah (God) in Arab languages. For Muslims, feet are considered unclean. They could not bear that shoes, which came in close contact with such unclean things, were decorated with Allah's name. Nike end up recalling all the shoes.

Other issues that need to be considered in selecting a communications tool include the following:

- Literacy levels in the target market: If your customers cannot understand written explanations, you may need to use pictures, videos, or sounds (radio) to convey your message (Hite & Fraser, 1988).
- Selection of a language in multilanguage countries: In any multilanguage country, a promotion in a single language risks alienating some of your target customers. A specialized advertising agency can provide guidance on this issue.
- Media infrastructure of the target country: Some mass media may reach only a small part of the country's target population. For example, the number of TV sets in Mexico is much lower than that in the United States.
- Credibility of different types of advertising: Some cultures hold a biased opinion toward advertising or toward the use of a particular medium. For example, in Eastern Europe, TV commercials have often been used to sell products generally considered too low quality to sell via other methods. Therefore the general population views any products advertised on TV as poor quality.

These issues are highly complex and can have serious implications. They generally are most relevant when using a mass medium. It is highly advised that companies wishing to utilize a mass medium should obtain the services of an advertising agency or a media consultant specializing in the company's target market.

Selecting a Marketing Communications Agency

Before you approach an agency, clearly define your goals for the agency's work: what do you need them to do, to communicate, to whom, and when? Also establish budgetary guidelines. There are two main types of agencies in addition to specialized consultants: advertising agencies and public relations agencies.

Advertising Agencies

Advertising agencies are the most common type of marketing communications firm. They range from very small firms who design ads and then place them in media, to large firms who offer a full range of marketing communications services, including consumer research, creation of advertising of all kinds, direct publicity, exhibitions, point-of-purchase advertising and in-store promotion, editorial publicity, package design, and so on. Such agencies are often in a position to give advice about marketing strategy as a whole.

Advertising agencies generally earn their income from a combination of commissions paid to them by the media and fees paid by the client for specific services. In addition to these general agencies, there are many advertising firms who specialize in particular fields, such as creation of ads, buying of space or time in media, or handling direct mail campaigns. You should be careful when dealing with advertising agencies: some advertising agencies tend to stress media advertising when other techniques may be more cost effective.

Public Relations Agencies

Public relations (PR) agencies are generally expert in press relations and other forms of PR, including arranging exhibitions. These firms (or individual PR consultants) charge a fee based mainly on time; often with a fixed minimum. For companies with little money to spend on publicity, a marketing-oriented PR firm may be your best choice, because on a small budget, media advertising will play only a small role. If you have only a very small budget, you may be able to use agencies or individual consultants for a particular purpose, such as for a mail campaign or store promotion.

Ideally you should retain the agency over a long period of time so that it can understand your market, your company, and your marketing problems. In that way it can help you develop a marketing communications strategy and then carry it out. Some agencies offer a combination of advertising and public relations strengths. Agencies will be happy to discuss their capabilities with you and help you make an informed decision as to whether they suit your needs. Your local chamber of commerce can provide resources directing you to advertising and public relations agencies. In addition, there are several national organizations of advertisers and public relations specialists that publish directories annually.

Implementation of Promotional Campaigns

After completing Steps 1 through 5, your company should be ready to begin implementing a marketing communications campaign. Because international promotional campaigns can demand significant financial and human investment, exporters are well advised to periodically evaluate the performance of their campaigns. An evaluation system should be set up to take into account the goals of the campaign (as articulated in Step 3) and the results, in both quantitative and qualitative terms. The feedback from each evaluation should then be recorded and utilized in planning future promotions.

CHAPTER 14

Export Costing

Upon completing this chapter you should

- understand general cost concepts and basic cost classifications;
- understand the different types of export costs;
- understand cost variability;
- be able to perform sensitivity analysis;
- be able to differentiate between relevant and irrelevant costs in decision making;
- be able to evaluate the importance of certain factors, other than the costs, in calculating the cost of goods for foreign markets.

Understanding Costs

Before analyzing the costs of an exporter, one should be familiar with the basic cost concepts and understand the importance of accurate cost information in planning and decision making.

Definition of Cost

Cost can be defined briefly as a sacrifice of resources. There are two types of costs: historical (accounting) costs and opportunity costs. Historical costs refer to those from past decisions and can be obtained from the accounting books of a firm. Opportunity costs are the benefits those costs that result from choosing one course of action rather than another. Therefore they are the estimated benefits from actions that could, but will not, be undertaken. Since opportunity costs are anticipations, they are forward-looking and therefore are more suited to our analysis of costs.

Importance of Cost Accounting in the Company Information System

The survival and success of any firm, whether oriented toward domestic markets or foreign markets, depends on how resource allocation is planned and controlled. Hence key decision makers must be properly informed about costs.

Cost accounting, the section of managerial accounting that involves the calculation and reporting of actual and predicted costs of products, services, or processes, is one of the tools that decision makers can utilize to acquire relevant information helpful for managing the inflow and out-flow of resources. Exporters should keep in mind that competitive price setting would be impossible without adequate cost information. However, accurate cost information by itself is insufficient for price setting. There are other factors involved, particularly external factors, some of which will be discussed in later sessions.

Need for Accurate Cost Information in Exporting

The need for timely, accurate cost information is vital for any firm, but it is particularly important in exporting. Some export-related costs such as product adaptation costs, distribution costs, and legal expenses are relatively clear and easy to obtain. However, a lack of accounting skills and knowledge of local costing systems appropriate to exporting in many developing countries make export trading more complicated and difficult than producing and selling in the domestic market only (Raymond, Tanner, & Kim, 2001). Furthermore, exporting to foreign markets involves other external factors such as currency exchange rates (Raymond et al., 2001), a lack of choices of transportation modes, and tariffs, increasing an exporter's need for accurate cost information.

Costs for Planning and Decision Making

The two most important objectives of estimating and calculating costs in exporting are planning and decision making. Adoption of courses of action and allocation of resources consistent with the long-term export goals and objectives of a firm require that cost data be collected in a consistent manner. Cost information is a vital ingredient in assessing and developing long-term (e.g., selecting countries to export to) and short-term plans. Cost analysis is also crucial in many situations where the firm has to make decisions concerning the future, such as adoption of pricing policies for particular markets and payments made to export staff (commission-based salary, fixed salary, or a combination; Cavusgil, 1988).

Cost Classifications

Cost analysis and identification will vary from firm to firm. What is a useful classification for one organization may not be for another. However, we can still distinguish between product costs versus period costs and direct costs versus overhead costs.

Product Costs Versus Period Costs

Product costs include all costs incurred in the manufacturing process of a product. Product costs are inventoried and written off only when the product is sold. Examples include direct materials costs, direct labor costs, and factory overhead. Period costs include all nonmanufacturing costs incurred to sell (export) the product. Administrative, distribution, and advertising expenditures are examples of period costs. These are written off in the period in which they are expensed. Both product and period costs are accounting costs and include fixed and variable (dependent on the units produced and sold) components.

Direct Costs Versus Overhead Costs

Direct costs are those costs that are easily traceable to the product, service, or process considered. Labor and materials are both direct costs. These types of costs are usually considered variable unless incurred under a contractual agreement (salaries for personnel responsible for the manufacture of the product would be a fixed labor cost).

On the other hand, overhead includes indirect labor (plant managers) and indirect materials (maintenance materials), as well as other types of general manufacturing costs that cannot be directly traced to units being produced, such as maintenance, depreciation, and insurance expenses.

Export-Related Costs

For a company that produces and sells for the domestic market, the cost of production is the most significant element of its total costs, whereas selling and distribution costs are rather insignificant. However, for an exporter, selling and distribution costs are likely to comprise a large portion of the final selling price, as exporting involves international transportation and tariffs, and possibly adaptation costs. In this section, three main additional groups of costs associated with exporting will be discussed: order-getting costs, order-handling costs of export overhead, and order-handling costs that are directly related to export orders.

Order-Getting Costs

Order-getting costs result from order-getting activities involving promotion, advertising, research, and direct selling. These costs can be further classified as repetitive and nonrepetitive order-getting costs. Repetitive costs include agency fees and commissions, sales commissions, and costs of continuing promotional activities. Nonrepetitive costs include research costs, initial product adaptation costs, and one-time major advertising campaigns. Furthermore, order-getting costs could be both volume determining (incurred in order to generate sales activity and to determine the volume of activity over time) and volume determined (generated as a result of a particular volume of export sales activity).

Order-Handling Costs: Export Overhead

During the early stages of exporting, a firm incurs very little additional administrative overhead. However, the firm quickly realizes that the special administrative and documentation requirements of exporting will require additional resources. Some firms, especially those heavily involved in exporting, have a separate export office responsible for activities related to sales processing and customer delivery.

It is imperative to organize and maintain accurate cost records of the activities of the export office and to recover these overheads within the pricing strategy used for exporting. In addition, if the firm is exporting to different markets or exporting different products, an allotment base might be needed for a relative profitability calculation of the different markets or products.

Finally, export overhead costs are likely to be fixed in the short term. For instance, salaries of export office staff, telephone charges, and depreciation of equipment will not change much based on the volume of orders or yearly fluctuations in export sales volume.

Order-Handling Costs: Direct to Export Orders

The determination of order-handling costs specific to export orders is one of the more complicated aspects of exporting because there are many elements to consider. For example, the terms under which the exporter quotes a price significantly impact the costs incurred. There are also many different options for transporting export goods—air, sea, multimodal (a combination of two or more modes of transportation)—which have varying cost effects. Basically there are five components of order-handling costs that are direct to exporting: packaging, labeling, marking, and strapping; loading and transportation; documentation charges and fees; finance, insurance, and duty costs; and miscellaneous other costs. Determination of these costs requires proper information collection and planning (Mariotti & Piscitello, 1995).

Packaging, Labeling, Marking, and Strapping Costs

Export packaging is any extra packaging required in addition to domestic requirements and therefore represents an extra cost burden. However, the amount of protective packaging varies according to the destination, transportation mode, and the product itself. It is important to record the export packaging costs separately from regular packaging costs so that effective cost control can take place, and so differences by country in duty rates for the packaging and the product itself can be taken into consideration.

Labeling, marking, and strapping costs are often neglected in cost calculations for export shipments. In regards to these costs, exporters should consider several issues:

- Labels should conform to the regulation of the importing country or the importers' requirements.

- The goods shipped must specify the country of origin in the language of the importing country.
- Strapping should only be used when the products are crated in such a manner that the straps support the crating, as they could damage the goods more than protect them in certain situations.

Loading and Transportation Costs

Freight costs can easily become the largest element of an export order (Morash & Clinton, 1997). In addition, other costs may be incurred depending on the transportation mode and nature of the good. In particular, internal transport and loading can be a very large cost element if the production facility is far from the nearest shipping port. Some of these costs include terminal charges for the handling of the cargo over the dock to the ship, initial cartage to get the merchandise to the dock, and special loading and unloading charges if the shipment is unusual.

Ocean freight still accounts for the majority of the world's trade, although increasing amounts of goods now go by air because of the unique advantages of air transportation (faster and safer transportation of goods). For example, some low-weight products subject to quick deterioration (such as fresh flowers) require air transportation. Ocean freight costs are dependent on several cost factors. First, freight rates are based primarily on volume, although weight is considered in rare cases. Second, shipping companies charge at the highest rated currency at the time of shipping. In addition, storage costs can depend on whether goods are stored on board, whether refrigeration or constant temperature is required, and whether there are special storage needs. Freight costs can also differ depending on whether conference or nonconference shipping lines are used. Shipping conferences maintain regular sailing schedules and shipping space on certain routes or in certain parts of the world and freight discounts are possible. There may also be a cost advantage in using "flag preference"—duty cost savings can sometimes be achieved by shipping on vessels of the customers' country. Finally, various surcharges may be imposed, such as a bunkers surcharge, where the shipping company issues a surcharge if fuel costs increase.

Documentation Charges and Fees

Many countries require that the exporter provide detailed information about its goods, which involves the preparation of a consular invoice, a document required by some foreign countries, describing the shipment of goods and listing information such as the consignor, consignee, and the value of the shipment. The exporter will incur charges for such documents and their translation, notarization, and correction (Cavusgil, Knight, & Riesenberger, 2008). Sometimes small exporters use the services of a forwarding agent, a specialized firm that provides advice on export procedures, prepares shipping documents, and books space on shipping lines. Forwarding agents typically charge a fixed cost based on a percentage of the freight charges. The costs of preparing documentation by the exporter itself should be taken into consideration.

Finance, Insurance, and Duty Costs

The most common cost elements in this category include the following:

- *Export duties.* Many countries charge export duties on specific or all commodities as a source of revenue to aid development.
- *Bank charges.* Banks can assist in the collection of money from customers and can be asked to hold documents until customer payment is made. For their services, banks charge a fee to their customers.
- *Financing charges.* If exporting occurs over a long period of time and the customer requires long-term credit, then the finance charges to extend credit over that period have to be added to costs.
- *Insurance.* This is a very complex area, each shipment is likely to require insurance for transport, as well as warehousing or storage.
- *Currency charges.* There will be costs associated with the conversion of currency.

Miscellaneous Costs

In determining the cost structure for a particular export order, other costs may be incurred depending on the situation, including

- costs of moving goods on arrival;
- inbound terminal charge or wharfage charge;
- additional storage costs.

Types of Costs

It is also important to understand how costs change with fluctuations in the volume of sales and production, a concept called cost variability. The basic principle of cost behavior is that as the level of activity in the firm rises, so do the costs. The problem is to determine for each item of cost in what ways and by how much costs change as the level of activity increases. There are four kinds of cost items to be considered: fixed costs, variable costs, step costs, and semivariable costs (Cavusgil, 1988).

Fixed Costs

A fixed cost is a cost that does not vary with the number of units produced or sold. They tend to be incurred through the passage of time and therefore are often known as period costs. Fixed costs must be incurred independent of the actual volume of sales and production because they maintain the operating capacity of the firm.

One important feature of fixed costs is that while total fixed costs remain relatively unchanged in response to changes in sales volume, fixed costs per unit will decline. Patent and trademark costs, an export manager's salary, and market research costs can be considered fixed.

Variable Costs

A variable cost is one that tends to vary directly with changes in production and sales volume. Direct materials and labor costs as well as indirect materials costs (in most cases) are variable. Unlike fixed costs, total variable costs increase as the level of activity increases. However, the variable cost per unit remains relatively constant.

Step Costs

These are some expenditures that are fixed over a range of output levels. For example, an export supervisor can manage a fixed number of export staff. As the level of export activity increases, a need for more employees may arise and therefore an extra supervisor might be needed. This situation is an example of a step function.

Semivariable Costs

These costs have both fixed and variable elements that combine to produce a total cost that varies with the level of activity, but not proportionately. Total labor costs associated with export salesmen might behave as a semivariable cost if they are paid a fixed salary and a percentage commission on export sales orders generated.

Caution With the Fixed/Variable Distinction

The distinction between fixed and variable costs poses a serious challenge for two particular reasons:

- The variability of costs depends very much on the range of the level of activity (such as export sales), while most fixed costs will only change for very large increases or decreases in activity level.
- In practice, variable costs per unit will change with volume changes. For example, the exporter can negotiate quantity on its direct materials purchases and therefore reduce its unit costs through quantity discounts.

Marginal Costing

Even though marginal costing plays an important part in export pricing strategies, it is a concept based on the idea of cost behavior. The idea is to observe the effect of marginal changes (one unit of change) in output and sales on costs. Most accountants who have already produced a fixed/variable cost breakdown for a firm will identify the cost of producing an extra unit of production as being the variable cost per unit. In many situations, this approach is quite appropriate and the marginal cost will probably be no more than the unit costs of direct labor, direct materials, and variable overhead costs.

It should be noted, however, that an extra unit of production can produce significant other cost changes. In our example of step costs, increases in sales volume necessitated the recruitment of an additional supervisor, which should also be considered as part of marginal cost.

Analyzing Costs

Once costs are classified into fixed and variable categories, managers can perform a cost-volume-profit analysis. There are essentially three tools that export managers can use to assess their performance: break-even point calculation, margin of safety, and contribution margin to sales ratio.

Break-Even Point Calculation

Break-even analysis is used to determine the level of sales volume at which revenues are equal to costs. Beyond this point, known as the break-even point, a firm starts making a profit. To find the break-even point, the following equation can be used:

$$\text{Break-even point} = \text{Fixed costs/Contribution margin,}$$

where fixed costs are the total fixed costs and contribution margin is the difference between the price and the variable cost per unit. The logic behind the formula is that the contribution margin is the net receipts per unit that are contributed toward covering fixed costs and providing profits.

Margin of Safety

It is sometimes helpful to know something about the relationship between target sales and break-even sales. For this purpose, we use the margin of safety. This measure is found using the following equation:

Margin of safety = (Target sales − Break-even sales)/Target sales × 100.

With the help of this measure, a firm can see how far its sales are from the sales amount that starts incurring a loss for the firm. The higher this value is, the less sensitive the firm is to sales fluctuations, as it has significantly more sales than the point where it starts experiencing a loss.

Contribution Margin to Sales Ratio

This is simply the ratio of the contribution margin (C) to sales price (S). A C/S ratio of 50% would indicate that for each additional dollar in sales, the firm earns 50 cents per unit that may be used for paying off fixed costs and making a profit.

Limitations on the Cost-Volume-Profit Analysis

Cost-volume-profit analyses give managers the ability to perform sensitivity analysis and ask simple what-if questions. However, there are some restrictive assumptions of sensitivity analysis that limit its usage:

- The price and variable cost per unit are assumed to be constant (assumption of linearity).
- It is a single-period analysis. All revenues and costs occur in the same period.
- It assumes a single-product firm. All fixed costs are incurred to produce a single product.

Costs and Managerial Decision Making

One of the primary reasons for collecting cost information is to guide decision making and planning in the firm. Therefore it is imperative that cost information be relevant to the decision. In this section we will discuss the determination of relevant costs, the irrelevance of sunk costs, and the effects of limiting factors on export decisions.

Determination of Relevant Costs

In determining the relevant costs of exporting, an exporter should consider factors such as price elasticity in the foreign market, capacity utilization rate, fixed costs to be incurred, the level of competition, and the characteristics of the current industry structure, including existing barriers to entry and threat of substitutes. In a highly competitive market where demand is price elastic, an exporter may accept a lower price for products relative to its domestic market (not to be confused with dumping). The key here is to look at export contribution margins, that is, to compare the export price with the marginal costs associated with exporting. Even if exporting seems unprofitable, it may turn out to be otherwise. For instance, if the exporter is committed to paying high fixed costs anyway and has excess capacity that the domestic market cannot absorb, selling at any price above variable costs will make a positive contribution and generate greater profitability for the firm.

On the other hand, the firm might be operating at full capacity supplying the domestic market. In this case the firm should consider any additional costs exporting would require, including increases in fixed costs and possibly variable costs (as efficiency might drop once capacity is exceeded). If the incremental revenue from exporting outweighs the incremental cost, exporting will be profitable. Of course, before making any decision, management should take into consideration expected future costs and revenues by discounting the future cash flows at the appropriate discount rate.

Irrelevance of Sunk Costs

Sunk costs are costs that were incurred in the past, cannot change, and are therefore irrelevant to decision making. Once the firm incurs such an expense, the cost becomes irrelevant for future decision making. Besides, sunk costs are not incremental cash flows. One problem with sunk costs is that they are often confused with fixed costs. While all sunk costs are fixed costs, not all fixed costs are sunk costs. The plant is a fixed cost, but it is not a sunk cost. When the operation of the firm ceases, the plant can be sold.

It is critical that every company carefully protect its intellectual property rights when expanding into foreign markets. Thus the exporter must secure its patents and trademarks (proprietary resources), resulting in sunk costs. Once these costs are incurred, patent and trademark costs cannot be changed by the decision to export or produce only for the domestic market.

Effect of Limiting Factors on Export Decisions

Sometimes exporters might be faced with a choice between two courses of action. For example, the decision to supply an export customer or a domestic market with its finished products. This is a situation where two decisions are mutually exclusive. One solution would be to look at the individual profitability of each action. However, individual profitability comparisons can be misleading. Hence it is best to look at contributions. Here is a numerical illustration:

Assume that IBC Company is to choose between supplying the domestic market or the export market. The limiting factor is machine hours. The total available amount is 300 machine hours. Production for the domestic and export markets each require 300 machine hours. Sales, total variable costs, and fixed costs for the domestic market and export orders are $5000 and $7000, $2300 and $4000, $1300 and $1700, respectively.

Calculations:

Domestic market profit = $1400
Domestic market contribution = $2700
Export order profit = $1300
Export order contribution = $3000
Domestic market contribution/machine hours = $9
Export order contribution/machine hours = $10

Solution: Choose to export.

We can see that the contribution of the export order based on the limiting factor (e.g., machine hours) is higher than that of the domestic market. However, if we were to choose simply by looking at the individual profitability, we would choose the domestic market option and forego a better investment strategy.

Factors That Affect Costs

The typical cost elements of exporting were discussed previously. However, there are other factors to consider when estimating the cost of exporting. These may cause the exporter to over- or underestimate its total costs and thus set an uncompetitive price for its goods. These additional factors to consider are terms of payment, inventory holding (carrying) costs, collection costs, and foreign *exchange risks* (Cavusgil, 1988).

Terms of Payment

Terms of payment should be considered when making a final export quotation. Although it does not need to be emphasized as part of the exporter's initial offering, the terms under which the agreement is written are part of the final cost variable. The biggest risk is the failure of the buyer (importer) to make the payment by the due date.

Inventory Holding (Carrying) Costs

Inventory carrying costs are neglected aspects of exporting costs. These costs include labor, insurance, interest on capital investment, and storage costs. The exporter should incorporate these ingredients into its cost allocations. The longer the export goods are carried as inventory, the higher the cost of exporting.

Collection Costs

Although payment in advance is the safest term for the exporter, it is ordinarily unpractical and risky for the buyer. Thus other payment methods, such as letters of credit, are often used. In such instances, collection costs can increase due to discrepancy charges, amendment fees, and other minimum fees on smaller transactions.

Foreign Exchange Risks

Sometimes an exporter might need to quote in currencies other than its domestic currency (e.g., a U.S. exporter quoting in yen). As a result, on the day of payment, the exporter might incur a foreign exchange (FX) loss if the quoted currency (in this case, yen) depreciates against the domestic currency (U.S. dollars). To reduce the FX risk, an exporter can hedge with four financial instruments: forward contracts, future contracts, swap agreements, and options.

Forward Contracts

A forward contract is a contract signed between two parties where the seller agrees to sell the anticipated foreign receipts (yen) at a planned forward date at a predetermined rate. Thus the exporter fixes the dollars to be realized. However, if the planned date is only a few days away, this is considered a spot sale instead of a forward contract. Forward contracts are usually done with a bank's foreign exchange department and require a credit line from a bank.

Futures Contracts

Futures contracts are very similar to forward contracts, but unlike forward contracts, futures contracts are fixed (the yen contract is for 12,500,000 yen for an equivalent amount of U.S. dollars converted at the predetermined rate) and have a limited number of maturity dates each year, typically at the end of each quarter. Another difference is that a bank credit line is not necessary. However, the exchange (secondary market where the futures are traded) might require that a margin account be maintained with a cash balance equal to a small percentage of the contract, usually about 1% to 2%. The trader can borrow the rest from the broker.

Swap Contracts

Swap contracts require a more complicated procedure where a series of forward contracts are placed together. In a swap contract, two parties agree to exchange (swap) cash flows in specific currencies at specified dates and rates. Usually one of the parties is a bank.

Options

An option contract gives one the right to buy (call option) or sell (put option) a foreign currency at the exercise price (striking price), a predetermined exchange rate at which the option owner can buy or sell the foreign currencies. The feature of an option that differentiates it from other financial instruments is that the option owner is not obliged to exercise the contract. For example, if one has a call option to buy US$20 for 2000 yen (the exercise rate is 100 yens/US$), he will not exercise it unless the market rate is above the exercise price. In addition, options, unlike other financial instruments, must be purchased up front (100% margin).

Many financial managers recognize that they have significant foreign currency risks that need to be managed. If foreign exchange rates move against them after a foreign currency sale is made, but before the foreign cash is converted to domestic currency (e.g., transaction exposure), an exchange loss may occur. The situation Automatic Feed Co., a U.S.-based company, faced when dealing with Volkswagen, from Germany, illustrates a good example of the need for sound FX risk management. At the time Automatic Feed was quoting the project, the German mark was trading for about DM1.50/$. On a $14 million project they were willing to pay DM21 million. As the project was being negotiated, the Maastricht Treaty was in the process of falling apart, leading to significant volatilities of many European currencies. As the dollar weakened to DM1.37/$, Automatic Feed's position improved. With the real appreciation of the mark against the dollar, which was very beneficial for the U.S. exporter, the project would have required a payment of about DM19 million if the contract terms included U.S. dollars as the payment currency. However, just as quickly Germany went into recession, the mark weakened to DM1.60/$, and their payment obligation reached more than DM22 million, reducing Automatic Feed's competitiveness. To minimize the impacts of market volatilities, firms like Automatic Feed would consider hedging by entering into a forward contract to sell the marks at the rate they contracted.

As this example shows, the relative value of the domestic currency of the exporter against the importer's currency (when the importer pays in its own currency) can have a significant impact on the competitiveness of exports. Furthermore, the higher the volatility of the exchange rate, the more difficult it is to predict the future exchange rates. Finally, it is difficult to hedge currencies before an order is received, and even if an order is received, the forward positions available in the market may not be long enough, say, 1 year.

Understanding Potential Export Costs

In this section, factors that should be considered as potential export costs, such as drawbacks, free trade zones, insurance, ambiguous words, and cost, insurance, and freight (CIF) term, will be discussed to help exporters reduce the potential risks and costs associated with their exporting activities.

Drawbacks

Usually the seller (exporter) pays the applicable duty charges unless some other agreement is signed between the parties. Consequently exporters should investigate whether their export qualifies for duty drawback (see Chapter 8 for further discussion). Duty drawback is a situation in which a duty is refunded, wholly or partially. The reason behind this is to encourage trade. For the United States, situations most commonly associated with drawbacks include the following:

- When an export item is manufactured in the United States with imported materials, the duties paid on the imported materials may be refunded as drawbacks, less 1%, which is retained by the U.S. Customs Service.
- When both imported and exported materials of the same kind and quality are used to manufacture items, either retained in the United States or intended for export, then 99% of the duties paid on the imported materials are refundable on the exports. This provision makes it possible for firms to obtain drawbacks without the hassle of maintaining separate inventory for domestic and imported materials.
- When an item is exported because it does not conform to specifications or was shipped without the consent of the consignee, then 99% of the duties paid on the items may be recovered.

- When imported materials are used to construct or equip vessels and aircraft built for a foreign account, 99% of the duties paid on the materials may be recovered, whether or not the vessels and aircraft are exported.

To obtain a drawback, a drawback proposal must be filed with a regional commissioner of customs. A list of U.S. drawback center locations can be found in Chapter 8.

Free Trade Zones

A free trade zone (see Chapter 8 for further discussion) is a port designated by the government of a country for duty-free entry of nonprohibited goods (Czinkota, Ronkainen, & Moffett, 2004). Merchandise may be stored, displayed, and used for manufacturing within the zone and reexported without duties being paid. Duties are imposed on the merchandise only when the goods pass from the zone into an area of the country subject to the customs authority. To encourage and facilitate international trade, more than 3,000 free ports, free trade zones, and similar customs-privileged facilities are currently being used in some 116 countries. It should be noted, however, that no retail trade may be conducted in a free trade zone.

Insurance

An important factor, both in terms of cost and potential risk exposure, is the cost of insurance that is part of a CIF quotation (see the appendix at the end of this chapter for popular terms of shipment suggested by International Chamber of Commerce; Incoterm, 2008). There can be real danger in quoting cost and freight (C&F) as compared to CIF. Making a C&F quotation implies that the importer will take out insurance on the shipment. However, there is the exporter's risk that the importer will fail to properly insure the shipment even though, in theory, it is the importer that bears the risk of loss once the goods clear the ship's rails.

If a claim arises that is not covered by insurance, the exporter might encounter difficulties even though the title has theoretically passed on to the buyer (importer). This is because the buyer will not want to pay for damaged or destroyed merchandise. Even a letter of credit might not protect the exporter unless a clean bill of lading is obtained to negotiate the letter of credit. An inexpensive solution would be to take out contingency insurance or a free on board (FOB) sales endorsement on the exporter's marine insurance, which applies only in the event the importer's coverage is missing or inadequate. This should also be discussed with the freight forwarder, who can usually provide this coverage if the exporter does not have his own marine insurance.

Safe CIF Quotation

Unless otherwise demanded by the importer, exporters are advised to quote CIF to the nearest seaport or airport. The importer can then easily ascertain charges within his own country, such as unloading charges, customs duty, and internal freight or cartage. That will give the importer a duty-paid, delivered-to-his-warehouse price.

Ambiguous Words

The use of ambiguous words on an export contract can be very dangerous, as it may lead to misunderstandings and erroneous cost calculations. Common examples are ton, FOB, and dollar. Ton can mean a short ton of 2,000 pounds, a metric ton of 2,204 pounds, a long ton of 2,200 pounds, or 400 pounds of salt. So exporters should never use the word "ton" without qualifying it further.

Free on board should never be used unless you specify what and where, such as "FOB ocean vessel at New York City." Finally, dollar has more meanings around the world than nearly any other word. A quotation for an importer in Hong Kong, such as "500 dollars per order," might be perceived as Hong Kong dollars. However, if the exporter's intent is to quote in U.S. dollars, a huge difference in value will result from this ambiguity.

Appendix: Terms of Shipment

Incoterms are international commercial terms used in shipping documentation that are recognized as the international standard. Incoterms explain how responsibilities for the goods and their carriage are allocated between the seller and the buyer.

EX (name of place). The named place is the point where the seller indicates to the buyer that terms of invoice have been met. All costs, including loading, are for the account of the buyer. For example, ex works is the price applied to the goods at the point of origin (manufacturing point) while ex ship is the price used when the goods are made available on board the ship.

FCA (free carrier). Focuses on goods being delivered to a carrier named by the buyer. It was adopted by Incoterms in order to clarify FOB, especially in the case of FOB air, and to solve the increasing problems and confusion created by the rapid growth of multimodal transportation, containerization, and special handling techniques.

FAS (free alongside ship). In the FAS quotation, the price charged to the buyer includes all charges to deliver the goods alongside the vessel.

FOB (free on board). FOB is the point at which, once the goods are on board the ship, the seller is released of all obligation and risk. The exporter is responsible for all costs necessary to put the shipment aboard a vessel in the named port. FOB is only applicable now for ocean and inland waterway transport.

CPT (carriage paid to). This term is used for any mode of transportation, and means the seller pays all freight until the named place is reached, where the buyer then assumes all costs.

CIP (carriage and insurance paid to). This is similar to CPT, except the exporter must provide insurance against damage and theft.

CFR (cost and freight). CFR was formerly designated as C&F. The exporter accepts the responsibility for paying the freight, as well as taking care of the loading and all incidental charges that may be necessary to obtain a clean bill of lading. It does not change the point in time that the buyer assumes the risk of loss, that is, when the goods cross the ship's rails.

CIF (cost, insurance, and freight). A pricing term that indicates that cost, insurance, and freight to the port of destination are included in the quoted price. The buyer is responsible for the transportation of the goods from the port to the buyer's inland location.

DAF (delivered at frontier). A term that ends the seller's responsibility as soon as the shipment arrives at the frontier of the destination. This term is used for transactions that require land transportation only. Unloading is the buyer's responsibility.

DES (delivered ex ship). This term is similar to DAF, but the seller's responsibility ends as soon as the shipment arrives at the port of destination. This term is used for transactions with ocean transport. Like DAF, unloading is the buyer's responsibility.

DEQ (delivered ex quay). This term is similar to DES but includes unloading as the seller's responsibility.

DDU (delivered duty unpaid). This term means the seller is responsible for all transportation to the destination point the buyer designated, with the import duty paid by the seller. However, unloading is the buyer's responsibility.

DDP (delivered duty paid). This term is similar to DDU, except the import duty is the buyer's responsibility.

CHAPTER 15

Pricing for Export Markets

Upon completing this chapter you should

- understand the importance of export pricing and its common issues;
- understand the best approach for setting prices worldwide;
- be able to consider variables in arriving at prices for foreign customers;
- be able to attach a level of importance to each variable;
- be able to identify the person responsible for setting export prices;
- understand why prices should vary across markets, across customer types, and over time;
- understand the role price plays in a company's international competitive strategy.

Challenges in Export Pricing

Export pricing is related to a large number of marketing strategy variables (Cavusgil, Knight, & Riesenberger, 2008). Among many other things, prices

- influence a customer's perception of value;
- determine the level of motivation that can be expected of intermediaries;
- have an impact on promotional spending and strategy;
- compensate for weaknesses in other elements of the marketing mix.

Price setting for international markets is far from a scientific process; rather it is through a trial and error that companies arrive at price levels that are both internally and externally acceptable (Calantone, Kim,

Schmidt, & Cavusgil, 2006; Raymond, Tanner, & Kim, 2001). Export managers often experience problems, which fall into three main categories: resource commitment to pricing, centralization of decisions, and production costs.

Resource Commitment to Pricing

Firms are hesitant to commit resources for in-depth investigations of export markets before price levels are determined. Some comments made by managers about export pricing are reflective of this problem:

- "Our firm simply will not supply the funds to conduct in-market research."
- "We devote far too many resources to research regarding product attributes and none to our competition's pricing structure."
- "We have no idea what real market demand is, and (HQ) won't support our efforts to collect primary data."
- "Quite simply we have no idea what inflation and exchange rates do to our price, and HR won't let us hire a specialist."

It is a common problem that exporters are less willing to invest resources in market research for export pricing even though price setting is one of their most important decisions. Export managers are advised to get as much primary data as possible before setting the price.

Centralization of Decisions

Centralization of export pricing decisions within the company leads to problems, as most markets require a certain degree of flexibility and responsiveness to local market conditions and developments. Some comments made by managers illustrate these problems:

- "We are restricted by headquarters to a pricing window that keeps us from being competitive."
- "We cannot change our prices quickly enough to react to the export market because too many people are involved in the pricing decision."

- "We set the product prices, but the division head won't let us change those prices more than once a year."
- "Our pricing system is antiquated, and senior management never gives us an accurate picture of total costs of the product."

Production Costs

High domestic production costs complicate export pricing issues. Selling in foreign markets adds costs to the product, leading to price escalation that might make your products uncompetitive in the chosen export market (Roberts, 1988). The following comments by managers point toward this problem:

- "The production costs alone of our product are higher than the competitive price in our export market. I can't compete once distribution costs are added on."
- "Our knowledge of the customer and his purchasing power, as well as our competition, are rarely integrated into overall strategy. We are expected to sell products far too expensive for our customers."
- "Our R&D division continuously places expensive variations on our product that our clients don't want and can't afford, despite our warnings."

In addition to these internal issues, there are a host of external factors that can influence your product's price in foreign markets (Cavusgil, 1988; Myers, Cavusgil, & Diamantopoulos, 2002). For example, in the middle of the sweeping price competition in Germany in the insurance industry, Allstate Insurance opened an office near Berlin in 1996. Allstate detected new opportunities arising from the deregulation of insurance rates in the German insurance industry. Benefiting from the deregulation, Allstate offered discounts to lower risk drivers and kept its own costs to a minimum, undercutting the competition by as much as 25%. Managers need to be aware of these types of external factors because your product's export prices play a critical role in the overseas marketing success of your organization. Ultimately prices do have a measurable impact on sales and also affect profitability. They often invite competitive reaction and, indeed, can be driven down by determined competitors.

Conversely, they can escalate to unreasonable levels because of tariffs, taxes, necessary increases in markups to cover rising costs, and so on. They can complicate a firm's marketing strategy in unforeseen ways when price variations among different markets lead to gray market imports. Finally, prices are one of the most flexible elements of the marketing mix because they can be changed quickly.

Factors That Influence Export Pricing

The internal and external factors that influence your firm's export pricing strategies can be categorized into four classes: firm- and management-related factors, product-based factors, industry-based factors, and export market characteristics (Cavusgil, 1988; Myers et al., 2002).

Firm- and Management-Related Factors

These firm and management factors are related to the internal strengths and weaknesses of your company (Cavusgil, 1988). They also account for the business strategy followed by your company and for the operational resources and configuration of your business. Company variables that impact export pricing decisions can be further classified into several categories, such as size and resources of the firm, international experience of the firm, use of information systems, number and locations of overseas production facilities, centralization of management decisions, and commitment of management to the export venture.

Size and Resources of the Firm

Larger firms tend to have access to greater resources and therefore have a greater ability to absorb the impact of export pricing decisions. This allows pricing below the costs of competitors. Such resources include not only tangible resources such as financial resources and human resources but also intangible resources such as information and general business experience.

International Experience

Companies with greater levels of international business experience tend to realize the inherent complexities associated with export pricing. Therefore more experienced firms consider export pricing as a problematic area than less experienced ones. Firms with international experience address export pricing issues effectively through a comprehensive export pricing strategy. This strategy addresses various elements of export pricing, which will be discussed later.

Use of Information Systems

Information systems provide management with inputs for decision making. Greater use of effective information systems allows a higher level of control over foreign market initiatives. In particular, market-based pricing requires the collection of market-specific information. Pricing is often accomplished by consulting salespeople and obtaining on-site opinions of alternative prices on volume and profit. Formal investigations such as market experiments and field tests also provide valuable information that allows firms to analyze the implications of different prices on the market. It is important to note that collecting such information is expensive, and the cost of data collection can influence a company's commitment to the export venture.

Number and Locations of Overseas Production Facilities

The locations and number of the firm's suppliers, manufacturing facilities, and subsidiaries will factor heavily into the pricing strategy. Production facilities established in locations other than the home country will introduce enhanced logistical, labor, and regulatory concerns into the decision-making process. Although firms that produce overseas seeking inexpensive wage rates may incur other costs and risks that affect final prices, multiple production facilities will eventually enable the firm to produce in markets where production costs are cheapest, allowing more flexibility in the pricing of its exports. By rotating production to the facility where inputs are the cheapest, managers can reduce costs and modify their prices as sales warrant.

Despite the proliferation of foreign-owned manufacturing facilities around the world, many companies only participation in the global market is by exporting products they make in their home countries. The usual reason is that the volume of their sales abroad is simply not large enough to justify foreign manufacturing.

Level of Internationalization

When production is kept at home, a company is tied to conditions prevailing in that market, a circumstance that reduces its pricing flexibility in its export markets. Economic and political developments at home, and even natural disasters such as major hurricanes, can force export prices up at a time when local producers in the overseas market or exporters from other countries are not similarly affected and can maintain low prices. One example might be a trade embargo observed by only a few governments. Because of the boycott, the supply of certain needed raw materials is reduced, driving up the cost of making some products. Competitive products made in nonboycotting countries would obviously enjoy a clear price advantage in export markets.

In contrast, companies that manufacture abroad often enjoy greater pricing flexibility both in the countries in which they are located and in export markets. In addition to being able to calibrate production to local demand and competitive conditions, these multinational corporations (MNCs) find it easier to respond to foreign exchange fluctuations.

Centralized pricing decisions typically focus on costs and profitability concerns. On the other hand, decentralized pricing incorporates concerns about competition to a greater extent than centralized pricing. Companies that sell to sophisticated customers have to allow greater responsiveness to customer demands and are therefore predominantly focused on decentralized pricing approaches.

Product-Based Factors

A specialized product, or one with a technological edge, gives a company price flexibility. In many markets there is no local production of the item, government-imposed import barriers are minimal, and importing firms all face similar price escalation factors. Under such circumstances, producers are able to remain competitive with little adjustment in price strategy.

Other product-based factors include input cost volatility of the raw materials of your products, the degree of standardization of your company's products, and the age of the product in terms of its position in the product life cycle. Input cost volatility leads to greater centralization of the pricing decision and use of foreign currencies to source raw materials from multiple locations. Standardized products have better coordinated prices across markets, and older and more mature products face higher levels of competition both in terms of the number of competitors and price. The age of the product in the domestic market affects an exporter's price decision. However, the stage of the product in the product life cycle could be less relevant in cases where no substitute products are available in foreign markets and thus consumers in the market view the product as a new, innovative product, in which case the product enters the market as a new product in a new product life cycle. This implies that the product life cycle in international markets can be extended from that in the domestic market.

Industry-Based Factors

There are several factors of export pricing that arise from the unique environments of the industry. Such industry-based factors include the competitive and regulatory intensity of the market environment.

Competitive Intensity of the Export Market

The level of competitive intensity within both the industry and export market will increase the need for responsive decision making (Roberts, 1988), dictating a fluid and simple pricing method by those familiar with the market and the customer. This quick response is only possible if lower level managers and sales representatives are given autonomy in the export pricing decision. These employees must be familiar with customers, distributors, and competitive levels within their areas of responsibility. This kind of familiarity results from significant exposure to the export market.

A relatively low level of price competition usually leads to administered prices and a static role for pricing in the marketing mix. In such instances, a "skimming" price strategy is often used. Eventually, however, as price competition develops and technological advantages shrink, specialized and highly technical firms must make more and more market-based exceptions to their previously uniform pricing strategies.

Impact of Suppliers on Export Pricing Decisions

Pricing strategies are also influenced by industry-specific factors, such as the number of suppliers, fluctuations in price, and the availability of alternative raw materials. In order to reduce uncertainty, a growing practice of companies is to negotiate fixed-price agreements with suppliers before making their own bids for major contracts.

Predatory Pricing by Competitors

Another problem for firms in some industries is predatory pricing by particularly aggressive competitors. Recently that strategy has been pursued mainly by new players hungry for market share, most notably those in just recently industrialized countries such as Taiwan, Korea, and China.

Regulatory Intensity of the Export Market

Import policies and trade barriers in foreign markets have a significant effect on export pricing decisions (Cavusgil, 1988; Myers et al., 2002). In markets where price escalation results from import barriers, firms may not be able to experience large profit margins due to the already inflated price of their product. Furthermore, with the increased tension between nations over trading policies, intellectual property rights, and nontariff barriers, antidumping legislation has become an important topic with strong ties to export pricing. Antidumping laws regarding specific products will affect the pricing decisions of the firm. A simple cost-plus price may result in a price too low for a heavily regulated market. High regulatory intensity may require more of a market-based pricing approach, whereby the firm is sensitive and responsive to additional costs added on by market-specific regulations.

In Germany, for instance, price fixing is still legal in some retailing segments, such as book publishing. A bestseller can be sold for a lower price at a big chain in the United States, but in Germany, the same book must sell for the same price no matter if it is at a corner store or a major retailer. The admittedly anticompetitive practice helps to explain why independent book stores proliferate in Germany. However, as competitive pressures have increased, an Austrian book chain, Librodisk AG, has asked the EU to scrap a law that makes all German-speaking countries subject to the prices set in Germany. If the proposition is agreed upon, then the whole fixed-price system will be in jeopardy.

Export Market Characteristics

The market an exporter is interested in will likely have factors that affect its export pricing. These characteristics include the length of the distribution channel, the sophistication level of customers, the regulatory and competitive intensity of the export market, and the foreign currency volatility associated with exporting to this market (Myers et al., 2002).

The Pricing Impact of Channels of Distribution

The distribution channels used by your company will influence international pricing, particularly export pricing. When a company is able to distribute its products through its own overseas subsidiaries, it has greater control over final prices, including the ability to rapidly adjust prices as well as obtain firsthand knowledge of market conditions.

An exporter working with independent distributors, however, usually finds that it can control only the landed price (the exporters price to the distributor). As one might expect, many exporters are concerned about the difficulty of maintaining price levels. Some firms report that distributors substantially mark up prices, up to 200% in some countries. The use of manufacturer's representatives gives a company greater price control, but this method is used less frequently by U.S. companies, which usually require a "full service" intermediary in the export market.

Direct selling to end users is necessary in many industries, especially those involving large systems or technical equipment. In the case of sales to government agencies, a protracted bidding process and negotiations preclude the use of list or other standard prices. Firms often attempt to establish more direct channels of distribution to reach their customers in overseas markets. Indeed, that is sometimes a motivation for establishing a company-owned subsidiary. By reducing the number of intermediaries between the manufacturer and the customer, the adverse effects of successive markups can be avoided.

The complexity and levels of distribution channels tend to impact product prices as well. Greater complexity and multiechelon channels lead to higher costs due to higher inventory levels and greater transaction costs. The nature of the relationship between the channel members and the exporter also affects export pricing strategy.

Environmental Factors That Affect Pricing Decisions

Pricing is affected by factors not immediately perceived as price related. For instance, climatic conditions in foreign markets may necessitate costly product or distribution modifications, and prices must be adjusted to cover these extra expenses. A maker of soft drink equipment must treat its machines intended for tropical markets to prevent rust corrosion, while an agribusiness must take into account climate, soil conditions, and the country's infrastructure before making any bid.

Economic and Currency-Related Factors

Economic factors such as inflation, exchange rate fluctuations, and price controls may significantly affect your export pricing (Myers et al., 2002). In particular, the value of the U.S. dollar in foreign markets draws the attention of many export managers. In fact, the dollar's unusual strength in the first half of the 1980s led a number of companies to introduce compensating adjustments as part of their pricing strategies. In contrast, during the first half of the 1990s, U.S. exporters enjoyed a much weaker currency, boosting their sales in international markets.

Some variables that affect the choice of the use of a particular currency for export sales are the competitive intensity of the export market, the resources of the exporter, the firm's international experience, and the number and locations of the firm's manufacturing facilities. Higher competitive intensity requires firms to respond in currency choices established by strong competitors. Firms with greater access to resources can better absorb the impact of foreign exchange fluctuations. Firms with greater levels of international experience understand the complexities of foreign exchange markets and can use these to their advantage. Finally, firms with multiple production and sourcing choices can take advantage of exchange rate movements by supplying different products to different markets from the most appropriate locations.

Since currency fluctuations are cyclical, exporters that find themselves blessed with a price advantage when their currency is undervalued must carry an extra burden when their currency is overvalued. Companies committed to serving international markets must be creative, pursuing different pricing strategies in different currency exchange rate conditions.

Locus of Export Pricing Decisions

Most exporters will be forced to make centralized pricing decisions, as they are typically involved in arm's length transactions with their foreign distributor or retailer. However, there are important lessons that can be gleaned from examining the approaches used by global companies. Market and customer responsiveness is a key element of success, and exporters might be able to build "feedback loops" into their pricing practices to allow information inputs from local markets to influence centralized pricing strategy formulation. Let's explore two possible scenarios: centralized pricing and decentralized pricing.

Centralized Pricing

International pricing decisions are centralized in most globalized companies. Reasons for this include the following:

- Increasing globalization of markets requires greater uniformity of prices across markets. The existence of different prices from country to country often leads to gray market imports (i.e., sourcing of a product from low-price countries by unauthorized intermediaries for sale in high-price countries). This results in the creation of another distribution channel parallel to authorized channels but not under the control of the manufacturer.

- Global companies encounter the same competitors in many markets, requiring globally coordinated competitive strategies. A fragmented strategy often leads to suboptimal results.

- In some companies, pricing is closely related to production volume planning. Since volume planning is usually done at the corporate level, it requires centrally directed prices.

- Typically the parent company wants to forecast its annual revenues worldwide. Therefore it must be able to estimate the sales of all its operations, including its overseas subsidiaries. This often dictates setting prices centrally or, at least, imposing some guidelines for the prices to be set by subsidiaries.

- Many firms seek tight control over pricing of their "global" brands. Companies typically aim for a homogeneous market segment with similar positioning from one market to another. To create a uniform image across national boundaries, not only the product but also the price must be consistent. The price is normally set by the corporate headquarters relative to the prices of competing local products in each market. The policy might state, for example, that the brand must always be premium priced relative to local products and that "premium" is defined as, say, 20% above the price of the most expensive locally produced item. Such a policy limits local autonomy in setting prices. An example of a global brand priced in this manner is Grand Metropolitan's Smirnoff Vodka. Gillette is another company that seeks a global brand image for its products.

- Important to a company's pricing policies and practices is the proximity of its overseas markets to one another. When markets are close geographically, a country subsidiary cannot set prices for its own market in isolation. No subsidiary can mark up the price to the point where the customer would import the product rather than buy it locally.

Centralized pricing management by the company or by a centralized or regional pricing office is often the only way to prevent subsidiaries from undermining one another's pricing programs.

Decentralized Pricing

If the local market is relatively poor, with most consumers at lower income levels, the local subsidiary may have to deviate from centrally determined pricing guidelines. The following factors are often responsible for a decentralized pricing process:

- *Specific local cost factors.* Value-added taxes and the cost of adapting a product to a particular market may demand greater price flexibility in some countries.
- *Transportation costs.* These vary widely from country to country owing to the nature of the distribution infrastructure, the extent of unionization in the transport industries, and local distribution laws.
- *Economic and financial conditions.* Interest rates and inflation often cause local divisions to deviate from corporate pricing guidelines. Local prices must reflect currency realities.
- *Capacity utilization.* A subsidiary with excess capacity in a local market may choose to lower prices to boost demand, while tight capacity may suggest an advantage in charging higher prices.

How do multinational firms resolve the conflicting needs for centralization and decentralization of pricing decisions? Typically the corporate office sets policy and issues general guidelines to which the overseas subsidiaries and distributors must adhere. The guidelines are usually written at the beginning of each fiscal year and sometimes more often if necessary. Pricing policies reflect both the general direction prices should take during the course of the year and the company's underlying export pricing strategy. For instance, an American manufacturing company's 1996 policy was that prices were not to rise more than 1% over 1995 prices. The company adopted this policy in an attempt to fend off its chief rival.

Once a broad pricing strategy is set by the company's home office, subsidiaries and distributors are allowed to make adjustments locally because of the considerations listed above. In some companies, the degree of pricing flexibility given to the subsidiary is precisely defined. For example, headquarters may allow local prices to deviate 5% to 15% from the centrally established prices.

How is pricing freedom transferred from headquarters to the subsidiaries? In practice, pricing freedom is transferred through three main mechanisms:

- A system of discounts on sales to intermediate customers
- Credit arrangements and terms of sale
- Transfer prices charged to subsidiaries

The company as a whole benefits as a result of a pricing system that is responsive to local needs. Similarly, credit terms and other variable conditions of sale have a direct impact on the final cost to subsidiaries and intermediate customers.

Finally, transfer prices charged to subsidiaries can also be adjusted to increase profits at the headquarters, or they may be lowered to increase the subsidiaries' pricing flexibility. Transfer pricing practices are discussed later in this chapter.

Dimensions of Export Pricing

Your company's export pricing strategy has several underlying dimensions: export pricing objectives, export price setting philosophy, export pricing determination, and export pricing implementation.

Export Pricing Objectives

These are the strategic and economic goals set by management in pricing the firm's products. These objectives are linked to the wider marketing and business strategies of the firm and are measured through profitability, market share, and return measures. As competitive levels in a market increase, firms move toward competitive prices in order to survive. This is an example of evolving pricing objectives. Your firm's pricing objectives will change as products move from introduction to growth to maturity, and finally start declining in sales. Typically mature products face higher price competition.

Export Price Setting Philosophy

The export price setting philosophy of your company is the set of principles that your management adheres to when establishing export prices. These principles are reflected in a variety of managerial and environmental factors:

- The competitive posture associated with export prices
- The locus of the control of export prices
- The frequency of the pricing review process
- The choice between flexibility and rigidity in export pricing procedures

The frequency of the pricing review process is a critical aspect of determining your firm's pricing strategy. Traditionally companies have followed the policy of an annual price review. This policy allows customers to lock in prices for their own costing and pricing purposes. There are two problems with this policy:

1. The certainty of a price review encourages forward buying by foreign distributors.
2. The volatility of international markets may require more frequent price reviews to maintain profitability.

Foreign exchange rate volatility and quickly shifting input costs along with high competitive intensity require an almost continuous price review process. However, if these elements are missing or are fairly stable, management can afford to review prices at regular intervals.

Approaches to Export Price Setting

Clearly there is no single approach to international pricing that is best for every company and every situation. What is important for the manufacturer to remember is that the suitability of prices must be examined at several levels in the international distribution channel: at the importer, wholesalers, retailers, and so on. In most companies, a product's price starts with a "floor price," which is the lowest possible price at which the product may be retailed or wholesaled (depending on the nature of the company). The floor price is derived from the total cost of bringing the product to market plus a corporate markup. Costs typically include research and development (R&D), raw materials, processing, transportation, distribution, marketing, and administrative overhead. Arriving at the correct floor price is not as easy as it seems. The process is complicated because of differences in cost accounting practices, company policies (such as whether or not to factor in domestic overhead), global manufacturing and sourcing factors, and so on.

Price setting approaches vary by company size, industry, product, and market type. However at a broader level, there are two distinct approaches to price setting: cost-based pricing, including rigid cost-plus pricing and flexible cost-plus pricing, and market-based pricing (Cavusgil et al., 2008). These major export pricing approaches are discussed below.

Rigid Cost-Plus Pricing

The complexity of export pricing has caused many managers to cling to rigid cost-plus pricing, a formula that ensures margins. However, this pricing strategy may push the final price unreasonably high so that the company becomes uncompetitive in major markets. The foreign list price is set by adding international customer costs and a gross margin to domestic manufacturing costs. The final price to the foreign customer includes administrative and R&D overhead costs, transportation, insurance, packaging, marketing, documentation, and customs charges, as well as profit margins for both the distributor and the manufacturer. Cost-plus pricing is a static element of the marketing mix since it does not reflect market environments to any significant extent.

Flexible Cost-Plus Pricing

This strategy sets list prices in the same way as the rigid pricing strategy but allows for price variations in special circumstances. For example, discounts may be applied to the final price, depending on the customer, the size of the order, or the strength of local competition (Roberts, 1988). Although there is more room to adapt export prices to local conditions, the primary objective of this approach is still to maintain profit margins. In this sense, this pricing strategy can also be viewed as an essentially static element of the marketing mix.

Dynamic Incremental Pricing

This method assumes that fixed costs are incurred regardless of the company's export sales performance. Therefore it seeks to recover only variable and international customer costs in export prices while adding in a partial overhead factor rather than a full overhead load. This approach enables the distributors to sell products at prices that dynamically reflect local market conditions. In some cases, local distributors try to expand their market share by maintaining prices at the lowest possible level. Most companies that use dynamic incremental pricing do so only under special circumstances. For example, one U.S. industrial MNC negotiates "one-shot" deals with its distributors, offering them low prices when it has a sufficient quantity of the product, when the sales potential is good, or when competitive pressure necessitates aggressive pricing.

In some cases, dynamic incremental pricing helps a company introduce a product to a market. Under this strategy, also known as "penetration pricing," the introductory or "market floor" price is the lowest possible. The objective is to gain as much market share as possible in the shortest time. Once the product attains a sufficient market share, prices tend to increase slowly. Over the past few decades, Japanese and Korean MNCs in particular have successfully used penetration strategies in the United States and other Western markets, often inviting dumping charges by local marketers. When carried to extremes, however, as when a company charges a price lower than the cost of making a product or the product's domestic price, penetration pricing may run afoul of local antidumping laws.

In penetration strategies, introductory prices start low and slowly rise, whereas with "skimming" a company introduces the product into the market at a relatively high price, often while limiting distribution. This can be an effective method for launching innovative, high-tech items, such as advanced consumer electronics or trendy products. A certain segment of the market will pay premium prices to be first to have such things, which are introduced amid great excitement, highly visible advertising, and extensive media coverage. As with a penetration strategy, the price slowly comes into line with the product's price in other countries. Dynamic incremental pricing also implies skimming when it coincides with a dominant market share position, as other companies cannot afford to ignore the price leader's practices. Several years ago, Cummins Engine reduced its prices dramatically in Europe, the Middle East, and the Far East to about 70% of its previous prices. This strategy was successful in limiting the inroads made by the company's Japanese competition.

Generally speaking, dynamic incremental pricing reflects as many pricing factors as possible while offering flexibility to local distributors. As a result, local prices with this strategy will vary from market to market, reflecting different costs and market environments. For instance, TCBY's franchisee, Top Green, exports Chinese-made TCBY products to stores in Hong Kong and other TCBY franchises in the Asia-Pacific region. Hong Kong products generally cost about 15% more than those sold in Guangzhou and other areas of the Guangdong Province and considerably more than those in Shanghai. A smoothie sold in retail stores, for example, is $1.44 in Guangzhou and $2.07 in Hong Kong. The retail price of a coated yogurt bar is $2.07 in Hong Kong, more than twice the price in Beijing and more than three times that the price in Shanghai, primarily to balance foreign exchange rates, transportation costs, cost of living, economic conditions, perceived value of the customers, and competitors' prices, among many other market conditions.

Transfer Pricing Practices

One of the thorniest problems multinational companies grapple with when they venture beyond their home country borders is transfer pricing (Czinkota, Ronkainen, & Moffett, 2004; Fowler, 1978), also known as "intracompany pricing." The prices at which units of the same company sell to each other have a far-reaching effect on the company's success because they influence everything from foreign subsidiary performance to executive compensation to tax obligations. There has never been a single "best" way to set transfer prices, one that satisfies both the parent company and its foreign affiliates (not to mention the tax collectors in all countries concerned). Nor does any system meet all the needs of production, marketing, and finance equally well.

Transfer pricing is the most important concern for MNCs. It is also an increasingly important issue for governments, which is evident in the quickening pace of transfer pricing legislation around the world. Governments are enacting tougher laws that require increased documentation of the fairness of values placed on goods and services exchanged among subsidiaries or between parents and their subsidiaries. As an illustration, consider a U.S. manufacturer of computer components that set up a company in Malaysia to take advantage of the country's lower labor costs and gain better access to computer manufacturers in Southeast Asia. Initially the U.S. parent owned all the intangible property, including proprietary designs and know-how, and the Malaysian subsidiary paid royalties for them. However, an arrangement was made whereby the parent's royalty income was phased out. The Malaysian company now possesses a cost-sharing arrangement with the parent and in return owns a share of the intangibles. The parent company saves more than $10 million annually on taxes alone. With such implications, MNCs are interested in managing transfer prices effectively. Further details about transfer prices are offered below.

Why Is Transfer Price Important?

Multinational companies attempt to manage their internal prices among their units primarily for two reasons. First, transfer pricing can become a vehicle for repatriating profits from those countries that have remittance controls. In the extreme case, funds may be blocked by the central bank, and transfer pricing may be the only means of getting earnings out of the country. Second, transfer pricing can be a way to shift profits out of high-tax countries into low-tax ones (Fowler, 1978). Underlying both objectives is the desire to foster companywide efficiency. While individual units may show poor performance, the company as a whole can achieve optimal results by means of careful transfer pricing. For this reason, MNCs typically centralize transfer pricing under the direction of the chief financial officer.

Common Transfer Pricing Approaches

Companies have a number of transfer pricing strategies available. Products can be sold to members of the same corporate family at cost or a variation of direct cost, at market prices, at inflated prices, or at some combination of these. Some MNCs use different transfer pricing methods for different purposes, accepting the cost and complexity of maintaining more than one system. Others opt for the simplicity of a single approach, accepting the inevitable deficiencies of whatever system they choose. The following bases are commonly used for transfer pricing:

- *Actual cost.* A firm's transfer price uses its actual manufacturing cost. With this method manufacturing facilities are treated as cost centers rather than profit centers, an approach that resolves many internal disputes over allocation of profits. However, it leaves the cost centers with little motivation.
- *Standard cost.* Unlike actual cost, which has the advantage of identifying efficiencies or inefficiencies in the supplying unit, the standard cost approach facilitates "management by exception" decision making, in which variations from standard cost signal the need for additional investigation and attention by management. A major shortcoming is that standard costing often requires management to make arbitrary assumptions and leaves the company vulnerable to expending time unproductively in debates on how to set the standards.
- *Modified cost.* This is useful in promoting the achievement of strategic objectives. For example, actual and standard costs are sometimes adjusted to encourage more extensive use of certain products or services. Companies that expect to have unused capacity for a time often lower their transfer prices in order to provide incremental contributions to the coverage of "sunk" costs. Among the modifications available are variable costs, marginal costs, and full absorption costs.

- *Market price.* Prevailing external market prices (arms length prices) are often viewed as the best transfer pricing mechanism for external reporting. Because this approach removes internal bias and facilitates validation, it appeals to outside parties, such as tax authorities. From a performance evaluation perspective, however, market prices may be unfair because they give the supplying business unit the entire profit on the transaction, including the benefit of any cost reductions due to global efficiencies. To equitably share the advantage of lower costs, transfer prices must be lower than market prices.

- *Modified market price.* Market prices can be adjusted to reflect specific characteristics of the goods or services involved. For example, they may be reduced to reflect lower marketing or distribution costs that occur in external markets. Ordinarily this will help resolve perceived inequities among supplying and receiving business units. However, a supplying unit that has no excess capacity will still feel unfairly penalized if the lower price cuts into the profits the unit would otherwise earn on external sales. In such a case, external profit is a relevant opportunity cost and it should be factored into the transfer price.

- *Negotiated price.* A negotiated price is determined by bargaining between the buying and selling units. Although some executives argue that this technique results in an arm's length transaction that is just as valid as an external market price, its use in evaluating the performance of subsidiaries has some risks. For instance, negotiators may fail to reach agreement, which could result in counterproductive and expensive procurement of goods or services from outside the firm. Another problem is that excessive internal competition can undermine the achievement of congruent goals among business units, resulting in a serious loss of cooperation.

- *Contract price.* A variation of the negotiated price method is a price agreed upon at the time the firm's business plan is adopted. Such a "contract" price eliminates variations that result from centralized sourcing decisions beyond the control of managers of foreign operations. One drawback of the method is that it does not pass on price hikes in raw materials to marketing units. As a result, it removes the marketing unit's incentive to recover any inflationary and foreign exchange losses through third-party pricing.

Factors That Influence Transfer Pricing

Many factors are involved in deciding which transfer price to use and whether to use different prices for reporting external and internal performance. Sometimes one issue is of overriding importance to a company, clearly dictating a particular pricing system. More often, however, a company's situation is mixed, making the choice highly complex and probably contentious. For most companies, the decision involves some combination of the considerations discussed below:

- *Local taxes.* Perhaps the most significant concerns in setting transfer prices are the local tax rate and pertinent tax regulations. The use of transfer pricing in local jurisdictions that have relatively lower corporate tax rates normally results in lower overall income taxes. Generally, lower transfer prices also mean lower import duties. Similarly, keeping transfer prices low can reduce local value-added taxes. An effective transfer pricing system should deal with changes in import duties, income taxes, and so on, in a way that minimizes overall tax exposure.
- *Currency fluctuations.* Transfer pricing should effectively consider fluctuations in currency exchange rates to minimize the impacts from volatilities on the profitability of the entire organization. A low transfer price can be given to a subsidiary that realized excessive profits from such currency market volatilities.
- *Inflation.* Transfer prices can be adjusted to balance the effect of local inflation. A low transfer price will help minimize the loss in value from inflation.
- *Subsidiary profits.* Still another use of transfer pricing is to manipulate the profit position of a subsidiary. For example, startups often require substantial corporate assistance, which can be provided in the form of lower purchase prices from or higher sales prices to other company units. In this way a

market niche can be carved out more quickly for the startup and its long-term survival guaranteed.

- *Expense accounting.* Transfer prices can also be used to advantage when the host government places restrictions on allowable deductions for expenses. Sometimes certain services, such as product development or strategic planning assistance, are provided to the subsidiary but cannot be charged because of restrictions. In this case, costs for those services can be recouped by increasing the transfer prices of components sold to the units.

- *Joint venture support.* Similarly, transfer pricing can help recoup expenses from a joint venture, especially if there are restrictions on repatriation of profits. Lowering the prices of products and services to a parent reduces the outflow of funds from the home country, while raising the prices of purchases from the parent shifts funds to the home country. When a government imposes local price controls, transfer pricing practices may again help. Higher transfer prices on exports of intermediate goods from a parent to a subsidiary in such a market may help support the case for an increase in the price of the final product.

- *Output capacity.* Subsidiaries with substantial excess production capacity can set transfer prices low enough to encourage additional internal consumption, but high enough to cover the supplying unit's variable costs.

Potential Problems of Transfer Pricing

As implied by the above discussion, the ability to control internal prices charged to subsidiaries affords the global corporation significant flexibility and overall efficiency. Nevertheless, these benefits often come at a cost:

- There is the complication of internal control measures. Manipulating transfer prices makes it very difficult to determine the true profit contribution of a subsidiary.
- Morale problems typically surface at a subsidiary whose profit performance has been made worse artificially.

- Because of cultural differences, some subsidiary management may react negatively to price manipulation.
- There are concerns about local regulations. Subsidiaries, as local businesses, must abide by the rules. Legal problems will arise if the subsidiary follows accounting standards that are not approved by the host government. Indeed, in many countries, transfer pricing practices are often subject to review by local authorities.

Export Pricing Implementation

The key issue exporters face in the implementation of export pricing is the challenge of coordinating prices across markets. Gray market imports present the most significant obstacle to price coordination in international markets. Certain products have to be adapted to meet local market requirements. This leads to unique products that have different prices. Containing these products within their designated sales territories might be a problem if there is an arbitrage opportunity for local traders. Another aspect of export pricing implementation is the locus of price decision making. Sophisticated customers demand price flexibility from salespersons and frontline employees rather than waiting for head office decisions.

Undoubtedly pricing will continue to gain significance for exporters over the coming decades. With intensified competition and interdependence of markets, export managers will find the management of prices even more challenging (Myers et al., 2002). The challenges will involve attainment of better coordination of worldwide prices by corporate headquarters, achievement of the delicate balance between corporate and local control of prices, quicker response to marketplace changes, avoidance of gray market or parallel importing activity, and development of alternatives to costly price competition. In addition, there are other challenges exporters often have to consider in export pricing.

The Role of Communications

The challenges associated with communications imply new or improved practices on the part of exporters. For example, an efficient, smooth, and rapid system of communication with subsidiary managers or distributors is essential. Those companies that operate in so-called global industries, such as telecommunications, construction equipment, and medical equipment, need to devise efficient mechanisms for monitoring competition worldwide and disseminating relevant information to the members of the corporate family in a timely manner.

Organizational Challenges

Pricing globally remains an organizational challenge. Increasingly it is an area in which input from various functional divisions and regions allows for better decision making. Nevertheless, many companies make critical pricing decisions without the necessary consultation with all units concerned.

Relationship Between Price and Other Marketing Variables

Export managers will also have to develop a better appreciation of the intimate relationships between price and other elements of the marketing mix. Pricing decisions cannot be reached in isolation from other dimensions of the sale, such as product quality, after-sales service, follow-up sales opportunities, credit terms, and so on. Price represents only one item in the bundle of benefits perceived by the customer. Interpreting customers' perceptions of product value continues to be a formidable but necessary task. Pricing decisions that are based on a good understanding of perceived value from the perspective of both the intermediaries and the final customers are more likely to be successful.

CHAPTER 16

Financial Aspects and Payments in Exporting

Upon completing this chapter you should

- understand the crucial financial aspects of exporting;
- be able to classify export financing needs;
- understand different sources of financing;
- understand the methods of payment and how to use them effectively;
- understand the basic mechanisms of international countertrade;
- be aware of the different types of insurance policies available.

Payment and financing arrangements for exporting are more complicated than those for selling in the domestic market. Exporters expect payment as quickly as possible and importers usually prefer delaying payment until they have at least received and resold the goods. Since the parties live in different countries, communication and coordination can be very challenging. Hence the ability of the exporter to resolve these obstacles, in terms of payment and financing, is crucial for the success of the export business. Major problems with payment and financing that challenge exporters could be any of the following three types: financing export transactions, receiving payment, and insurance (Cavusgil, Knight, & Riesenberger, 2008).

Financing Export Transactions

The use of effective export finance techniques provides additional export marketing advantages. An exporter may need preshipment financing to produce or purchase the product or to render service or postshipment financing of the resulting transaction (account) or accounts receivable.

Preshipment Financing

This form of financing is particularly important for small and medium-size exporters who might not have sufficient internal financial resources to meet production expenditures. Usually preshipment financing is in the form of a bank advance, overdraft, or loan against confirmed orders from the customer.

Postshipment Financing

Exporters often need to finance transactions not only prior to the shipment but also after the shipment. Postshipment financing can be arranged through various financial institutions, including commercial banks, merchant bankers, insurance companies, and other financial institutions.

Postshipment financing may be on a short, medium, or long-term basis. Short-term financing involves loans that are due in 1 year. The financing institution may provide up to 90% of the free on board (FOB) value of the contract. Medium-term financing is usually used for consumer durables and light capital goods. Medium-term loans are for 2 to 5 years. Finally, long-term loans are for heavy capital goods, infrastructure, and so forth. These loans may be for 10 years or more and may require government participation. They normally comprise 70% to 80% of the FOB value of the contract. Interest rates are typically 7% to 8% per year.

An exporter can finance his international transactions (extending credit to the importer and financing himself) through internal and external sources. However, small and medium-size exporters usually need external export finance mechanisms. The main focus of this chapter will be external sources of financing.

Determinants of the Export Finance Decision

There are many important factors to consider in making decisions about financing. Exporters have to consider the creditworthiness of the buyer, the costs of financing, and the length of financing, among others, in determining financing decisions (Czinkota & Ronkainen, 2002).

Obtaining Credit Information On Potential Buyers

The first determinant of the export financing decision for both the exporter and the financial institution involves the availability of credit information on potential buyers. Buyers must be identified as to their willingness and ability to make payments. Credit information on foreign firms can be obtained through a variety of sources, including bank credit reports, local credit agencies, country risk assessment ratings, and the collection experiences of other exporters.

Cost of Different Financing Methods

The cost of different financing methods is another factor exporters should consider in making financing decision. Different financial institutions offer varying interest rates and fees. Depending on the objectives of the financing, exporters need to consider interest rates and fees in the total cost of the financing. For instance, if it is short-term financing, programs that require fewer fees may be more attractive. However, for mid- to long-term financing, interest rates may play a determining role. Furthermore, the amount of financing could affect your decision to pick one program over another. The costs associated with different methods of financing, as well as their effect on profitability, should be well understood.

Length of Time That Financing Is Required

Costs increase as the financing term increases. As mentioned before, there are short-, medium-, and long-term loans. The exporter should choose the most appropriate term required to complete the transaction. The most appropriate loan term will vary depending on the type of product, which determines the term of payment as well as the duration of payment. The term of payment may depend on negotiations between the seller and buyer. This means the term of payment being negotiated could affect the financing term.

Private Sources of Financing

There are two major sources of export financing: private sources and non-private sources. The major private sources of financing include commercial banks, factoring, confirming, and forfeiting (Cavusgil et al., 2008).

There are different courses of action, costs, and benefits associated with each of these.

Commercial Banks

Exporters need to finance their export sales until payment is received. The exporter should first consider its local commercial bank as a source of financing. There are four basic factors that any exporter should consider in selecting a bank for overseas transactions:

- The efficiency and experience of the bank's international division
- The exporter's relationship with the bank
- The availability of the bank's foreign branches, correspondents (especially in the case of letters of credit), or representative offices
- The export credit and financing policies of the bank

Banks generally make fewer term loans abroad than they do domestically. It is not uncommon, particularly when making loans with a relatively long maturity, for a commercial bank and a bank abroad to participate with a bank located within a third country in making the loan.

Many exporters have similar financing needs for both international and domestic transactions. Thus the willingness of banks to finance exporting depends on the certainty of repayment. Exporting loans may be secured or unsecured. Since it is the prudent policy of commercial banks to minimize risk exposure, a large portion of export loans are made on a secured basis. Collateral usually takes the form of a shipment document, warehouse receipt, and banker's acceptance. A commercial bank holds the titles of these pledging assets until collection of payment from the importer on behalf of the exporter. Unsecured loans might take the form of authorization of the exporting firm to draw drafts on commercial banks up to a predetermined amount or merely signing a note supported by a loan agreement.

If the draft is drawn for 180 days, rather than a "sight draft," which can be paid upon receipt, the exporter must make additional arrangements to finance the export transaction. This leads to the creation of banker's acceptance. The draft is changed into an acceptance once the word "accepted" has been stamped across the face of the draft and the signature of a bank officer who has been authorized to sign such documents has been obtained. In addition, the draft must contain a brief description of the transaction that gave rise to it. The banker's acceptance can either be held until it is due and presented to the accepting bank for payment or it can be discounted for immediate cash. The maturity of a banker's acceptance typically has a maximum of 180 days.

Factoring

Another kind of financing method that can successfully serve exporters is the factor. Export factoring is the process whereby a financial institution purchases export receivables on a nonrecourse basis, with notification to the importer. The factor is then responsible for collection and any relevant credit risk without recourse to the exporter. Thus the exporter can save collection expenses and reduce its credit risk.

Export factoring begins with the evaluation of the creditworthiness of each importer. If the factor considers the importer creditworthy, the factor may agree to assume the loss in case the importer defaults. However, if the importer is not creditworthy, the factor may simply take responsibility for payment collection, leaving the exporter to assume any credit risk. Advantages of factoring include the following:

- Entire credit and collection operations can be shifted to the factor. This can result in a sizable savings to the firm.
- More timely and effective cash management may result.
- Firms can secure fast, short-term financing.

On the other hand, factoring has several drawbacks. Currently there is limited geographic coverage of factoring. Furthermore, it is not easy to locate institutions offering export factoring. An exporter who plans on utilizing the factoring service should know that the factor is not responsible for default caused by reasons beyond the financial inability of the importer. For example, the factor is not responsible when the importer is able but refuses to pay. Factoring is also more costly than commercial bank refinancing. Factoring fees include a 3% margin to cover paper-work, collection, and insurance costs. Cash advances from the factor are not free. Interest rates for cash advances are typically 3% to 5% above the current prime rate.

Confirming

Another source of private financing for exporting is confirming. Confirming is a financial service wherein an independent company confirms an export order in the seller's country and makes payment for the goods in the currency of that country. Confirming has been used extensively by European firms and is relatively new to U.S. exporters. Confirming can cover practically the entire exporting process, including transportation, packaging, customs duties, and broker fees. By paying approximately 3% of the invoice value, an exporter's order can be confirmed and paid in his own currency without having to deal with concerns such as international shipping documents and financial and political risk insurance. The exporter can expect payment for his goods within 3 or 4 days of shipment. The disadvantages of confirming are similar to those of factoring. And with its array of services, confirming can be even more expensive than factoring.

Forfaiting

Forfaiting involves the sale, at a discount, of longer term accounts receivable or promissory notes from foreign buyers. These instruments may also carry the guarantee of the foreign government. There are four parties in a typical forfait transaction: the forfaiting house; the guarantor (most often a bank in the country of the importer), who provides the guarantee in the form of an avail; the exporter; and the importer. The forfait can be comprised of the unpaid portion of a contract or 100% of the sale. Finally, forfaiting may be done either with or without recourse to the exporter, and therefore the specific arrangements should be verified by the exporter.

Nonprivate Financing Sources

Besides private sources of export financing, there are also nonprivate agencies that support exporters financially. In the U.S., the Export-Import

Bank (Eximbank), Foreign Credit Insurance Association (FCIA), Private Export Funding Corporation (PEFCO), and Cooperative Financing Facility (CFF) can be sources of export financing.

Export-Import Bank

The U.S. Eximbank, founded in 1934, is an independent agency of the U.S. government specializing in curtailment of predatory export financing practices. Eximbank has the main objective of enhancing U.S. exporters' ability to compete financially with exporters of other countries (Eximbank, 2008). Eximbank's direct loans are relatively limited to large sales volumes. There is no short-term financing of less than 180 days. For medium-term financing, the range is from 180 days to 10 years.

Eximbank can assist exporters in many ways (see Chapters 6 and 8). First, Eximbank can offer guarantees of loans and revolving lines of credit made by more than 300 U.S. banks and their foreign branches. It can loan to commercial banks to finance export shipments. Eximbank normally discounts export receivables and banks' payment obligations. Financing offered by Eximbank can be extended to an importer, and in many cases it can be transferred from the importer to the end user. Finally, Eximbank can issue long-term loans in the form of direct loans to foreign importers or loan guarantees to commercial banks. Eximbank is constantly expanding its services in foreign trade through practices such as cutting interest charges and extending loan maturities. For more information on Eximbank's various services for small businesses, including export financing, visit their Web site at http://www.exim.gov/smallbiz/index.html.

Foreign Credit Insurance Association

The Foreign Credit Insurance Association (FCIA), Eximbank's insurance arm, is designed to assist exporters by assuming most of the commercial credit risk, as well as political risk, that may be incurred by exporters. The coverage offered on both short- and medium-term export sales is designed to assist exporters in expanding sales abroad by protecting them against nonpayment by foreign buyers and facilitating the financing of credit sales.

The FCIA assures exporters and their financing institutions that the major part of a credit, granted by an exporter on his commercial bank to a foreign buyer, will be paid even if the related bill has not been settled by the buyer. Not only is a policyholder insured against most credit and political risks inherent in exporting and foreign trade, but the holder is also able to arrange more favorable financing of export receivables because of the security provided by the insurance. Should default occur on the foreign receivables, the assigned bank asks the insured exporter to file a claim with FCIA. After verifying the validity of the loss under the policy terms, FCIA will pay the claim to the insured exporter and the assigned bank.

Private Export Funding Corporation

The Private Export Funding Corporation (PEFCO) is owned by a group of commercial banks and industrial corporations in cooperation with Eximbank. It provides additional sources of capital to supplement that of commercial banks and Eximbank in the financing of longer term exports (beyond 5 years). All PEFCO loans are approved by Eximbank, and both the interest and principal are unconditionally guaranteed. Individual commitments by PEFCO range from $1 million to $100 million. More information on PEFCO's programs can be found on its Web site at http://www.pefco.com.

Cooperative Financing Facility

To provide more easily accessible financing for small and medium-size sales of U.S. products, Eximbank has directed significant resources into its Cooperative Financing Facility (CFF). Through CFF, Eximbank makes lines of credit available to foreign financial institutions and U.S. banks with foreign branches to finance a portion of the cost of exports, with the remainder of the funds coming from the foreign financial institution's own resources. Transactions normally are initiated by the foreign buyer acting on his own initiative or at the suggestion of the U.S. exporter. CFF helps arrange the cooperation of financial institutions abroad or of U.S.

banks with foreign branches to extend loans to U.S. exporters at their own risk.

Methods of Export Payment

There are several basic methods of receiving payment for products sold abroad. As with domestic sales, a major factor that determines the method of payment is the amount of trust in the buyer's ability and willingness to pay. While domestic sales are usually made on open account and cash in advance, export sales utilize other payment methods in addition to those used in domestic sales. Ranked in order from most secure to least secure (for the exporter), the basic methods of payment are cash in advance, letter of credit, collection draft, open account, and consignment sales (Cavusgil et al., 2008).

Cash in Advance

The ideal form of payment for any exporter is to receive cash with the order. With this method of payment, money is received before the goods are delivered, and accordingly no risk is involved. Even payment by check may result in a collection delay of 4 to 6 weeks. However, it is unlikely that the cash in advance method can be used unless the product being sold is heavily in demand or custom made, as the buyer has to bear the risks associated with this method of payment.

Letter of Credit

Letters of credit (LCs) are the most popular form of payment in international transactions. Due to the inherent risks associated international transactions for both the seller and the buyer, LCs became popular especially between parties without previous transaction experience. That is, an LC establishes trust between the parties by involving both the buyer's and seller's bank. An LC is issued by a bank to a creditworthy customer (the importer) to assure a seller (the exporter) that if the exporter conforms to all details specified in the LC, payment will be made by that bank even if the importer defaults. The bank acts as a third party, examining documents to ensure that they are in order prior to payment.

Payment under a documentary LC is based on a document, not on the terms of sale or the condition of the goods sold. Before payment, the bank responsible for making payment verifies that all documents are exactly as required by the LC. If a discrepancy exists, it must be rectified before payment can be made. Thus the full compliance of documents with those specified in the LC is mandatory. If the buyer has no right of inspection and no right of rejection, this type of document is known as an irrevocable LC. It is used by exporters for two main reasons:

- The importer may not meet the credit standards of the exporter and therefore the exporter may demand bank obligation to eliminate credit risk.
- If the exchange situation in the importer's country indicates that a delay might occur in the transfer of payment to the exporter's country, the exporter may insist on an irrevocable LC.

There is also a revocable LC option under which either party may unilaterally make changes. However, this is rarely used because of the high risk inherent to the exporter. If a revocable LC is used, the buyer can, at will, cancel the order at the exporter's expense.

A Typical Letter of Credit Transaction

Following are the basic steps in a typical LC transaction (Cavusgil et al., 2008).

1. After the parties agree on the terms of a sale, the importer arranges for its bank to open an LC.
2. The importer's bank assesses the trustworthiness of the buyer for the LC.
3. The importer's bank prepares an LC (usually irrevocable), which includes all instructions to the exporter concerning the shipment.
4. The importer's bank sends the LC to the exporter's bank for confirmation.
5. The exporter's bank prepares a letter of confirmation to forward to the exporter along with the LC.

6. The exporter carefully reviews all conditions in the LC. The exporter's freight forwarder should be contacted to make sure that the shipping date can be realized.

7. The exporter arranges with the freight forwarder to deliver the goods to the appropriate port or airport.

8. Once the goods are loaded, the freight forwarder completes the necessary documentation.

9. The exporter (or the forwarder) presents this documentation to the exporter's bank, indicating full compliance.

10. The bank reviews the documents. If they are in order, the documents are mailed to the importer's bank for review before being sent to the buyer.

11. The importer (or his agent) receives the documents that are necessary to claim the goods.

12. A draft, which may accompany the LC, is paid by the exporter's bank at the time specified or may be discounted at an earlier date.

Potential Issues With a Letter of Credit

The exporter should be careful about the following potential issues associated with LCs:

- Even if high charges incurred for shipping, insurance, or other factors are documented, the correspondent bank will pay only the amount specified in the LC. Hence the exporter should carefully prepare quotations for prospective customers.

- Upon receiving an LC, the exporter should carefully compare the terms of the LC with those of his pro forma quotation. If the terms do not precisely match, the LC may become invalid and the exporter may not be paid.

- The exporter must provide documents to show that the goods were shipped by the date specified in the LC. Otherwise the exporter may not be paid. Exporters should check with their forwarders to make sure that no unusual condition has arisen that may delay shipment. Similarly, documents must be presented by the date specified for the LC to be paid.

- International LCs are usually governed by uniform customs and practices or by International Chamber of Commerce (ICC) Publication No. 400 in case some dispute occurs.
- Exporters should always request that the LC specify that partial shipments and transshipment will be allowed. Doing so prevents unforeseen last-minute problems.

Documents That Accompany a Letter of Credit

There are a few documents that are commonly associated with LCs. The most common documents that will accompany an LC before it is payable include the following:

- Bill of lading (see Chapter 17): a document that establishes the terms of a contract between a shipper and a transportation company under which the freight is to be moved between specified points for a predetermined fee. Usually prepared by the shipper on forms issued by the carrier, it serves as a document of title, a contract of carriage, and a receipt for goods.
- Packing list: a list showing the number and types of items being shipped, as well as other information needed for transportation purposes.
- Invoice (see chapter 17): a required commercial document that contains the name and address of the shipper, seller and consignee (the importer) identification, reference numbers (such as an LC confirmation number), order and shipping dates, modes of transportation, description of goods, and payment terms..
- Certificate of inspection (see chapter 17): a document certifying that the merchandise was in good condition immediately prior to its shipment.
- Marine insurance: insurance that compensates the owners of goods transported overseas in the event of loss that cannot be legally recovered from the carrier. It can also cover air shipment.

Costs for a Letter of Credit

If an importer has no import credit record, it will be required to put up 100% of the LC amount in cash or other marketable securities. As the importer builds a credit record, the bank will grant the firm credit terms for the LC, provided the buyer signs a promissory note backed by sufficient collateral. Payment terms will vary from bank to bank and based on the creditworthiness of the importer and the amount of money requested. Credit terms for an LC typically run from 30 days to 90 days.

Collection Draft

The collection draft method is similar to the LC. In order to minimize the risks incurred by the importer and the exporter, a bank acts as an intermediary between the parties. With collection drafts, the exporter ships the goods and the exporter's bank sends the bill of lading and other specified shipping documents to a bank in the importer's country. The importer's bank will not release the bill of lading to the importer until the goods are paid for. That is, the transfer of merchandise title will take place only upon receipt of full payment. Once the importer makes payment, it can pick up the goods. The buyer's bank sends the importer's payment back to the exporter.

To complete this type of deal, the seller must draw up a draft. There are three types of drafts: sight drafts (the draft is payable as soon as the goods arrive); time drafts (the seller extends credit to the buyer, payable in 30 days, 60 days, or 90 days, for example, to pay for the goods from the date the buyer picks up the goods and accepts the draft); and clean drafts (the shipping documents are sent to the buyer at the same time as the goods and the buyer must pay after receiving the goods).

Open Account

Open accounts are used when the seller has adequate credit data about the importer. It is a procedure where an exporter ships goods to a buyer for payment at a later date. Under this form of payment, the buyer has the right to inspect and be compensated for defects. Payment can be delayed by the buyer until goods in receipt are satisfactory.

Sales made on open account carry certain risks. The absence of documents and banking channels may make legal enforcement of claims difficult to pursue. For example, since documents that verify the indebtedness (such as draft) are unavoidable, export receivables may be harder to finance. Also, the exporter may need to pursue collection abroad, which is more difficult and costly.

Consignment Sales

In international consignment sales, the exporter (consignor) retains title to the goods and agrees to wait for payment until the goods have been sold in the consignee's country. However, this is very risky because the consignee may return the goods at any time and without liability. Also, there may be difficulty in ensuring that the consignee observes the terms of the agreement. Hence, with this method, the exporter has the greatest risk and the least control over the goods and may be forced to wait a long time before getting paid.

There are some critical factors to consider when making consignment sales abroad. These include the following:

- Creditworthiness of the consignee
- Stability of the country
- Ensuring the party who is responsible for property risk insures the merchandise until it is sold and payment is received

Collection Problems

In exporting, collection problems involving bad debts can be more easily avoided than corrected once they arise. Just as in a company's domestic business, exporters sometimes face problems with importers who default on payments that result in bad debts. When these problems occur in international trade, obtaining payment can be both difficult and expensive, even when the exporter has insurance against commercial credit risk. Thus exporters should try to avoid these problems through methods such as credit checks, safe payment methods (cash in advance, LCs), and credit risk insurance.

In the case of credit checks, banks are often able to provide credit reports on foreign companies, either through their own foreign branches or through a correspondent bank. The U.S. Department of Commerce's World Trade Data Reports (WTDRs) provide useful information for credit checks. For a nominal fee, WTDRs can be requested on any foreign company. The report contains financial information and also identifies other U.S. companies that do business with the firm. The service is provided by district offices of the Department of Commerce. Your nearest district office can be found on the Department of Commerce's Web site (http://www.commerce.gov/services).

The simplest and least costly solution to a payment problem is to contact the customer and try to negotiate. If negotiations fail, the exporter should request assistance from his bank and legal counsel. The exporter and importer may agree to either take their dispute to an arbitration agency or to take legal action (litigation). Arbitration is often faster and less costly; disputing parties are allowed to select their own neutral, someone (or agency) who knows their industry, products, or culture. The ICC handles the majority of international arbitrations and is usually acceptable to foreign companies because it is not affiliated with any single country. For more information, including contact information, exporters are advised to visit the ICC Web site (http://www.iccwbo .org/policy/arbitration).

The exporter and importer rarely use the same currency. Thus the payment is made either in one of the parties' domestic currency or in a mutually agreed on currency that is foreign to both parties. One of the inherent risks of foreign trade is the volatility of future exchange rates with respect to the exchange rate that was available when the price was quoted. If the denominated currency is not the exporter's currency and the exporter is not properly protected, a devaluation in the denominated currency against the exporter's domestic currency will result in a loss for the exporter. For example, if the buyer has agreed to pay 100,000 yen, with an exchange rate of 100 yen per U.S. dollar, the exporter would receive $1,000. If, however, the yen later decreases in the value to be worth 110 yen per U.S. dollar, the exporter would receive $909, incurring a loss of $91. Of course, if the yen appreciates against the exporter's currency, the exporter will profit. However, exporters are usually not speculators and prefer to avoid risks. One way to avoid foreign exchange (FX) risk is to quote prices in one's own currency. This shifts the FX risk from the exporter to the buyer. Other methods that help exporters reduce this type of risk were discussed in Chapter 12.

Finally, exporters should be aware of problems of currency convertibility. Not all currencies are freely or quickly convertible into other currencies. Exporters are strongly advised to ensure that the currency the payment will be made in is convertible before signing an export contract.

Countertrade

International countertrade is a trade practice where a supplier (in this case, the exporter) agrees, as a condition of sale, to undertake specified courses of action to accept payment in a form other than a monetary instrument, including the importer's final goods or services, or other regional products (Choi, Lee, & Kim, 1999; Egan & Shipley, 1996; Fletcher, 1998; Paun & Shoham, 1996). Countertrade has rapidly grown as a method of carrying out sizable international trade transactions as a result of

- two energy crises during the 1970s, which brought many countries a large balance of payments disequilibrium;
- government requirements for approval of larger transactions, particularly in Eastern Europe, Indonesia, and Malaysia, to balance an import with an export;
- the lack of FX to pay for imports in developing countries such as India and China.

Exporters consider countertrade a necessary cost of doing business in markets where exports would otherwise not occur. The following section explores the types of countertrade, its procedures, and its costs and benefits.

Types of Countertrade

There are several types of countertrade used in international trade. Common types of countertrade include following (Cavusgil et al., 2008):

- *Barter.* Trade in which merchandise is exchanged directly for other merchandise without the use of money. Barter is an important means of trade with countries using currencies that are not readily convertible.

- *Compensation.* A modern version of barter in which both of the exchanged products are valued in specific currencies and are invoiced in those same currencies. Compensation permits unbalanced transactions with payments partly in currency and partly in product.

- *Counterpurchase.* The primary form of countertrade today, in terms of volume, as practiced by multinational corporations and large established countertrade firms. In a counterpurchase deal, the exporter signs a separate, second contract to buy an agreed-upon amount of other products in return for concluding an export contract.

- *Buyback.* Similar to a counterpurchase. However, it is typically a part of negotiations for turnkey projects. Buyback is an agreement to purchase or distribute the end result of the project or supplies sold to the importer. Although the sales contract for the supplies, machinery, equipment, or project might make reference to the buyback arrangement, it is important that this be included in a separate contract and does not affect payment for the initial transaction.

- *Offset.* A practice in which the country of the importer of capital goods requires that its manufacturers be permitted to produce parts to be included in those capital goods.

Countertrade Versus Corporate Barter

Corporate barter is a variation of barter, which describes large-scale brokered barter between corporations. One of the main reasons behind the growing demand for corporate barter is the fact that in the international marketplace, product life cycles can move much quicker than anticipated. One way to minimize potential inventory problems is to adopt a conservative production run. However, this strategy may turn out to be detrimental to the livelihood of companies, especially around the holidays (e.g., Christmas). Corporate barter is a remedy for those who do not want to face an undercapacity problem. Through corporate barter, manufacturers are able to utilize their underperforming assets to acquire the media, goods, and services they need to run their businesses.

There are close parallels between countertrade and corporate barter. Thus some of the explanations for countertrade may help explain the growth of corporate barter. Whereas a firm uses international countertrade when there is a shortage of foreign exchange reserves, a manufacturer who is unable to find a cash buyer may be prepared to sell to a corporate trader for trade credits—the medium of exchange in corporate barter—rather than to make no sale at all. In turn, the corporate trader may be able to find customers for the manufacturer's goods who can supply other services in lieu of money. Media Resources International, a corporate barter company in New York, helped Volvo of North America sell automobiles to the Siberian police force at a time when Siberia had no cash to pay for them. Media Resources International arranged to accept payment in oil, which was then sold for cash on the world market. It then bought spot TV advertising credits equal to the value of the cars.

A second explanation for countertrade that may also account for corporate barter is that parties may view the deal as a marketing opportunity. Sharp Electronics wanted to reward its top electronics dealers with an incentive program without spending cash. In exchange for surplus inventory, a corporate barter company in Stamford, Connecticut, Icon International, arranged for 50 staterooms for 100 passengers on a major Mediterranean cruise line for Sharp's dealers. Another example is Volkswagen USA, which was saddled with hundreds of cars of a model that was about to be discontinued. Global Marketing Resources took the cars, with the manufacturer's approval and remarketed them into channels preapproved by its dealer group. In exchange, Volkswagen received from Global Marketing Resources some second-quarter spot television advertising in an aggregate amount equal to the full dealer cost of the automobiles.

A third explanation might be the desire to disguise prices or loss in value. One academic study conducted to explain the reasons for the growth of corporate barter concluded that corporate barter is primarily used as a way to implement secret price cuts without the risk of spoiling the long-term market, thereby increasing competitiveness, sales, and capacity utilization. For instance, assume that Shaver Company has an outdated inventory valued at $100,000. Liquidation of the inventory will probably bring in $20,000, and therefore result in an 80% loss on goods manufactured. However, a corporate barter company can buy the goods for $100,000 in trade credits. Shaver Company can then use those credits to acquire goods and services for its operations.

Benefits of Countertrade and Corporate Barter

There are several advantages that are common to countertrade and corporate barter:

- *Reduce cash expenses.* Barter (trade) credits, the medium of exchange in a barter, constitute additional sources of revenue and therefore can be used against business costs previously paid in cash. Whereas corporate barter reduces cash expenses for corporations, countertrade helps importers preserve scarce hard currency and improve the balance of trade for the importing country.
- *Increase company competitiveness.* Through countertrade, the company can reach more markets to sell its products, particularly in developing countries, and hence increase its sales potential.
- *Referral business.* It has often been said that "word of mouth" is the best form of advertising. Bartering can be used as a stepping stone or marketing tool using these "word of mouth" principles.
- *Allows for disposal of declining products.* Through countertrade, a company can sell its outdated products and dispose of its inventory.
- *Provide a source of attractive inputs.* Countertrade and barter can be used to obtain a steady, long-term supply of raw materials at a low cost.

Export Insurance

Insurance is necessary in international trade because of the inherent risks that are present in any export transaction. A company can insure against commercial credit risks, political risks, and shipping risks.

Commercial Credit Risk

Commercial credit risk insurance covers losses due to nonpayment by the buyer. Generally a loan officer will not finance foreign accounts receivable of an exporter without insurance, no matter how thoroughly the buyer's credit has been checked. FCIA, a private insurance group that operates as Eximbank's agent, is the best place to apply for receivables insurance (FCIA, 2008). Private insurance also exists, but it is very limited.

In order to receive coverage from FCIA, the exporter must first apply for an FCIA policy, which can be done through almost any insurance broker. However, a broker who specializes in international insurance would be preferable. Insurance can be also obtained directly through one of the several regional offices of FCIA. FCIA insurance protects 90% (98% in the case of agriculture) of foreign receivables against commercial loss and provides 100% protection for political risks.

Some of the policies offered by FCIA for small and new-to-export firms include the following.

Umbrella Policy

An umbrella policy must be obtained through an "administrator," who is defined as any qualified party such as a banker, an export trading company, a sales agency, or an insurance broker. An umbrella policy is a third-party-administered policy that places the burden of fulfilling the insurance contract on the administrator. The exporter must apply for an umbrella policy just as for all other policies, and both the administrator and FCIA must agree to accept the exporter before a policy is issued. To obtain approval, the exporter must not have had export credit sales of more than $3 million over the last 2 years and cannot have held a FCIA policy during the last 2 years. However, once an umbrella policy is issued there are no limits as to continued eligibility. Please visit Eximbank's Web site (http://www.exim.gov/products/insurance) or call 202-565-3946 for additional information.

New-to-Export Policy

A new-to-export policy is intended for the exporter with little or no history in exporting. Exporters should meet Small Business Administration

(SBA) guidelines; that is, any employer having less than 500 employees. These policies cover 95% of commercial risk (as opposed to 90% in the case of an umbrella policy). The policy offers a lower premium than is usually found in regular insurance policies. If bank financing of receivables is important to the exporter, the most advantageous feature of this policy is the hold-harmless agreement that FCIA provides to the exporter's bank. This agreement between FCIA and the bank states that if the exporter assigns the coverage of the receivables to the bank, in the event of a claim, FCIA will pay the bank the amount under consideration, including failure by the exporter to perform according to the terms of the policy. Of course, FCIA retains recourse against the exporter if the loss is a result of exporter nonperformance.

Short-Term and Medium-Term Single-Buyer Policies

Short-term and medium-term single-buyer policies are among several new policies introduced in 1986 to allow exporters to insure their receivables against loss due to commercial and specified political risks. Short-term policies provide 90% to 100% coverage, with coverage of 98% for agricultural goods. The duration of these policies is 180 days (360 days in the case of agricultural goods). For more information, please visit Eximbank's Web site (http://www.exim.gov/products/insurance/single_buyer.cfm). The medium-term policy refers to contracts or receivables in excess of 180 days and up to 5 years. It is applicable to exporters of capital and quasi-capital goods and project-related services. The coverage is 100% for political risks and 90% for commercial risks (95% for small businesses). For more information, please visit http://www.exim.gov/products/insurance/medium_term.cfm.

Insuring Political and Country Risk

Even if the importer is creditworthy and reputable, there is still political risk that an exporter needs to take into consideration. Political risk refers to war, currency fluctuations, inconvertibility, and expropriation (the seizing of property without permission) by the state. Watch for political unrest, high interest rates, high inflation, and major trade deficits. For political risk assessment in the country you are interested in, exporters are also advised to check the information available at the Political Risk Insurance Center Web site (http://www.pri-center.com/country/index.cfm).

If you are insured with FCIA, political risk is automatically covered. However, you can buy country risk coverage only, excluding commercial credit risk, from private insurance companies that prefer to cover country risk only. A list of private institutions and brokers for political risk insurance policies is available at the Political Risk Insurance Center Web site (http://www.pri-center.com/directories/index.cfm).

Cargo Insurance

Exporters should be aware of the risks to their cargo while it is in transit. These risks include fire, storm, collision, pilferage, leakage, and explosion. Goods traveling abroad must be insured against loss or damage at each stage of their journey so that whatever mode of transportation is being used, neither the exporter nor the buyer suffers any loss.

Either the exporter or the buyer will be liable for the goods in transit. For example, in an FOB contract, the transfer of ownership is at the point where the goods pass over the ship's rail. In theory, the exporter insures the goods up to that point and the importer takes responsibility from then on. However, in practice, the buyer generally buys insurance to cover the entire journey. Under a cost, insurance, and freight (CIF) contract, the exporter takes out ocean insurance even though his ownership and responsibility for loss or damage ends when the goods are placed on the vessel. Here are some suggestions for cargo insurance.

How to Insure?

Insurance can be arranged through an insurance broker or an insurance company. An insurance policy is issued when goods are insured, but it is also common to use a certificate of insurance as evidence of insurance. Individual policies for a single shipment are rarely used by active exporters. Exporters normally insure under long-term policies, known as open cover. These contracts may run for a fixed time or indefinitely until canceled. The open cover gives the exporter automatic, continuous coverage so the exporter does not have to arrange for protection every time it makes a shipment.

On a CIF contract, the exporter sends the certificate of insurance to the customer to be claimed at the port of destination if the goods have been damaged on the ship. It is common practice to insure for 10% more than the CIF value of goods in order to allow for problems involved in replacing the goods and waiting for the claim to be paid.

Average Terms

The protection offered by marine insurance (insurance that compensates the owner of goods transported overseas by air or sea in the event of loss that cannot be legally recovered from the carrier) is usually defined by its average terms. The word "average" in insurance means partial loss. Partial loss, in turn, can mean the total loss of part of the insured cargo or simply damage to all or part of it. There are two ways in which the term average is used. Particular average loss is a partial loss suffered by part of the cargo. General average loss is loss that affects all cargo interests on board the vessel as well as the ship itself.

Types of Cargo Insurance

There are three important types of cargo insurance:

- Free of particular average (FPA): the minimum coverage in general use. It covers losses due to a ship or aircraft being totally lost. FPA covers total loss only. However, it may also cover partial losses resulting from perils at sea and in the air, but only in the event that specified disasters occur to the ship or aircraft.
- With particular average (WPA): insures against the goods being damaged in transit, but not because the ship was in danger. Partial loss is normally covered with losses above a stated percentage of the insured cargo value. In practical terms, the additional coverage one gets with WPA terms, compared to FPA, is a protection against damage from seawater caused by "heavy weather."

- All risk: insures against most risks except the risk of force majeur (war), unless the exporter has specifically asked for this to be included. All-risk coverage is the broadest kind of standard coverage. However, all-risk coverage does not, as its name suggests, really cover all risks. It excludes coverage against damages caused by war, strikes, riots, and so on. It covers only physical loss or damage resulting from external causes, such as damage from hooks, rain, theft, shortage, nondelivery, leakage, and breakage.

Airfreight Insurance

Previously the focus has been primarily on marine insurance applicable to sea transportation. However, the popularity of airfreight has been increasing for the last three decades due to its high reliability and the speed of service offered by air transportation. Lacking the long history of marine insurance, the rules for airfreight insurance are quite different. The average fees for airfreight insurance are about 50 cents per $100 of declared value, generally to a maximum of some kind, dependent upon the carrier. Air carriers can be held liable for losses due to negligence but only to the limit of their liability. This is currently slightly more than $9.07 per pound of shipment (or $20.38 per kilogram).

An exporter can also request airfreight insurance from the carrier, the cost of which is charged with airfreight costs. This covers all risks, excluding war, which carries an additional premium. It does not cover other modes of transportation involved before or after the insured flight. This approach is usually cheaper than paying the additional valuation charges. In addition, liability does not have to be proven. If, however, marine insurance is available, it will likely be the best overall insurance and should be utilized for airfreight as well.

CHAPTER 17

Managing Export Operations

Upon completing this chapter you should

- understand the differences between various modes of international shipment;
- understand the importance of using a freight forwarder in exporting;
- understand the proper ways of packing and labeling export goods;
- be able to recognize and use various documents required in international transactions;
- understand the restrictions and controls on exporting;
- understand cargo insurance.

After the sale is made, the exporter needs to efficiently manage the flow of export goods. This requires an understanding of various documents, tariff systems, foreign exchange risks, exchange controls exerted by the government, packing, methods of payment, and other factors that need to be properly accounted for when moving goods across countries. In the previous chapters, methods of payment and foreign exchange risks were explained in detail. Thus our main focus throughout this chapter will be on the remaining aspects of the export process following an export order, including shipping, packing, and marking; export licenses and export documentation; export and import restrictions; and insurance.

International Shipping

International shipping has three critical stages. First, export goods must be packaged for international shipment, with the correct export permits (licenses), documentation, and marine insurance verified. Next, the goods need to be transported over land from the manufacturer to a port. Finally, the goods must be moved by ship, train, or plane to a foreign port where they go through customs and arrive at the buyer's warehouse. In international shipping, exporters have several options, including ocean carriers, rail, motor, air carriers, and intermodal shipment.

Ocean Carriers

An exporter can use any of three types of ocean carriers (David, 2004):

- *Conference lines.* Some ocean carriers join together in an ocean freight conference to establish common shipping rates and conditions. To participate in such a conference, a line must agree to abide by the rules of that conference. These rules cover vessel performance in the broadest sense, adherence to published schedules, and rates to be charged by the type of good or service. Often, if the exporter signs a contract to ship all of his goods on member lines, it is offered reduced rates.
- *Independent lines.* These lines operate on their own, as they have not agreed to be bound by a set of rates or a particular schedule. Schedules are less rigid than those of conference carriers, and the smaller the line or less frequent its services, the less reliable it may be. Independent lines usually offer lower rates than conference lines. Two of the leading schedules are published weekly. For the West Coast, exporters can use the *Pacific Shipper* (https://www.pacificshipper.com; Tel: 954-628-0058). For the East and Gulf Coast, the leading publication is the *Shipping Digest* (http://www.shippingdigest.com; Tel: 954-628-0058). Each principal seaport or port region has one or more publications that update shipping schedules and contain carrier advertising. Similar information appears in *The Journal of Commerce* (http://www.joc.com).
- *Nonvessel Operating Common Carrier (NVOCC).* An NVOCC is a third-party company that contracts with a shipping line for a certain number of containers over certain named routes for a period of time, generally 1 year. By acquiring this container capacity volume, the NVOCC receives a discount similar to a quantity discount in purchasing. This space is then

sold to shippers of smaller lots at rates they would generally be unable to obtain from either conference or independent lines. NVOCCs have altered ocean freight pricing structures and competition. As these companies specialize in specific routes, it may take time to find routes that are viable for your shipments. Generally, using an NVOCC will result in less frequent service or end-of-the-line service in high-volume seasons, when freight capacity is in high demand.

Ocean freight rates can be obtained from the various steamship lines or freight forwarders. These rates are usually based on a 1 ton weight or a 1 ton volume (1,000 kg or 1 cubic meter, respectively), whichever produces higher revenue. In some cases, prices are quoted on a per-unit or per-piece basis, as is the case with oranges, which are packed in a standard carton accepted by the industry. The rate may also be quoted with a currency adjustment factor. This is an automatic adjustment added to the tariff and related to the destination country.

Rail and Motor

Rail transport is one of the most cost-efficient methods of moving bulky goods or commodities from inland points to the export point. Cost reduction innovations in rail service have begun to make these services more cost effective for the exporter. For instance, in addition to the well-known standard boxcar, railroads have developed container-based innovations. Two types of freight rates exist for rail services: the carload or full carload lot (CL or FCL) and the less than carload lot (LCL). Rates are calculated per 100 pounds, with LCL rates being higher than CL rates.

The alternative to rail for inland movement of goods is trucking. Intrastate carriers, which are regulated by state regulatory commissions, must file a request for tariff (rate to be charged) with the particular commission to change rates. Interstate carriers must also submit tariffs, effective for 24 hours, to the Interstate Chamber of Commerce (ICC). Independent truckers operate on a contractual basis and do not file tariffs, so it is often helpful to ask for a rate from an independent trucker before going to an intrastate or interstate carrier.

Because of deregulation, trucking companies are able to vary their charges as market conditions change. The services of freight forwarders or freight brokers can be used for arranging a truck line. Charges are generally "per container" from the point of pickup to the destination. However, the basis of the charges (cubic feet, cubic meters, cubic yards, or weight) can be determined by the customer.

Nearly all types of goods can be moved by trucks, and rates will generally vary by the type of good the exporter is shipping. Trucks are often more expensive than trains, but they provide flexibility in terms of timing and routing that may not be available through rail service.

Air Carriers

Air transportation is often overlooked because it is perceived to be too expensive compared with other modes of transportation. However, airfreight is highly beneficial when the exporter needs to get goods to market quickly or when the remaining part of an order must be filled. Many perishable goods move by air, particularly fresh flowers and seafood.

Airfreight service can be arranged through either a carrier or a freight forwarder and is quoted on a weight or measure basis with break points. When quoted in kilograms (2.2 lb/kg), freight rate breaks occur at 45, 100, 200, 300, 400, and 500 kg. Goods can also move in containers, with the LD3 (3,200 lb), LD7 (10,000 lb), and A container (higher cube version of LD7) being the most common sizes. There are minimum charges for air cargo depending on the location and shipment. Discounts are available for volume and can be negotiated with the carrier or the forwarder. Contracts are generally unwritten but exist as understandings between the shippers (exporters) and their carriers. In addition, there are nominal handling costs that cover the cost of handling air export documentation.

Intermodal Shipment

An exporter might also consider using a combination of the transportation modes described above. This is called intermodal shipping, where more than one form of transportation is used in moving goods from their origin to their destination. Intermodal strategies facilitate intercontinental shipping in terms of cost, speed, and even documentation.

International Freight Forwarder

A freight forwarder is an excellent source for international traffic handling (Davies, 1981). The freight forwarder acts as an agent for exporters in moving cargo to overseas destinations. Forwarders are familiar with the import rules and regulations of foreign countries, all modes of transportation, export regulations, and the documentation connected with foreign trade (Cavusgil, Knight, & Riesenberger, 2008; Davies, 1981). They can also assist exporters in computing freight costs, port charges, consular fees, and special documentation fees, all of which will help in preparing the price quotation for the importer. In addition, a forwarder can provide routing and scheduling information, prepare all necessary shipping documentation, handle shipping insurance, and arrange for warehouse storage.

As freight forwarding is a particularly important role, it is imperative that the exporter select the right forwarder. When selecting a freight forwarder, you should first identify the forwarders that your competitors are using. Other sources of information are the district office of the Department of Commerce (http://www.commerce.gov/Services), various online sources (e.g., http://www.forwarders.com), telephone directories, the international departments of major banks, and small business associations.

Selection of a Freight Forwarder

As discussed in Chapter 6, the selection of a good freight forwarder is very important. Thus the exporter should thoroughly inquire about prospective forwarders before choosing the right one. Reliability is a key issue. In handling the export of nonhazardous lubricating oils and greases, Shell Oil Co. uses freight forwarders to do all their documentation and arrange transportation. An intensive selection process was used to choose the three forwarders the firm currently uses. The selection process was more qualitative than price-based. The freight forwarder's background, locations, and its personnel were all closely examined before selection. It was also important to check the financial stability of every service provider.

Shell's finance department did a Dun & Bradstreet retrieval (the *D&B Business Background Report* provides useful information on a company's history, operations, special events, and the business background of its management) to examine the provider's financial condition for the last reporting period and the most recent 5-year period. Finally, before getting down to the selection process, an exporter needs a basic understanding of what freight forwarders do and how they will fit within their organization.

For a further discussion, please refer to Chapter 6. Also, please see the appendix at the end of this chapter for a sample evaluation form for freight forwarder candidates.

Working With a Freight Forwarder

Exporters should consider the following in selecting a freight forwarder:

- The exporter should not rely solely on the forwarder for freight quotations. Due to deregulation, fierce competition, and frequent changes in shipping roles, it is recommended that several different bids be obtained. For large shipments in particular, the exporter may also need to check with the carrier directly. For a fair rate comparison, the exporter must ensure that all of the services being considered are equal.

- In order to remain in control of their collections, exporters should request that the forwarder send all documents to them for verification before presentation and in some cases may prefer to forward documents to the bank themselves. Of course, this is feasible only if the exporter has the staff and the skills.

Export Packing and Marking

Goods must be packed and labeled properly to make sure they arrive at their destination in good condition. Export shipments require a great deal more handling than domestic shipments. Packing that is adequate for domestic shipments often falls short when goods are transported overseas, where they may be subject to unusual handling or sent to parts of the world with extreme climates. Here is a good example.

With only 3 days remaining before the World Cup race in Australia, 49 of the 50 solar-powered cars scheduled to compete had arrived by sea. The SolarCat team was still applying solar panels to their racecar. The car had not moved from Philadelphia, and given the limited time remaining, the SolarCat team had no choice but to ship the fragile car by air. Complicating matters was the fact that the car would be returned by sea, subjecting both the car and its packing to very different transportation environments. The SolarCat car was scheduled for multiple customs inspections when leaving and reentering the United States and when entering and leaving Australia. Repeated container dismantling, typical of inspections, could damage the contents and reduce the effectiveness of the packing.

A design team from ActionPak and Hardy-Graham worked around the clock to design and construct a unique shipping solution. Using the patented "Hardy-Built" fastening system developed by Hardy-Graham, Inc., packaging designers assembled a shipping container that could accommodate repeated openings and closings when customs inspections were required. With a single screwdriver, customs officials were able to remove the cover quickly and safely. They could also easily remove side panels if necessary without damaging the container or the car. After the contents were confirmed, the cover or side panel could be quickly refastened without nails, screws, or adhesives and the shipment could continue on its journey.

To withstand the rigors of air and sea travel, ActionPak created a wooden deck based on military specification MIL-C-104B, complete with 4-in. by 4-in. headers (10 cm by 10 cm) and beveled rubbing strips to minimize friction for easy ground movement (ActionPak, 2008). The rigid deck was designed to accommodate a lift truck for entry from all four sides. For further protection, the entire car was encased in a protective shell using a process called cocooning. Cocooning minimized the impact from vibrations to maintain body integrity and to keep the delicate solar cells firmly in place. In addition, without heavy lifting equipment available at the desert race site in Australia, the SolarCat team needed a way to load and unload the car safely. ActionPak devised and installed a reusable wooden ramp that travels with the car inside the container. The ramp allowed the team to roll the car off and onto the container base without any lift trucks, hoists, or heavy equipment.

Factors to Consider for Export Packing

The four critical considerations for export packing are to avoid breakage, minimize weight, keep moisture out, and prevent pilferage. The product, mode of shipment, and destination factors (time, climate, etc.) determine the selection of packing materials necessary to protect the goods. Exporters want to protect their cargo against as many hazards as possible. At the same time, they want to use the lightest weight cartons or packing available.

Exporters must also consider the mode of shipment. Rail and ocean vessels require heavier packing than a shipment by air, and containerized cargo on a ship will not require packing as heavy as that required for noncontainerized cargo. Using noncontainerized cargo increases shipping risks, which include breakage due to "heavy weather," damage by heavy or leaking cargo placed on top, being dropped in loading and unloading, and pilferage.

Moisture is a potential problem in transportation, particularly in the case of shipment by ocean and rail, even if the vessel is equipped with air conditioning and humidity control. The goods might be unloaded in the rain, which poses a big problem, particularly if the foreign party does not have a covered storage facility.

Packing the Goods

Unless the importer requests special packing, we recommend the following practices:

- The exporter should use containers. Containers vary in size, material, and construction. However, most containers are made of aluminum, so they are lightweight, durable, and rust-proof. They can accommodate most cargo, but are best suited for standard package shapes and sizes. The use of containers reduces the risks that were briefly described in the preceding section.

- Regardless of size, containers should be packed in such a way that weight is evenly distributed. This will provide proper bracing within the container. Please note that containers should be filled to capacity and sealed.
- Goods should be packed on pallets to ensure greater ease in handling.
- Packages and packing filler should be made of moisture-resistant material.
- To avoid pilferage, containers should not be marked with the contents or brand name of the goods.
- Since some countries charge a customs duty based on gross weight of the cargo, the weight of cartons and packing should be kept to the minimum level necessary to get the goods to their destination without damage.
- Exporters might get better results if they consult with their forwarders and carriers about port condition and the facilities to be encountered so that packing can be adjusted accordingly.

Marking

Exporters should adhere to the importing country's regulations on containers and marking for goods being imported or risk incurring severe penalties. The container must have markings that conform to the data on the export documents or it will be considered deception by the importing country's customs officials. Specific markings and labels are used on export shipping cartons, containers, and pallets for the following reasons:

- To meet shipping regulations
- To ensure proper handling
- To conceal the identity of the contents
- To help receivers identify shipments

Most exports require the country of origin or manufacture. Because the size, language, and importance of this mark (e.g., made in USA) may vary in different countries, obtaining updated information on regulations in the importing country is vital. The types of markings that appear besides the country of origin or manufacture include the following:

- Shipper's mark
- Gross and net weight (in kilograms or pounds)
- Number of packages and the size of the carton (inches or centimeters).
- Handling marks (international pictorial symbols)
- Cautionary markings such as "this side up" or "use no hooks"
- Port of entry
- Labels for hazardous materials (universal symbols)

To avoid misunderstandings, export markings must be legible. Letters are generally stenciled onto containers in waterproof ink. Markings should appear on three faces of the container, preferably the side, end, and top, and old markings must be removed. Also, any special handling instructions must be included on the container. Finally, it is recommended to write in the language of the country of destination.

Export Documents

Every export sale requires a series of documents to prove that

- the order has been shipped to the buyer;
- the freight has been prepaid if prepayment was one of the terms of sale;
- the quality meets the standard required;
- the shipment is insured as agreed in the sale contract;
- the exporter is licensed to export.

These documents must be completed in such a way that the title passes to the buyer at the time stated in the sales agreement. The exporter must also be aware that the importer must be in possession of all necessary documents so that the shipment can be discharged and clear customs in the importer's country. Poorly completed documentation results in three main types of costs:

- The cost of interest charges incurred by exporters as a result of delay in receiving payment
- Bank charges for amending documents such as letters of credit, telephone bills resulting from calls made to rectify the problem, and courier charges for sending replacement documents
- Reluctance of the importer to do further business with the exporter.

Export documents can be prepared by the exporter, a freight forwarder, a commercial bank, the exporter's agent, or a trade specialist. However, because of the vast amounts of documentation that can be required, it is best to utilize the expertise of a freight forwarder who is highly specialized in export documentation. The necessary documentation varies from order to order and country to country. Export documents must be precise, as even slight discrepancies may prevent the merchandise from being exported. After gaining some export experience, the management of the exporting company may gain the expertise to handle these operations in house. The necessary documents include an export license (if required), commercial invoice, packing list, certificate of origin, insurance certificate, certificate of inspection, ocean bill of lading, air waybill (if applicable), letter of credit (LC; if used), and bill of exchange (draft).

Export License

For various reasons, including national security, foreign policy, and resource supply levels, countries control the export of goods and technical data through the granting of licenses. In the United States, export licenses are either individually validated or general, depending on the goods being exported, the destination, the buyer, and the final use purpose. In most cases, no license is required (NLR) to export goods from the United States. However, in some cases, an individually validated export license (IVL) is required. Chapter 8 discusses the process to determine whether or not you need an export license.

Export Declaration

The export declaration serves as the principal means to control exportation. It provides a statistical measure of the quantity of goods exported and determines whether all necessary regulated requirements are being met, including an export license. Required information concerning shipment includes the names and addresses of the principals involved, the destination, and a full description of the goods, together with the declared value. Of course, if specific licenses are required to ship a particular commodity, the export license must be presented with the export declaration. In the United States, an export declaration is required for any shipment from the United States worth more than $2,500 (along with the license, if required).

Commercial Invoice

The commercial invoice contains information similar to the domestic invoice:

- Name and address of the foreign buyer
- Quantity of each item
- Description of the goods
- Unit price
- Extended price
- Discounts
- Net amount payable

Additional information unique to exporting also includes

- marks that identify the shipment, destination, buyer, and other information;
- name of the carrying vessel (if possible);
- consignee, which may be the buyer, the shipper, the buyer's customs broker, or another party;
- exporter's invoice or order number;
- weight and any special instructions concerning weight;
- total amount invoiced, accompanied by an indication of the sales price terms (e.g., free on board [FOB] and cost, insurance, and freight [CIF]);
- consular statement.

Increasingly, invoices made out in the English language are acceptable. However, some countries insist that imports be invoiced in their own language. In the absence of a separate contract of sale, the invoice, although not a contract itself, will take on added importance as confirmation of the terms of the arrangement between the parties. Finally, the commercial invoice must contain details that correspond exactly with the LC to avoid delays in payment or even lawful default.

Packing List

The packing list is included with the shipment list. It typically contains information on the following:

- Number of packages in the shipment
- Package numbering
- Gross and net weight of each package
- Dimensions of the package
- Quantity of goods contained in each package

In addition, the names of the shipper and the consignee may be coded in order to reduce the possibility of pilferage and theft.

The packing list is valuable to the carrier when deciding how to load the cargo. It is an essential document for customs authorities when performing inspections, as well as for the customer in identifying the contents of the shipment. When a shipment consists of one simple product in a standard pack, it may be possible to incorporate the packing information in the invoice. However, as a general rule, it is better to provide the financial and packing information separately, in the invoice and packing list, respectively.

Certificate of Origin

The certificate of origin is a document that declares the nature of the goods and their place of manufacture. It is normally completed by the exporter, but often must be on a form prescribed by the importing country. A certificate of origin may be required even though the commercial invoice contains all of the necessary information. In some cases, the importer's country requires that the certificate be endorsed by the exporter's local chamber of commerce or the local embassy or consulate of the importing country. If the importing country does not have a representative in the country of export, it is normally necessary to send the document for endorsement to the trade authority in the importing country.

The country of origin of the goods may influence the liability for duty or the rate of the duty to be charged by the importing country. Therefore it is important that the certificate of origin be completed accurately in accordance with the regulations of the importing country.

Insurance Certificate

Nearly all export shipments are insured. Typically the method of payment or terms of the sale require insurance on the goods. As a result, it is necessary to have an insurance certificate indicating the type and amount of coverage. The insurance certificate refers to the insurance policy and describes the quantity and value of the goods and the terms of the insurance provided by the insurance policy. An insurance certificate can be considered written evidence of political and commercial loss coverage, as well as being one of the essential documents that must be properly endorsed and submitted to the bank for collection of payment.

If the exporter is in doubt as to whether a particular shipment is insured by the consignee (the importer) or the agent, and if it is not possible to obtain written confirmation before shipment, then the exporter should arrange insurance even at the risk of insuring the goods twice. It should be noted that in most cases the liability of the carrier is limited by the conditions of the agreement. Hence the exporter should not depend on the carrier's liability in case of loss or damage.

The insurance certificate is usually issued by the insurance company of the exporter. However, when the exporter ships through a forwarder, the forwarder will issue the certificate. The certificate is a negotiable document and must be endorsed before submission to the bank.

Certificate of Inspection

Some importers and countries require a certificate of inspection attesting to the specifications of the goods shipped. The certificate of inspection certifies the quantity and quality of the goods and their conformity to the order. As a normal practice, a request for goods inspection is clearly written in the LC. Exporters should be cautious if the importer or the importer's agent has an inspection right, because this requirement might render the LC revocable. Or if there are no time requirements as to when an inspection must occur, the importer or agent could simply fail to inspect and therefore the LC cannot be negotiated. However, if properly used, a certificate of inspection helps the exporter avoid claims after arrival of the goods. It also permits the exporter to deal with problems before shipment, when it is much easier and cheaper to rectify problems.

If the inspection is "standard export inspection," the shipper or shipping company will nominate a standard inspector. However, the exporter can hire a "private weights and measures" inspection company to conduct an accurate inspection of the goods. A phytosanitary and health inspection certificate is another type of certificate attesting to the absence of disease and pests. This type of certificate may be required for certain agricultural and food products.

Ocean Bill of Lading

The bill of lading is regarded as the most important and well-known document in the international transaction area. It is a receipt and contract for shipment between the owner of the goods (the exporter) and the carrier. It serves as evidence that a shipment has been made. Once the carrier or freight forwarder completes the bill of lading, they become bound to forward the goods to the agreed destination in the same condition as they were received. There are two types of bills of lading:

- *Straight bill of lading.* This type of bill of lading is nonnegotiable. A straight bill of lading allows only the appropriate person specified in the bill of lading to pick up the goods. This is usually the preferred type of bill of lading for beginning importers, as it offers the buyer the most protection by prohibiting the release of the goods to anyone but the party specified in the documentation.

- *Shipper's order bill of lading.* This type of bill of lading is also called a negotiable bill of lading. It can be bought, sold, or traded while the goods are in transit and is used for LC transactions. The customer usually needs the original or a copy as proof of ownership to take possession of the goods.

A bill of lading is frequently referred to as being either clean or foul. A clean bill of lading means that the items presented to the carrier for shipment were properly packaged and free from apparent damage when received. A foul bill of lading means that the shipment was received in damaged condition. Thus a bill of lading serves as a firsthand mediator to any possible dispute on shipment. The bill of lading is also a certificate of ownership or title to the goods. When written to order, it serves as a negotiable instrument through which title is transferred from the exporter to the importer. While an air waybill (discussed in the following section) cannot be effectively consigned to the shipper due to the short time between pickup and delivery of the goods, an ocean bill of lading can be consigned to the order of the shipper, thereby controlling the shipper's interest in the merchandise.

Air Waybill

An air waybill is the carrying agreement between the shipper and the air carrier. It is prepared by the airfreight forwarder, usually with information from the shipper's invoice and packing list. In contrast to the ocean bill of lading (discussed in the preceding section), the air waybill is a non-negotiable instrument and serves as a shipping contract and receipt to the shipper. It certifies that the airline has accepted the goods as listed on the air waybill and has agreed to carry the goods to the airport of destination in accordance with the conditions of the contract. If the shipment requires prepayment, the freight forwarder pays the airline for the freight costs and bills the shipper.

Letter of Credit

The letter of credit (LC) is essentially the purchase of bank credit in favor of the seller by the buyer. The bank issuing the LC assumes the credit risk of the buyer. The exporter can draw a draft against the bank issuing the credit and receive payment with presentation of the proper shipping documentation. As opposed to the previously mentioned documents, the LC is initiated by the importer.

The LC is the key to trouble-free international trade, as it gives the seller an assurance of payment for the goods within the time agreed in the contract. It is also the document with more inherent problems than any other. This is not the result of any inherent weaknesses in the LC. Problems usually arise due to a lack of attention to details and carelessness in dealing with the document. This can result in a failure to comply with the conditions under which it was issued.

The value for exporters in being paid under an LC is that once they comply with the terms specified (e.g., providing the required documents), they can turn to their bank for payment rather than the importer. However, the exporter's bank cannot make payment unless it is fully satisfied that the terms have been met. See Chapter 15 for a more detailed discussion of LCs.

Bill of Exchange (Draft)

In international transactions, bills of exchange are important documents of payment. A bill of exchange, which is very similar to an ordinary check in appearance, is an instrument used as a formal demand for payment in a business transaction. Bills of exchange are written evidence of a contract between the exporter and the consignee in which payment data for an export shipment is specified.

Bills of exchange are handled through the use of sight or time drafts drawn by sellers on foreign buyers. The major difference between the use of the LC and the bill of exchange is that the former involves the credit of one or more banks. In the bill of exchange, the exporter assumes all risks until the actual payment is received. The exporter assumes not only commercial risk but also the risk of sudden foreign exchange restrictions. Therefore it is not uncommon in international trade for the bill of exchange to be used in conjunction with an LC. An LC provides a guarantee that the bill of exchange will be honored.

The typical procedure followed is for the exporter to draw a draft on the buyer and present it with the necessary documents to the bank for collection. Upon receipt of the draft, the exporter's bank forwards the draft along with the necessary documents to a correspondent bank in the buyer's country. The buyer is then presented with the draft for his acceptance and immediate or later payment. With his acceptance of the draft, the buyer receives the properly endorsed bill of lading, which is used to acquire the goods from the carrier. There are a number of draft classifications. The most basic classifications are the sight draft and time draft (see Chapter 15 for more information).

In making a sale on sight draft terms (also called documents against payment), the exporter makes the shipment to the importer and delivers all relevant documents to his bank for collection. A sight draft requires that acceptance and payment for the goods be made upon presentation of the draft and other required documents even before the arrival of the goods. These required documents are the bill of lading, packing list, commercial invoice, and any other documents mentioned in the contract. Usually the importer will wait until the ship is unloaded to pay for the goods, which may result in delays. However, the exporter can require that the collecting bank "protest nonpayment." Protest means that in the event of nonpayment or nonacceptance, the bank must make a formal presentation through a notary. Protest is not a very common occurrence, as it may embarrass the buyer (through advertising of protest) and hamper good customer relations.

When a sale is made on time draft terms (also called documents against acceptance), the exporter agrees to accept the importer's promissory note in payment for his shipment. In this case, the importer will not necessarily be motivated to sign the draft before the shipment arrives. However, the exporter can protect himself by tying the time to the bill of lading date, the date of the draft, or some other specific date that will prevent the importer from extending the time by inaction. When a time draft is drawn on a buyer and is accepted by the buyer, it is called a "trade acceptance." This can be used for financing purposes under some conditions. A trade acceptance is a promise to pay within a certain number of

days, usually 30 to 110 days, upon the acceptance of the documentation. Finally, it is very important not to confuse a banker's acceptance (see
Chapter 15), which carries the credit of a bank, with a trade acceptance.
When a time draft drawn under an LC is accepted for payment by a bank
(banker's acceptance), that bank obligation can be sold at a discount to
a third party, such as another bank. In fact, the banker's acceptance is a
highly marketable time draft.

Export and Import Restrictions

In the process of exporting, firms may face many restrictions and controls
on their activities:

- Export restrictions: restrictions that come from an exporter's
  home country
- Import restrictions: restrictions imposed by the importing
  country

Export Restrictions

It is required that certain kinds of goods be accompanied by a permit or
license before they can be exported (ITA, 2008). Arms, nuclear energy
materials, gold, narcotic drugs, natural gas, and electric energy are some
examples of goods that might require a specific license for exporting (ITA,
2008). Issuing export licenses is an effective way to regulate the nature of
external trading relationships. The government can restrict the export of
certain items by not granting export licenses or by limiting the quantity
to be exported. The extreme case is where there are specific problems concerning the exporting of certain products. For example, the U.S. controls
the exporting of products that are considered to have military value.

The most comprehensive restriction occurs when one country prohibits all trade with another. This situation usually arises from political reasons. Consequently firms cannot do business in those particular
foreign markets. A good example is the economic sanctions placed by
certain Western European governments against South Africa in the mid-
1980s. Other countries that are currently under U.S. sanctions include
the Balkans, Belarus, Burma, Ivory Coast, Cuba, Democratic Republic of

the Congo, Iran, Iraq, Liberia, North Korea, Sudan, Syria, and Zimbabwe. More specific information on U.S. sanction programs can be found at http://www.ustreas.gov/offices/enforcement/ofac/programs.

Import Restrictions

Of more importance than export restrictions are import restrictions imposed by the foreign country. Restrictions on imports can take the form of import licensing, tariffs, quotas, unfavorable exchange control, stringent quality inspections, and extra taxes. An exporter should be familiar with these restrictions so that necessary steps can be taken before it is too late.

Tariffs

Tariffs (duties) are taxes on imports (or export tariffs if they collected by the exporting country). Tariffs serve two main purposes: raising tax revenues (revenue tariff) and protecting domestic industries (protective tariff). A protective tariff can also be used to bring the price level of imported goods up to that of domestic substitutes. For example, the European Union raised the tariff on video cassette recorders (VCRs) from 8% to 14% in 1986 in response to the growing dominance of foreign competitors in the VCR industry. Since they are designed to protect domestic industries, protective tariffs tend to be relatively higher than revenue tariffs. However, tariffs can have other purposes, including punishing foreign firms, industries, or countries (punitive tariffs); offsetting the effects of subsidies foreign competitors receive from their governments (countervailing tariffs); or to prevent the dumping activities of foreign firms (antidumping duties).

If a tariff is assessed on a per-unit basis (usually per unit weight), it is known as a specific duty. When duties are collected on the appraised value of the imported goods, they are called ad valorem duties. Finally, if both a specific duty and an ad valorem duty are charged on the same product, the combination is known as a compound duty.

There are some controversial issues concerning tariffs. For instance, raw materials can enter industrial markets free of duty. However, if processed, those same raw materials (such as coffee beans) have a tariff assigned to them. This is a disadvantage for nonindustrial countries, who often have to pay higher effective tariffs. Another controversial issue has to do with the burden of paying tariff costs. There is evidence that luxury goods are protected relatively less than inexpensive goods (furs vs. cheap footwear), which raises prices on a larger portion of items purchased by low-income consumers than by high-income consumers.

Quotas

Quotas are specific provisions limiting the amount of foreign products that can be imported. Japan maintains quotas on 25 agricultural products, most of which are not produced in Japan. In some countries, quotas are imposed on exports as a component of national planning. The amount of import product restriction is an important determinant of the competitiveness of domestic producers. For many Western countries, quotas are being used both commercially (to conserve foreign exchange) and diplomatically (to ensure a specific distribution of importation from allied countries). There are three general quota categories:

- Absolute quotas: These are the most restrictive quotas, which limit absolutely the amount that can be imported. The most extreme case is an embargo.
- Tariff quotas: These permit the importation of limited quantities at low rates of duty, with any excess amount subject to a substantially higher rate.
- Voluntary quotas: These are known as voluntary export restrictions (VERs) and are utilized to protect domestic companies until they have had time to make the adjustments necessary to regain external competitiveness.

Exchange Controls and Permits

An exchange permit is a crucial instrument of any importing country. In effect, exchange permits conserve the value of a currency in another country in settlement for the goods imported. The essentiality of the exporter's goods to the importing country determines whether or not the exporter can affect a favorable exchange rate. Nonessentials and luxuries may not be allowed to enter certain countries without favorable exchange rates. Given that exchange controls limit the amount of foreign currency that an importer can obtain to pay for the goods imported, it is the job of the importer to obtain the exchange permit. However, the exporter should not sit back and wait until the importer secures a permit. The exporter may need to facilitate the exchange process, particularly when his country's currency is scarce and direct currency exchange is hard to obtain. Also, the transaction may involve more than two countries. The goods may have to be exchanged for other goods before they can be exchanged for the agreed currency.

Exchange control can be a very complicated task for exporters, particularly those with little or no previous experience. Well-informed sources such as local commercial banks or local agencies of the Department of Commerce can provide assistance. In addition to these sources, help from a freight forwarder is highly recommended.

Import License

Some countries require that potential importers secure permission from governmental authorities before conducting an international transaction. This requirement is known as an import license. To obtain an import license, a company may have to send samples to regulatory agencies in advance. A license requirement can restrict imports directly (by denial of permission) or deter trade due to the cost, time, and risk involved in the process.

Qualitative Controls

These controls also limit the profitability of exporting, but they are far less restrictive than quantitative controls such as duties and quotas. Foreign products can be imported with few exceptions, provided that the exporter accepts a lower profit margin. A good example of qualitative controls is standards. Countries set certain standards for classification, labeling, and testing. Labeling is required to provide information about the origin of the goods. However, labels increase production costs. The main purpose of a testing standard is to protect the safety of the population in the importing country. However, exporters have long argued that such practices are sometimes imposed to protect domestic producers.

Extra Taxes

Some countries have excise or processing taxes on certain products. Although such taxes are intended to generate revenues from domestic sources, they can also have some specific objective. For example, the European "road tax," an annual charge based on size, weight, or horsepower, serves as a means of discriminating against larger American cars. In some countries, including Indonesia and Korea, there is a luxury tax that is geared toward increasing the price of certain luxury goods to deter consumption (Guerin, 2003).

Another form of taxation that is of importance to exporters is the "border tax" levied on imports by European countries (Demaret & Stewardson, 1994; Willard, 1997), which are in addition to tariffs. A border tax adjustment imposed by a country is intended to place a tax burden on imports equivalent to that imposed on domestic products. The purpose of such a tax is to put domestic goods and imports on the same competitive basis.

Cargo Insurance

Export shipments are usually insured against loss, damage, and delay in transit by cargo insurance (Badger, Bugg, & Whitehead, 1994). Cargo insurance (or so-called marine insurance) can cover all modes of transportation. In the previous chapter we briefly discussed the major types of insurance policies, including marine insurance. In this chapter we will provide more details on cargo insurance.

Cargo insurance can provide protection to cover all transport risks from the time the goods leave the exporter's warehouse or factory until they reach the final destination specified by the importer. In its most basic form, such insurance provides the means to reimburse the owner of goods being transported overseas for any loss or damage incurred for which the carrier cannot legally be called upon to make payment. For international shipments, the carrier's liability is frequently limited by international agreements, and the coverage is substantially different from domestic coverage. In addition to legal owners, nonowners (the exporter is a nonowner as soon as the title of ownership passes to the foreign buyer) often have an interest in seeing that a shipment is adequately protected.

Acquiring Cargo Insurance

The basic steps that the exporter should follow in acquiring cargo insurance are as follows. The exporter first chooses a marine insurance company or insurance agency. Then, the exporter obtains an open policy (see Chapter 15), which is the master contract between the exporter and the insurance company. The insurance company provides rate quotes based on the list of products and possible importing countries provided by the exporter. Otherwise, rates can be quoted one by one as the exporter requests them before pricing his goods. Once the exporter agrees to the quote, it signs a contract with the insurance company or the agency involved. However, it is recommended that the exporter ask the insurance company whether it only issues policies. If they only issue policies, then for each shipment the exporter must complete an application form to be delivered to the insurance company so that a policy can be prepared and sent to the exporter. This is a very time-consuming process that exporters should be aware of. If the insurance company issues certificates, the exporter is given an allotment of them. The certificates are stamped with the number used on the open policy. Usually there are three pages in a certificate: the first page is the insurance certificate, the second page is mailed to the insurance agency or company, and the third page is for the exporter's files. Thus the exporter possesses the insurance certificate immediately after the shipment is made. This is particularly important when the payment is going to be made through an LC, which requires that all necessary documents, including the insurance certificate, be available and presented to the designated bank by the expiration date.

Who Needs and Pays for Cargo Insurance?

A critical factor in determining the party who needs the insurance is the insurable interest (Garratt & Marshall, 1996; Ingram, 1985; Loshin,

2007). Insurable interest depends upon which firm will benefit most from the safe arrival of the cargo or will be injured most by its loss, damage, or delay in transit (Badger et al., 1994). Either the exporter or the buyer pays for the cargo insurance. The party responsible for purchasing the insurance should be specified in the terms of sale. Even if the terms of sale make the importer responsible for the insurance, the exporter should not assume that adequate insurance has been obtained. Insufficient coverage may result in a loss for the exporter due to "heavy weather," rough handling of the cargo during loading and unloading, or any other unexpected hazards. Thus the exporter may want to provide additional insurance to obtain the proper level of coverage.

Types of Policies

In Chapter 15 we discussed three basic types of cargo insurance policies: free of particular average, with particular average, and all risks. However, none of these policies covers loss by war, strikes, riots, or expropriation. They explicitly state that they are "free of capture and seizure" and also "free of strikes, riots, and civil commotion." For additional premiums, clauses covering these specific perils can be substituted in the policy. These can be added to the space called "endorsement" on the insurance certificate. For most of the world, these two endorsements have a very low premium. Insurance premiums are always stated per $100 of coverage. To increase any rates stated in any open policy, the insurance company must give advance notice, which is usually 30 days.

War Clause

The war clause covers goods only while they are on board. If they have not been unloaded within 15 days of arrival at the port of destination, this coverage ends. If transshipment is required, the goods must be aboard the second vessel within 15 days of arrival at the intermediate port or coverage ceases.

Strikes, Riots, and Civil Commotion Clauses

This is also called the "strike clause." It covers loss, damage, or theft by strikers, rioters, or anyone participating in labor unrest. Spiteful damage is also insured. However, the strike clause does not pay for damage covered by the standard war clause. The strike clause insures the goods from the time they leave the exporter's warehouse or factory until they arrive at the importer's warehouse. Export goods are not covered for delay, even if such delay is caused by strikers.

Other Clauses

Besides the war and strike clauses, other clauses include the following:

- *Termination of adventure clause.* Provides coverage if the voyage is ended or interrupted before the final destination is reached.
- *Transit clause.* Lists the points of the voyage, such as warehouse to warehouse, between which the insurance is in effect.
- *Change of voyage clause.* Continues coverage, for an extra premium, if the voyage is changed.
- *Seaworthiness admitted clause.* Guarantees that the insurer will not try to avoid a claim on the grounds that the vessel was not seaworthy.
- *Both to blame clause.* Covers the insured party against any claim it may have as a result of collision, regardless of blame.
- *Sue and labor clause.* Guarantees the insured party reimbursement of expenses incurred to protect cargo from further loss or damage.
- *Not to insure clause.* Prohibits the insured from assigning any right of recovery in the policy to the vessel owners, dock owners, or any other party connected in any way with the adventure.

How Much to Insure

While export insurance must be, at a minimum, 110% of the CIF value in order to comply with typical LC provisions, as well as general customs, the importer can request more insurance coverage due to increases in the value of the shipment at the time of arrival (resulting from an increase in the general price levels or some other reason). The value of the estimated insurance premium is included in the calculation of 110% of CIF value, along with transportation costs and all other costs.

How to File a Claim

This stage of the insurance process is crucial. Throughout this section we will assume that the exporter is the insured party. When a possible claim situation occurs, the exporter should act with "reasonable dispatch"— how the owner would act if no insurance were carried. In short, unless the claim is for a total loss (e.g., the ship sinks), the exporter must take every possible action to protect the goods from further loss or damage. The steps to be taken can be summarized as follows:

1. Do everything to minimize the loss. For instance, if export goods are canned food and they have been subjected to seawater, then the exporter must immediately get them to a place where they can be dried to prevent rusting.
2. Notify an insurance agent of the loss at the first opportunity.
3. Make a claim against the carrier (or any other party that could be fully or partially blamed). Put the claim in writing and send a copy of it to the agent.
4. Follow the instructions of the inspector appointed by the insurance company to determine the cause of the damage or loss.

The exporter must take all protective steps possible unless notified of "constructive total loss" by the agent or the inspector. In the case of a claim for total loss, the exporter should submit the following documents (plus any other documents requested by the inspector):

- Original insurance policy or certificate that is endorsed
- Bill of lading, usually one negotiable copy and three nonnegotiable copies
- Original shipper's invoice
- A copy of the claim against the carrier or any other party to blame, as well as a copy of the replies
- If possible, a master's protect—a document that certifies to anything that may have contributed to the loss, such as "heavy weather"

When approved, a total loss claim is settled by full reimbursement to the extent of insurance coverage. On the other hand, when the claim is for partial loss, that is, particular average (see Chapter 15 for more information), the exporter should submit the documents listed above for total loss, plus the following:

- The report of the inspector confirming the loss and giving details of its extent
- A copy of the packing list
- Port of customs landing certificate
- If possible, a copy of the ship's ex-tackle report

With a particular average claim, the insurance company does not pay the difference between the amount of the insurance and the value of recovery from the sale. Rather, it pays a percentage of the insurance, which is found by comparing the net amount lost by the sale of the damaged shipment to the wholesale price of the goods if they had arrived undamaged on the date of arrival. If a claim arises for loss of part of a shipment, the procedure is much simpler, particularly if the goods are all similar. For example, if 20% of the containers, containing exactly the same items, are destroyed, then 20% of the insurance coverage is paid. However, if the damaged goods are not identical, the valuation becomes more complicated. Invoice values of the goods are then applicable to determine the amount of reimbursement.

A general average claim differs from a particular average claim in the sense that the aim is to spread the value of the losses suffered among all parties involved in the export process. The amount each will have to contribute is based on a percentage calculated by dividing the value of the individual interest by the value of the total adventure.

When a general claim is filed, an inspector is appointed as soon as the vessel reaches port. Then the value of the shipment is carefully calculated from the wholesale price of each type of good, less customs duties, any other taxes, and handling charges. Unless the insurance amount equals or exceeds the value of the shipment (fully insured), no guarantee will made by the insurer. That is one of the reasons that 110% of the CIF value is insured.

Regarding payments on claims, the insurer will usually ask that the exporter sign a subrogation form, giving the insurer ownership of the damaged or lost cargo, which is necessary before the insurer begins taking legal action against any other party that may have been responsible for the loss or damage.

Appendix: Freight Forwarder Evaluation Form

Suppose you are considering several freight forwarders. The criteria below can be used to evaluate the candidates on a five-point scale:

- very unfavorable (1)
- unfavorable (2)
- neutral (3)
- favorable (4)
- very favorable (5)

	CANDIDATE A	CANDIDATE B	CANDIDATE C
Reputation			
Knowledge			
Financial stability			
Specialization (in certain product areas or shipment methods)			
Responsiveness and attention to details			
Location (relative to carriers and your plant)			
Capacity (staff size)			
Facility (warehouse)			

The higher the total score, the more favorable the freight forwarder.

References

Aaby, N.-E., & Slater, S. F. (1989). Management influences on export performance: A review of the empirical literature 1978–1988. *International Marketing Review, 6*(4), 7–26.

ActionPak. (2008). *Export packing services – Industrial crating.* Available at http://www.actionpakinc.com/export_packing_containerization/export_packing_containerization.htm

Agarwal, S., & Ramaswami, S. N. (1992). Choice of foreign market entry mode: Impact of ownership, location, and internalization factors. *Journal of International Business Studies, 23*(1), 1–27.

Aksoy, S., & Kaynak, E. (1994). Export behavior of produce marketers. *International Marketing Review, 11*(2), 16–32.

Badger, D., Bugg, R., & Whitehead, G. (1994). *International physical distribution and cargo insurance.* Hemel Hempstead, Hertfordshire, UK: Simon & Schuster.

Bello, D., & Lohtia, R. (1995). Export channel design: The use of foreign distributors and agents. *Journal of the Academy of Marketing Science, 23*(2), 83–93.

Bello, D. C., & Williamson, N. C. (1985). Contractual arrangement and marketing practices in the indirect export channel. *Journal of International Business Studies, 16* (Summer), 65–82.

Boddewyn, J. J., Soehl, R., & Picard, J. (1986). Standardization of international marketing: Is Ted Levitt in fact right? *Business Horizons, 29* (November–December), 69–75.

Bowersox, D. J., & Closs, D. J. (1996). *Logistical management: The integrated supply chain process.* New York: McGraw-Hill.

Bowersox, D. J., Closs, D. J., & Cooper, M. B. (2002). *Supply chain logistics management.* New York: McGraw Hill.

Bowersox, D. J., Closs, D. J., & Stank, T. P. (1999). *21st century logistics: Making supply chain integration a reality.* East Lansing: Michigan State University and Council of Logistics Management.

Burton, E. N., & Schlegelmilch, B. B. (1987). Profile analysis of non-exporters versus exporters grouped by export involvement, 1978–1988. *Management International Review, 27*(1), 38–49.

Buzzell, R. (1968). Can you standardize multinational marketing? *Harvard Business Review, 46* (November/December), 102–113.

Calantone, R., Kim, D., Schmidt, J., & Cavusgil, S. T. (2006). The influence of internal and external firm factors on international product adaptation strategy and export performance: A three-country comparison. *Journal of Business Research, 59*(2), 176–185.

Cavusgil, S. T. (1985). Guidelines for export market research. *Business Horizons, 28* (November–December), 27–33.

Cavusgil, S. T. (1988). Unraveling the mystique of export pricing. *Business Horizons, 31*(3), 54–63.

Cavusgil, S. T. (1993). Preparing for export marketing. *International Trade Forum, 34*(6), 92–100.

Cavusgil, S. T. (1997). Measuring the potential of emerging markets: An indexing approach. *Business Horizons, 40*(1), 87–91.

Cavusgil, S. T., Deligonul, S., & Zhang, C. (2004). Curbing foreign distributor opportunism: An examination of trust, contracts, and the legal environment in international channel relationships. *Journal of International Marketing, 12*(2), 7–27.

Cavusgil, S. T., Knight, G. A., & Riesenberger, J. R. (2008). *International business: Strategy, management, and the new realities.* Upper Saddle River, NJ: Prentice Hall.

Cavusgil, S. T., & Zou, S. (1994). Marketing strategy–performance relationship: An investigation of the empirical link in export market ventures. *Journal of Marketing, 58* (January), 1–21.

Cavusgil, S. T., Zou, S., & Naidu, G. M. (1993). Product and promotion adaptation in export ventures: An empirical investigation. *Journal of International Business Studies, 24*(3), 479–506.

Cho, D. S. (1987). *The general trading company: Concept and strategy.* Lexington, MA: Lexington Books.

Choi, C. J., Lee, S. H., & Kim, J. B. (1999). A note on countertrade: Contractual uncertainty and transaction governance in emerging economies. *Journal of International Business Studies, 30*(1), 189.

Craig, S. C,. & Douglas, S. P. (1999). *International marketing research: Concepts and methods* (2nd ed.). New York: John Wiley & Sons.

Czinkota, M. R. (1991). International information needs for U.S. competitiveness. *Business Horizons, 34* (November–December), 86–91.

Czinkota, M. R. (1994). A national export assistance policy for new and growing businesses. *Journal of International Marketing, 2*(1), 91–101.

Czinkota, M. R., & Ronkainen, I. A. (2002). *International marketing.* Mason, OH: Thomson/South-Western.

Czinkota, M. R., Ronkainen, I. A., & Moffett, M. H. (2004). *International business* (7th ed.). Cincinnati, OH: South-Western.

David, P. (2004). *International logistics.* Cincinnati, OH: Atomic Dog Publishing.

Davies, G. J. (1981). The role of exporter and freight forwarder in the United Kingdom. *Journal of International Business Studies, 12*(3), 99–108.

Deligonul, S., Kim, D., Roath, T., & Cavusgil, E. (2006). The Achilles' heel of an enduring relationship: Appropriation of rents between a manufacturer and its foreign distributor. *Journal of Business Research, 59*(7), 802–810.

Demaret, P., & Stewardson, R. (1994). Border tax adjustments under GATT and EC law and general implications for environmental taxes. *Journal of World Trade, 28*(4), 5.

Donnelly, J. H., Jr. (1970). Marketing notes and communications: Attitudes toward culture and approach to international advertising. *Journal of Marketing, 34* (July), 60–68.

Egan, C., & Shipley, D. (1996). Strategic orientations towards countertrade opportunities in emerging markets. *International Marketing Review, 13*(4), 102.

Eximbank. (2008). Export credit insurance. Available at http://www.exim.gov

Farley, J., & Lehmann, D. (1994). Cross-national "laws" and differences in market response. *Management Science, 40*(1), 111–122.

Fatt, A. C. (1967). The danger of "local" international advertising. *Journal of Marketing, 31* (January), 60–62.

FCIA. (2008). Trade credit and political risk insurance. Available at http://www.fcia.com/productsForCompanies.html

Fletcher, R. (1998). A holistic approach to countertrade. *Industrial Marketing Management, 27*(6), 511.

Fowler, D. J. (1978). Transfer prices and profit maximization in multinational enterprise operations. *Journal of International Business Studies, 9*(3), 9–26.

Garratt, R., & Marshall, J. M. (1996). Insurable interest, options to convert, and demand for upper limits in optimum property insurance. *Journal of Risk and Insurance, 63*(2), 185.

Guerin, B. (2003). Indonesia redefines luxury. Available at http://www.atimes.com/atimes/Southeast_Asia/EA17Ae03.html

Hall, E. T. (1990). *Beyond culture.* New York: Anchor Books.

Hill, C. W. L. (1997). *International business.* Chicago: Irwin.

Hill, J., & Still, R. (1984). Adapting products to LDC tastes. *Harvard Business Review, 62* (March–April), 92–101.

Hirsch, M. L., Jr. (1994). *Advanced management accounting.* Cincinnati, OH: South-Western.

Hite, R. E., & Fraser, C. (1988). International advertising strategies of multinational corporations. *Journal of Advertising Research, 28* (August–September), 9–17.

Hofstede, G. (1980). *Culture's consequences: International differences in work related values.* Beverly Hills, CA: Sage.

Incoterm. (2008). Incoterm. Available at http://en.wikipedia.org/wiki/Incoterm

Ingram, J. D. (1985). Insurable interest: Who can question it? Do waiver and estoppel apply? *Insurance Counsel Journal, 52*(4), 647.

Inkpen, A., & Beamish, P. (1997). Knowledge, bargaining power, and the instability of international joint ventures. *Academy of Management Review, 22*(1), 177–202.

IRS (2008). General instructions for foreign sales corporations. Available at http://www.irs.gov

ITA. (2008). Export.gov. Available at http://www.export.gov

Jain, S. (1989). Standardization of international marketing strategy: Some research hypotheses. *Journal of Marketing, 53* (January), 70–79.

Jain, S. (1996). Problems in international protection of intellectual property rights. *Journal of International Marketing, 4*(1), 9–32.

Katsikeas, C. S., Bell, J., & Morgan, R. E. (1998). Editorial: Advances in export marketing theory and practice. *International Marketing Review, 15*(5), 322–332.

Katsikeas, C. S., Piercy, N. F., & Ioannidis, C. (1996). Determinants of export performance in a European context. *European Journal of Marketing, 30*(6), 6–35.

Kim, D., & Cavusgil, S. T. (2006). Does online information disclosure matter to etailers? A cross-cultural study. *International Journal of Internet Marketing and Advertising, 3*(1), 89–104.

Kim, D., Cavusgil, S. T., & Calantone, R. J. (2006). Information system innovations and supply chain management: Channel relationships and firm performance. *Journal of the Academy of Marketing Science, 34*(1), 40–54.

Kluckholn, F., & Strodtbeck, F. (1961). *Variations in value orientations.* San Francisco: Row Peterson.

Kogut, B. (1988). Joint ventures: Theoretical and empirical perspectives. *Strategic Management Journal, 9*(4), 319–332.

Kotabe, M., & Czinkota, M. R. (1992). State government promotion of manufacturing exports: A gap analysis. *Journal of International Business Studies, 23* (Winter), 637–658.

Levitt, T. (1983). The globalization of markets. *Harvard Business Review, 61* (May–June), 92–102.

Loshin, J. (2007). Insurance law's hapless busybody: A case against the insurable interest requirement. *Yale Law Journal, 117*(3), 474.

Mariotti, S., & Piscitello, L. (1995). Information costs and location of FDIs within the host country: Empirical evidence from Italy. *Journal of International Business Studies, 26*(4), 815–841.

Mentzer, J. T., DeWitt, W., Keebler, J. S., Min, S., Nix, N. W., Smith, C. D., et al. (2001). Defining supply chain management. *Journal of Business Logistics, 22*(2), 1–25.

Miller, M. M. (1993a). Executive insight: The 10-step road map for success in foreign markets. *Journal of International Marketing, 1*(2), 89–106.

Miller, M. M. (1993b). Executive insight: A road map for creating profitable operations in foreign markets—A case study. *Journal of International Marketing, 1*(4), 91–102.

Morash, E. A., & Clinton, S. R. (1997). The role of transportation capabilities in international supply chain management. *Transportation Journal, 36*(3), 5–17.

Myers, M. B., Cavusgil, S. T., & Diamantopoulos, A. (2002). Antecedents and actions of export pricing strategy: A conceptual framework and research propositions. *European Journal of Marketing, 36*(1/2), 159–188.

Nakata, C., & Sivakumar, K. (1996). National culture and new product development: An integrative review. *Journal of Marketing, 60* (January), 61–72.

Nakata, C., & Sivakumar, K. (2001). Instituting the marketing concept in a multinational setting: The role of national culture. *Journal of the Academy of Marketing Science, 29*(3), 255–275.

Osland, G. E., & Cavusgil, S. T. (1996). Performance issues in U.S.-China joint ventures. *California Management Review, 38*(2), 106–130.

Paun, D. A., & Shoham, A. (1996). Marketing motives in international countertrade: An empirical examination. *Journal of International Marketing, 4*(3), 29.

Peter, J. P., & Donnelly, J. H. (2007). *Marketing management: Knowledge and skills.* Boston: McGraw-Hill/Irwin.

Raju, P. S. (1995). Consumer behavior in global markets: The A-B-C-D paradigm and its applications to Eastern Europe and the Third World. *Journal of Consumer Marketing, 12*(5), 37–56.

Raymond, M. A., Tanner, J. F., Jr., & Kim, J. (2001). Cost complexity of pricing decisions for exporters in developing and emerging markets. *Journal of International Marketing, 9*(3), 19–40.

Roberts, A. (1988). Setting export prices to sell competitively. *International Trade Forum, 24*(3), 10–13.

Steenkamp, J.-B., ter Hofstede, F., & Wedel, M. (1999). A cross-national investigation into the individual and national cultural antecedents of consumer innovativeness. *Journal of Marketing, 63*(2), 55–69.

Szymanski, D., Bharadwaj, S., & Varadarajan, P. R. (1993). Standardization versus adaptation of international marketing strategy: An empirical investigation. *Journal of Marketing, 57* (October), 1–17.

Walters, P. (1986). International Marketing Policy: A Discussion of the Standardization Construct and Its Relevance for Corporate Policy. *Journal of International Business Studies,* 17 (2), 55-69.

Wikipedia. (2008). *Berne Convention for the Protection of Literary and Artistic Works.* Available at http://en.wikipedia.org/wiki/Berne_Convention_for_the _Protection_of_Literary_and_Artistic_Works

Willard, K. L. (1997). Book review: Fundamental tax reform and border tax adjustments. *Journal of International Economics, 42*(3–4), 507.

Zhao, H., Luo, Y., & Suh, T. (2004). Transaction cost determinants and ownership-based entry mode choice: A meta-analytical review. *Journal of International Business Studies, 35*(6), 524–544.

Zou, S., & Cavusgil, S. T. (1996). Global strategy: A review and an integrated conceptual framework. *European Journal of Marketing, 30*(1), 52–69.

Zou, S., & Stan, S. (1998). The determinants of export performance: A review of the empirical literature between 1987 and1997. *International Marketing Review, 15*(5), 333–356.

Zou, S., Taylor, C. R., & Osland, G. E. (1998). The EXPERF scale: A cross-national generalized export performance measure. *Journal of International Marketing, 6*(3), 37–58.

Index

CPSIA information can be obtained at www.ICGtesting.com
Printed in the USA
BVOW04s1006220115

384486BV00020B/285/P